Raising the Fleet

Raising the Fleet

THE PEARL HARBOR SALVAGE OPERATION, 1941–1944

A PICTORIAL HISTORY BY **Ernest Arroyo** AND **Stan Cohen**

In less than two hours a vital part of the Pacific Fleet lay in shambles. But like the Phoenix of Egyptian mythology, the Pearl Harbor that was consumed by fire on the 7th of December 1941, would rise from the ashes to become the hub of operations for America's victory in the Pacific Theatre of Operations in World War Two. NA 80G-32691

WITH EDITED EXCERPTS FROM
Pearl Harbor: Why, How, Fleet Salvage and Final Appraisal
by Vice Admiral Homer Wallin

Front cover photo is of the capsized *USS Oklahoma*. USN 80-6-182695

PHOTO CREDITS
NA—National Archives, Washington DC
USN—US Navy Archives
EA—Ernest Arroyo Collection
PHP—Pacific Historic Parks
PHPC—Pictorial Histories Publishing Company Collection
HA—Hawaii State Archives
NH—Naval History and Heritage Command
All other photos are credited to their source

Library of Congress Cataloging-in-Publication Data

Names: Arroyo, Ernest, author. | Cohen, Stan, author. | Wallin, Homer N.
   (Homer Norman), 1893-1984. Pearl Harbor.
Title: Raising the fleet : the Pearl Harbor salvage operation, 1941-1944 : a
   pictorial history / by Ernest Arroyo and Stan Cohen ; with edited excerpts
   from Pearl Harbor: why, how, fleet salvage and final appraisal, by Admiral
   Homer Wallin.
Other titles: Pearl Harbor salvage operation, 1941-1944, a pictorial history
Description: First edition. | Missoula : Mountain Press Publishing Company,
   [2018] | Includes bibliographical references.
Identifiers: LCCN 2017058974 | ISBN 9780878426843 (pbk. : alk. paper)
Subjects: LCSH: Pearl Harbor (Hawaii), Attack on, 1941. |
   Warships—Salvaging—Hawaii—Pearl Harbor. | Warships—United
   States—History—20th century. | Shipwrecks—Hawaii—History—20th century.
Classification: LCC D767.92 .A773 2018 | DDC 940.54/26693—dc23
LC record available at https://lccn.loc.gov/2017058974

PICTORIAL HISTORIES
AN IMPRINT OF MOUNTAIN PRESS PUBLISHING COMPANY

PRINTED IN CANADA

MP Mountain Press
PUBLISHING COMPANY
P.O. Box 2399 · Missoula, MT 59806 · 406-728-1900
800-234-5308 · info@mtnpress.com
www.mountain-press.com

TABLE OF CONTENTS

INTRODUCTION

There have been countless books written on the attack on Pearl Harbor over the last 75 years. Most have concentrated on the causes, pre-attack preparations, the many conspiracy theories and the results of the attack. Most of the books have some information, photos and maps on the post-attack salvage operation, but mostly as an afterthought to the main theme of the book—the attack itself.

My first book on the attack, originally titled *East Wind Rain*, now entitled *The Attack on Pearl Harbor* has one small chapter on the salvage operation with photos of the fantastic job done in the months after the attack by the navy and shipyard crews to get the ships back into service.

It was truly a miracle, first that the Japanese did not destroy the shipyard facilities and oil storage tanks and second that all but three of the major ships sunk or damaged during the attack eventually made it back into combat. Even the battleship *USS West Virginia* made it into Tokyo Harbor for the surrender ceremonies in September 1945.

I have published books on the battleships at Pearl Harbor by authors M. J. Smith and Harvey Beigel, with the exception of the *USS Arizona*. The *USS Oklahoma*, which was the largest salvage operation at Pearl Harbor would make a complete book on its own.

Not wanting to "reinvent the wheel," I have used quite a bit of text from my own publications and edited portions of the definitive book on the subject: *Pearl Harbor, Why, How, Fleet Salvage and Final Appraisal* by Vice-Admiral Homer N. Wallin. It was published in 1968 by the Naval History Division and is in the public domain. David Madsen has also written a book devoted to the salvage operation: *Resurrection, Salvaging the Battle Fleet at Pearl Harbor,* published by Naval Institute Press in 2003.

Raising the Fleet follows the genera of my other World War Two books, which is mainly photographic with captions and some narrative portion. I hope this book will give the average reader an appreciation of one of the most important aspects of World War Two naval history and as a memorial to all the military personnel and civilians who took part in this noble effort to get America back into the war.

Most of the photographs are from Ernest Arroyo and Pictorial Histories' collections and from the Naval Historical Archives and National Archives in Washington, DC and other sources acredited. I want to thank Ernie for his invaluable help as my co-author. Also I want to thank the staffs of the National Park Service and the Pacific Historic Parks (formerly the Arizona Memorial Museum Association) for their help.

In conclusion, this edition is dedicated to all participants involved in this great effort. We also cannot ignore the other great shipyard effort on the damaged *USS Yorktown* in May 1942 to get the ship back in service for the pivotal Battle of Midway, changing the course of the war in the Pacific.

—Stan Cohen
co-author

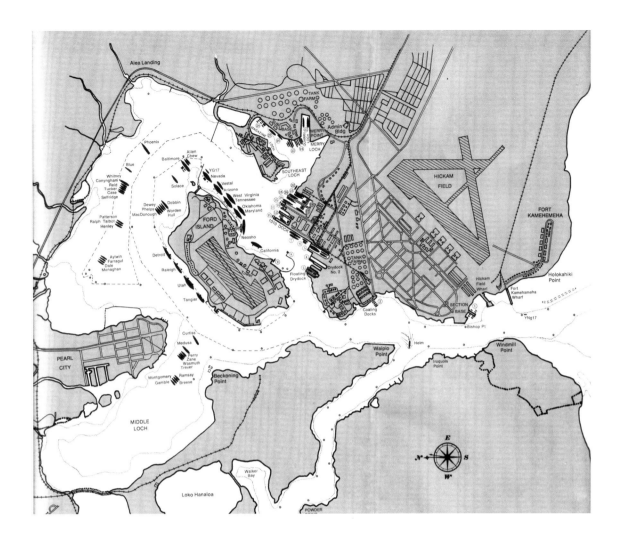

THE REPORTER WHO BROKE THE FIRST NEWS OF THE ATTACK

Frank Tremaine was a young reporter based in Honolulu as the Pacific bureau manager for United Press, a forerunner of the UPI. On the morning of the attack he was awakened by explosions and antiaircraft fire. From the window of his house he saw black smoke coming from Pearl Harbor, seven miles away.

Tremaine made several hurried phone calls to military officials before sending a cable to the UP offices in San Francisco and Manila, before he even got dressed: "Flash—Pearl Harbor under aerial attack. Tremaine." In the meantime his wife, Kay, was relaying his notes along with her own eyewitness account by phone to the San Francisco office.

Although Tremaine's report was the first account by a civilian correspondent, he was scooped by the official announcement from the White House, transmitted a few minutes earlier.

Frank Benjamin Tremaine was born in 1914, grew up in Pasadena, California, and graduated from Stanford University in 1936. He soon joined UP in Salt Lake City. He worked for the UP in the Pacific and reported the Japanese surrender on the *USS Missouri*. He was UP's first bureau chief in Japan. He also covered the Korean War, plus other postings around the world before coming to New York in 1952. He was named a senior vice president in 1972. Tremaine retired in 1980 and died on Dec. 7, 2006, at age 92.

SUMMARY OF
THE PEARL HARBOR ATTACK

TIME OF ATTACK: Sunday, December 7, 1941

0755 First wave of Japanese aircraft attacked
0845 Second wave of Japanese aircraft attacked
0945 Japanese aircraft broke off the attack

JAPANESE AIRCRAFT:

Total Japanese aircraft: 353 plus 79 held in reserve or for combat air patrol. The 353 used in the attack were divided into two waves. The first wave consisted of 40 torpedo planes, 49 level bombers, 51 dive bombers, and 43 fighters for a total of 183 aircraft. The second wave of 167 aircraft consisted of 54 level bombers, 78 dive bombers, and 35 fighters.

U.S. PERSONNEL CASUALTIES:

	Killed	Wounded	Total
Navy	1,998	710	2,708
Army	233	364	597
Marines	109	69	178
Civilians	68	35	103
Total	2,408	1,178	3,586

UNITED STATES SHIP DAMAGE

SHIP	REMARKS	DATE REJOINED FLEET
	BATTLE SHIPS	
ARIZONA	Sunk, total loss, on bottom at Pearl Harbor	
CALIFORNIA	Sunk, raised, repaired, modernized	May 1944
MARYLAND	Damaged, repaired, modernized	Feb. 1942
NEVADA	Heavily damaged, grounded, raised, repaired, modernized	Dec. 1942
OKLAHOMA	Capsized, total loss, raised, sold for scrap, lost at sea under tow to scrap yard	
PENNSYLVANIA	Damaged, repaired	March 1942
TENNESSEE	Damaged, repaired	March 1942
WEST VIRGINIA	Sunk, raised, repaired, modernized	July 1944
	CRUISERS	
HELENA	Heavily damaged, repaired	June 1942
HONOLULU	Damaged, repaired	Jan. 1942
RALEIGH	Heavily damaged, repaired, overhauled	July 1942
	DESTROYERS	
CASSIN	Heavily damaged, rebuilt	Feb. 1944
DOWNES	Heavily damaged, rebuilt	Nov. 1943
HELM	Damaged, continued on patrol, repaired	Jan. 1942
SHAW	Heavily damaged, repaired	June 1942
	MINECRAFT	
OGLALA	Sunk, raised, repaired	Feb. 1944
	AUXILIARIES	
CURTISS (AV-4)	Damaged, repaired	Jan. 1942
SOTOYOMO (YT-9)	Sunk, raised, repaired	Aug. 1942
UTAH (AG -16)	Capsized, on bottom at Pearl Harbor	
VESTAL(AR-4)	Heavily damaged, beached, raised, repaired	Feb.1942
YFD-2	Sunk, raised, repaired	May1942

AIRCRAFT DAMAGE

	Lost	Damaged
U.S.Navy	92	31
Army Air Corps	77	128
Total	169	159

U.S. SHIPS PRESENT AT PEARL HARBOR
(or within 3 miles of Oahu)

Rear Admiral Husband E. Kimmel was the Commander-in-Chief of the U.S. Pacific Fleet.

Battleships	8	Submarines	4	Repair (AR)	3
Heavy Cruisers	2	Tender (AD)	2	Oilers	2
Light Cruisers	6	Tender (AV)	6	Ammunition	1
Destroyers	30	Tender (AS)	1	Fleet Tugs	3
Minecraft	23	Sub. Rescue	1	Stores	3
Misc. Aux.	3	Gunboat	1	Hospital	1
Net Vessels	6	Ferryboats	2	Yard Tugs	9
PT Boats	12	Yard Oilers	5	Garbage Lighters	3
Yard Patrol	1	Water Barges	3	Repair Barges	3
Seaplane Derricks	4	Torpedo Test Barge	1	U.S. Coast Guard	6
Floating Dry Dock	1	Chinese Junk	1	Pile Driver	1
		Dredge	1	Misc. Yard Craft	19
				Total	178

JAPANESE SHIPS ASSIGNED TO "HAWAII OPERATION"

Type	Name	Lost	
CV	AKAGI	June 5, 1942	Midway
	KAGA	June 4, 1942	Midway
	SHOKAKU	June 19, 1944	Philippine Sea
	ZUIKAKU	Oct 25, 1944	Leyte Gulf
CVL	HIRYU	June 5, 1942	Midway
	SORYU	June 4, 1942	Midway
BB	HIEI	Nov. 13, 1942	Guadalcanal
	KIRISHIMA	Nov. 15, 1942	Guadalcanal
CA	CHIKUMA	Oct. 25, 1944	Leyte Gulf
	TONE	July 24, 1945	Kure
CL	ABUKUMA	Oct. 27, 1944	Surigao Strait
	KATORI	Feb. 17, 1944	Truk
DD	AKIGUMO	Apr. 11, 1944	Celebes Sea
	ARARE	July 5, 1942	Aleutians
	HAMAKAZE	Apr. 7, 1945	S. of Kyushu
	ISOKAZE	Apr. 7, 1945	S. of Kyushu
	KAGERO	May 8, 1943	Solomons
	KASUMI	Apr. 7, 1945	S. of Kyushu
	SAZANAMI	Jan. 14, 1944	Yap
	SHIRANUHI	Oct. 27, 1944	Leyte Gulf
	TANIKAZE	June 9, 1944	Tawi Tawi
	URAKAZE	Nov. 21, 1944	Formosa
	USHIO	Surrendered at Yokosuka Naval Base	

SUBMARINES Place and Date Sunk

I-1	Jan. 29, 1943	Guadal canal	I-9	June 11, 1943	Aleutias
I-2	Apr. 7, 1944	New Ireland	I-10	July 4, 1944	Saipan
I-3	Dec. 10, 1942	Guadal canal	I-15	Nov. 2, 1942	Solomons
I-4	Dec. 20, 1942	New Britain	I-16	May 19, 1944	Solomons
I-5	July 19, 1944	Guam	I-16A	Dec. 7, 1941	Pearl Harbor
I-6	July 14, 1944	Marianas	I-17	Aug. 19, 1943	Noumea
I-7	June 20, 1943	Aleutians	I-18	Feb. 11, 1943	Solomons
I-8	Mar. 31, 1945	Okinawa	I-18A	Dec. 7/8, 1941	Pearl Harbor

I-19	Oct. 18, 1943	Gilbert Island	I-26	Oct. 10, 1944		Leyte
I-20	Oct. 1, 1943	New Hebrides	I-68	July 27, 1943		Bismarks
I-20A	Dec. 7, 1941	Pearl Habor	I-69	Apr. 4, 1944		Turk
I-21	Nov. 29, 1943	Tarawa	I-70	Dec. 10, 1941		Ne of Oahu
I-22	Oct. 1, 1942	Solomons	I-71	Feb. 1, 1944		Solomons
I-22A	Dec. 7, 1941	Pearl Habor	I-72	Nov. 11, 1942		Guadalcanal
I-23	Jan. 28, 1942	Operations	I-73	Jan. 27, 1942		W.of Midway
I-24	July 27, 1943	New Ireland	I-74	Apr. 3, 1944		Turk
I-24A	Dec. 8, 1941	Bellows Fld.	I-75	Feb. 5, 1944		Marshalls
I-25	Sept. 3, 1943	New Hebrides				

(-A indicates Midget Sub)

OILERS Place and Date Sunk

AKEBONO MARU	Mar. 30, 1944	Palau
KENYO MARU	Jan. 14, 1944	Palau
KOKUYO MARU	July 30, 1944	Sulu Sea
KYOKUTO MARU	Sept 21, 1944	Manila Harbor
NIHON MARU	Jan. 14, 1944	Bismarcks
SHINKOKU MARU	Feb. 17, 1944	Carolines
TOEI MARU	Jan. 18, 1943	Rabaul
TOHO MARU	March 23, 1943	Makassar Strait
SHIRIYA	Sept. 21, 1943	95 Mi. N E Keelung

(Accompanied USHIO and SAZANAMI as the Midway
Neutralization Force.)

SUMMARY OF JAPANESE FORCES:

The Japanese Attack Force was commanded by Vice
Admiral Chuichi Nagumo in the Akagi.

Aircraft Carriers, Heavy	4	Aircraft Carriers, Light	2
Battleships	2	Heavy Cruisers	2
Light Cruisers	2	Destroyers	11
Submarines	30	Oilers	9
Midget Submarines	5		
		Total	67

JAPANESE LOSSES on December 7, 1941

Ships and Aircraft	Personnel
29 Aircraft	55
5 Midget Submarines	9
Total	64 Plus one POW

AWARDS FOR HEROISM ON DECEMBER 7, 1941
MEDAL OF HONOR

BENNION, Mervyn, Captain	WEST VIRGINIA
FINN, John W., ACO	NAS KANEOHE BAY
FLAHERTY, Francis C., Ensign	OKLAHOMA
FUQUA, Samuel G., LCdr.	ARIZONA
HILL, Edwin, Chief BOSN	NEVADA
JONES, Herbert C., Ensign	CALIFORNIA
KIDD, Isaac C., Rear Admiral	ARIZONA
PHARRIS, Jackson C., Gunner	CALIFORNIA
REEVES, Thomas J., CRM	CALIFORNIA
ROSS, Donald K., MACH	NEVADA
SCOTT, Robert R., MM1/C	CALIFORNIA
TOMICH, Peter, CWT	UTAH
VAN VALKENBURGH, Franklin, Captain	ARIZONA
WARD, James Richard, S1/C	OKLAHOMA
YOUNG, Cassin, Commander	VESTAL

NAVY CROSS	51	DISTINGUISHED SERVICE	
SILVER STAR	53	CROSS	4
NAVY AND MARINE		DISTINGUISHED SERVICE	
CORP MEDAL	4	MEDAL	1
DISTINGUISHED FLYING		BRONZE STAR	3
CROSS	1		

SHIPS AT PEARL HARBOR LOST DURING WWII

ARIZONA BB-39	Dec 7, 1941	PERRY DMS-17	Sept. 13, 1944
BLUE DD-387	Aug. 23, 1942	REID DD-369	Dec. 11, 1944
GAMBLE DM 15	Feb. 18, 1945	THORNTON AVD-11*	May. 2, 1945
GREBE AM-43	Jan. 2, 1943	TUCKER DD-374	Aug. 4, 1942
HELENA CL-50	July 6, 1943	UTAH AG-16	Dec 7, 1941
HENLEY DD-391	Oct. 3, 1943	WARD DD-139	Aug. 4, 1942
HULL DD-350	Dec. 18, 1944	WASMUTH DMS-15*	Dec. 29, 1942
JARVIS DD 393	Aug. 9, 1942	WORDEN DD-352	Jan. 12, 1943
MONAGHAN DD-354	Dec. 18, 1944	PT-22*	June 11, 1943
NEOSHO AO-23	May 11, 1942	PT-28*	Jan. 12, 1943
OKLAHOMA BB-37	Dec. 7, 1941		

* Not due to enemy action

SHIPS AT PEARL HARBOR 7 DECEMBER 1941
Oldest:
In Service:	SOTOYOMO (YT-9)	1903
In Commission:	USS VESTAL (AR-4)	October 4, 1909

Newest:
In Service:	ASH (YN-2)	July 1, 1941
In Commission:	USS PELIAS (AS-14)	September 5, 1941

Last:
Out of Service:	NOKOMIS (YT - 142)	May 1, 1973
Out of Commission:	USCGC TANEY (PG-37)	December 7, 1986

Most Battle Stars:
USS NEW ORLEANS (CA-32) 17
USS SAN FRANCISCO (CA-38) 17
At Tokyo Bay September 2, 1945:
USS WEST VIRGINIA (BB-48)
USS DETROIT (CL-8)

EXTRACT FROM A LETTER FROM ADMIRAL NIMITZ TO ADMIRAL DAVID L. McDONALD,
Chief of Naval Operations, dated 3 April 1965

"Several times in recent weeks I have been quoted- correctly - that ' as bad as our losses were at Pearl Harbor on 7 December 1941 - they could have been devastatingly worse - had the Japanese returned for more strikes against our naval installations, surface oil storage, and our submarine base installations. Such attacks could have been with impunity as we had little left to oppose them. Furthermore - I have been correctly quoted in saying that it was God's divine will that Kimmel did not have his fleet at sea to intercept the Japanese Carrier Task Force that attacked P.H. on 7 December 1941. That task force had a fleet speed of at least 2 knots superior to our speed - and Kimmel could not have brought the Japanese to a gun action unless they wanted it. We might have had one carrier but I doubt if LEXINGTON could have joined in time - picture if you can - 6 Japanese carriers working on our old ships which would be without air cover - or - had the Japanese wanted to avoid American air attacks from shore - they could have delayed the action until out of range of shore based air. Instead of having our ships sunk in the shallow protected waters of P.H. they could have been sunk in deep water - and we could have lost ALL of our trained men instead of the 3,800 approx. lost at P. H. There would have been few trained men to form the nucleus of the crews for the new ships nearing completion. Not only were the ships of the enemy task force faster - they were more modern - and the Japanese main fleet under Yamamoto was in the rear - in support - if needed. Nagumo - the commander of the P. H. Attack Force - missed a great chance by not following up his attack...

Warmest regards and best wishes -

C. W. Nimitz

REPORTS OF DAMAGE RECEIVED, DECEMBER

1st Report Dated 12 December, 1941

PEARL HARBOR, T. H., December 12, 1941

Secret
From: Commander-in-Chief, United States Pacific Fleet.
To: The Chief of Naval Operations.
Subject: Damage to Ships of the Pacific Fleet resulting from Enemy Attacks at Pearl Harbor, 7 December 1941.
References:
(a) Cincpac Secret Desp. 072244 of December 1941.
(b) Cincpac Secret Desp. 081015 of December 1941.
(c) Cincpac Secret Desp. 100220 of December 1941.
(d) Cincpac Secret Desp. 102043 of December 1941.

1. The following report relative to damage sustained by ships of the Pacific Fleet resulting from enemy attacks on 7 December 1941 is submitted. This amplifies reports submitted by references (a) to (d) inclusive:

(a) Battleships.

ARIZONA sunk at berth as result of aircraft torpedoes and heavy bombs which exploded forward magazines. Ship is considered to be a total wreck.

CALIFORNIA sunk at berth as a result of hits by two or more aircraft torpedoes; also received one large bomb hit amidships which caused serious fire. Recommendations regarding salvage and repairs will be forwarded later.

NEVADA damaged by heavy bombs, possible mine in the channel and aircraft torpedoes. Beached across from hospital point to prevent sinking after an attempt to sortie. Batteries intact and manned though no power is on the ship. Recommendations regarding salvage and repairs will be made later.

OKLAHOMA capsized at berth as a result of receiving three or more hits by aircraft torpedoes. Recommendations regarding salvage will be made later.

PENNSYLVANIA slightly damaged by bomb hit, starboard side of boat deck while in drydock number 1, Navy Yard, Pearl Harbor. Repairs have been completed and ship is ready for service.

MARYLAND damaged by bomb hit on forecastle and near miss. Ship was moved to the Navy Yard on 11 December and is expected to be fully ready for service 13 December.

TENNESSEE received one heavy bomb through turret top which did not explode, but put 2 rammers out of commission. Also one bomb hit aft which cracked one 14" gun. Heat from the *Arizona* fire melted and ignited paint in after portion of the second deck which was badly burned out. Ship is now heavily wedged to mooring by reason of the *West Virginia* leaning against her. Steps are being taken to dynamite the mooring to permit the removal of the *Tennessee*. Repairs are proceeding and it is estimated that by 14 December ship will be ready for service less one 14" gun.

WEST VIRGINIA sunk at berth as result of four aircraft torpedoes and one bomb hit. There is considerable damage from fire. Recommendations regarding salvage and repairs will be made later.

(b) Cruisers

HELENA damaged by bomb hit from frame 30, starboard side, opening up side under armor belt for distance of about 50 feet. Number one and two fire rooms and forward engine rooms flooded. Ship is now in drydock #2, Navy Yard, Pearl Harbor to effect repairs to make seaworthy. It is estimated that new shell and framing will be completed within two weeks and ship will be able to operate with two shafts and with all gun batteries in commission. It is recommended that ship proceed to Mare Island for completion of repairs to hull and machinery.

HONOLULU damaged by near miss at approximately frame 40 port side. Hole approximately 20 feet by 6 feet underwater. Ship being docked in drydock #1 today and it is estimated that work will be completed to make her fully effective by 16 December.

RALEIGH damaged by one aircraft torpedo which flooded forward half of machinery plant. Also hit by small bomb forward which penetrated three decks and went out ships' side and did not explode. It is proposed to dock the *Raleigh* following completion of the *Honolulu* to effect underwater repairs to make seaworthy. Recommendations as to whether all repairs to make the ship fully serviceable should be undertaken at Navy Yard, Pearl Harbor or a mainland navy yard, will be forwarded later.

(c) Destroyers

CASSIN and DOWNES damaged by bomb in number one drydock, Navy Yard, Pearl Harbor ahead of PENNSYLVANIA. Bomb hit *Downes* exploding her torpedoes warheads and causing serious oil fire. *Cassin* was damaged by fire and was knocked off drydock blocking and fell over on *Downes*. *Downes* appears to be total loss except for salvageable parts and materials. Recommendations regarding salvage and repairs to *Cassin* will be forwarded later.

SHAW hit by bomb while docking on floating drydock. Forward part of ship and floating drydock badly damaged by fire resulting from oil and powder. After part of ship not seriously damaged. Recommendations regarding repairs will be forwarded later.

(d) Auxiliary vessels.

OGLALA sunk by aircraft torpedo and near miss by bomb at ten-ten dock at Navy Yard, Pearl Harbor. Recommendations regarding salvage and repairs will be forwarded at a later date.

UTAH damaged and capsized as a result of hits by aircraft torpedoes. Recommendations regarding salvage and repairs will be forwarded later.

CURTISS damaged by enemy plane out of control which flew into crane mast and by bomb which exploded damaging hangar space causing fire which destroyed all radio equipment. Ship is entirely seaworthy. Repairs are [4] proceeding and ship will be ready for operations less one amidships crane by 15 December.

VESTAL damaged by a bomb hit aft while at berth at Pearl Harbor, is undertaking repairs with own repair force. It is estimated that the ship will be fully ready as a repair ship by 17 December. Docking may not be required.

2. It is believed that the sinking of the *Oklahoma*, *Nevada*, *California* and *West Virginia* is in large part due to the ships having been in condition X-RAY. Had time been available to set condition ZED before receiving damage, progressive flooding might have been avoided.

—H. E. KIMMEL
Copy to:
Buships Buord

An aerial view of the dry docks taken three days after the attack shows the damaged battleship Pennsylvania *with the heavily damaged destroyers* Cassin *and* Downes *in Dry Dock One at the bottom. The adjacent Dry Dock Two has the torpedoed cruiser* Helena, *the first ship to enter the new dock. Next is the unfinished Dry Dock Three and above that the badly damaged destroyer* Shaw *in the sunken Floating Dry Dock YFD-2.* NA 80G-387577

FOLLOW UP REPORT DATED 21 DECEMBER, 1941

UNITED STATES PACIFIC FLEET
U. S. S. PENNSYLVANIA, Flagship

PEARL HARBOR, T. H., December 21, 1941.

Summary of damage sustained by ships of Pacific
Fleet from enemy attacks at Pearl Harbor, 7 December 1941

Ship DAMAGE INCURRED AND CAUSE	REPAIRS PROCEEDING AND PROPOSED
ARIZONA Sunk at berth. Aircraft torpedoes and heavy bombs exploding forward magazines.	Propose caisson the ship and make recommendation thereafter.
CALIFORNIA Sunk at berth. Two or more aircraft torpedoes and one large bomb hit amidships causing fire Part of A. A. Battery still manned and available	Propose caisson ships, repair to make watertight and return to mainland for complete repairs. (Tow.)
MARYLAND Bomb hit frame 14, penetrated and exploded, holing shell, decks and bulkheads forward of fr. 24.	NYPH repairing shell to make seaworthy. Decks, bulkheads to be completed at NYPS.
Nevada Heavy bombs, aircraft torpedoes and possibly a mine in channel. Beached across from Hospital Pt. A. A. batteries still manned and available.	Propose float ship (caisson may not be required), repair to make watertight and return to mainland yard for complete repairs. (Tow.)
OKLAHOMA Capsized at berth. Three or more aircraft torpedoes.	Propose right and float ship (caisson may not be required) repair to make watertight and return to mainland yard for complete repairs. (Tow.)
PENNSYLVANIA Bomb hit starboard side boat deck.	Repairs completed.
TENNESSEE One heavy bomb (dud) through turret top. One medium bomb aft cracked 14" gun. Fire aft 2nd deck due to heat from ARIZONA. Electrical circuits 2nd deck aft damaged by fire. [2]	NYPH repairing shell to make seaworthy and habitable. NYPS complete habilitation, renew gun, and watertight integrity.

WEST VIRGINIA
Sunk at berth. Four aircraft torpedoes and one heavy bomb hit. Considerable damage by fire. (Tow)

Propose caisson ship. Repair to make watertight and return to mainland for complete repairs.

HELENA
Forward fire and enginerooms flooded by aircraft torpedo. Some machinery badly damaged.

NYPH repairing shell to make sea worthy. Propose return to NYMI for complete repairs. (On two shafts).

HONOLULU
Bomb. Near miss frame 40, port. Flooded five magazines handling room II turret. Damaged electrical circuits in flooded spaces.

NYPH proceeding with complete repairs.

RALEIGH
One aircraft torpedo, and small bomb (dud) which penetrated three decks and ship's side aft. Forward engineroom and forward firerooms flooded and damaged.

NYPH to make repairs to make seaworthy when HONOLULU is undocked. Propose return to NYMI (on 2 shafts) for complete repairs.

CASSIN and DOWNES
Drydock No. 1 ahead of PENNSYLVANIA. Bomb hit DOWNES exploding her torpedo warheads and causing serious fire. CASSIN knocked off blocks and fell over on DOWNES.

Propose upright, patch and float out CASSIN for possible repairs to return to full or limited service. Further recommendations later.

SHAW
Bombed while docked on floating drydock. Forward part of ship and floating dock badly damaged.

Propose float and reconstruct for ward part return to mainland yard for complete repairs, possibly under own power.

OGLALA
Sunk by aircraft torpedo and possibly near miss by bomb.

Salvage doubtful. Recommendation later.

UTAH
Capsized and sunk by aircraft torpedoes. [3]

Recommendations resalvage and repairs later.

CURTISS
Enemy plane out of control flew into crane mast. One bomb exploded in hangar space. All radio equipment destroyed. Ship entirely seaworthy.

NYPH, replace radio and effect necessary repairs to hangar space.

VESTAL
Bomb hit aft holing shell. Beached.

Repairs proceeding by own repair force. May not require docking.

PREFACE

FROM PEARL HARBOR: WHY, HOW, FLEET SALVAGE AND FINAL APPRAISAL
BY VICE ADMIRAL HOMER N. WALLIN

Ever since the successful completion of Fleet Salvage at Pearl Harbor in 1942, I have frequently been importuned to write a comprehensive report of that gratifying outcome of the Pearl Harbor disaster. However, in view of other work and avocations, and especially because of the immensity of the task, if it was to be authentic, I was negatively inclined,-at least until a more propitious time.

It was not until the early part of 1965 that the Director of Naval History, Rear Admiral Ernest M. Eller, U.S. Navy, Retired, persuaded me to take the pen in hand. His argument was that the Pearl Harbor Salvage Operation should be made a matter of historical record, and could in addition serve as a ready reference book for any future work of that nature; also that he knew of no other person who could write a reasonably authentic account with the data and information still available. So, in a way, I was "Hobson's Choice" if the work was to be done at all.

Fortunately, I had rather complete files covering the work, inasmuch as through the years I had become some sort of "pack rat" on technical records pertaining to my specialty of ship design, construction, and repair. Although I had turned over most of these files and photographs to the Bureau of Ships of the Navy Department, they were returned to me when I agreed to undertake the writing job.

Despite the fact that nearly a quarter of a century has elapsed since the event a great portion of the impact of my experiences at Pearl Harbor and the salvage work is still quite clear in my memory. At that time I was Material Officer on the staff of Vice Admiral William S. Pye, commander of the Battle Force of the Pacific Fleet. Therefore the handling of the damage sustained by ships of the fleet immediately became of first concern to me as an existent responsibility. Within a short time I was relieved of all other duties and ordered to full time work as Fleet Salvage Officer.

Ever since those days I have at times pondered the events which occurred before and after the Japanese air raid, and have often wished that the American people might have obtained a more correct understanding of the "Whys and Wherefores." It bothered me greatly when, following the attack, so many Americans and so much of our news media took a "Who dunnit" attitude toward the disaster and seemed to be more anxious to blame military negligence and inattention to duty rather than to gain a right appraisal of the panorama of events. Perhaps it is an element of human nature to accuse individuals and to find scapegoats whenever distasteful events occur.

Consequently, with the knowledge of one who was on the scene at the time, and of one willing to undertake a vast amount of research from official and other sources, I agreed to proceed with the salvage write-up,—provided I could at the same time pinpoint the situation which pertained in the fleet and in our relations with Japan at that period.

In order to do this with some semblance of authenticity I have reviewed a goodly portion of the testimony given before the Roberts Commission in December 1941 and January 1942, the Hart Investigation in 1944, the Hewitt Inquiry of 1945, the Naval Court of Inquiry of 1944, the Army Investigation in 1944, the Congressional Investigation of 1945, and the State Department releases published in 1953. This latter has been drawn upon freely as it is the official report of the United States' Foreign Policy from 1931 to 1941 inclusive, and is entitled "Peace and War." Also I have read a considerable number of books and reports on the Pearl Harbor attack, some written by Japanese participants. Virtually all of this information has the advantage of hindsight so far as evaluation is concerned and is therefore of inestimable value in piecing together a momentous event which requires retrospection as a primary ingredient.

Homer N. Wallin, Ensign, graduated from the Naval Academy class of 1917. After World War I he earned a Master's Degree for Naval Architecture and Marine Engineering at MIT in 1921. Prior to 7 December 1941 he was material officer on the staff of Commander Battle Force, Pacific Fleet. On 9 January 1942, now Capt. Wallin, was appointed Salvage Officer-in-Command of the Salvage Division, Navy Yard Pearl Harbor. USN

The Pearl Harbor episode brought forth multitudinous opinions and convictions, some highly emotional and some pertaining to personalities. Others were based on cold logic and technical facts. In the over-all we must all agree that the event which set off a cruel and bloody war is fraught with many lessons and guideposts for the future. I have endeavored to pinpoint a few of these which are particularly worthwhile, and have striven honestly to be fair to all persons who were involved in any way either before, during, or after the event.

The final appraisal of the Pearl Harbor attack is given in Chapter XV. It reveals indisputably that the Japanese government made a great mistake in attacking Pearl Harbor, as it did also in other aspects of the struggle for dominance in the Pacific. There is now no doubt that the attack resulted from the gross unpreparedness of the American military forces, as was attested by the 1945 statement of President Truman and the 1965 statement of Admiral Nimitz.

I am indebted to the Director of Naval History and his staff for invaluable assistance throughout, and of course for general guidance. That office has furnished much valuable data and information such as official damage reports from the Bureau of Ships, descriptions of rehabilitation work from various naval shipyards, pertinent excerpts from ships' logs, and so forth.

Also, I am most grateful to the Commandant of the Thirteenth Naval District, Rear Admiral William E. Ferrall, U.S. Navy, and his staff for much assistance, including office space and equipment, some secretarial work, and a widespread spirit of cooperation and helpfulness.

HOMER N. WALLIN
Vice Admiral, USN (Retired)

MAJOR PARTICIPANTS OF THE
PEARL HARBOR SALVAGE OPERATION

FLEET ADMIRAL CHESTER WILLIAM NIMITZ was born in 1885 near a hotel built by his retired sea captain grandfather in Fredericksburg, Texas. The former hotel is now home to the National Museum of the Pacific War. Nimitz wanted to go to West Point, but with no appointments available at the time he was selected for an appointment to the Naval Academy in 1901.

He left high school to enter the Academy Class of 1905. It was many years later, after he had become a Fleet Admiral that he was awarded his high school diploma. At the academy he was an excellent student and graduated with distinction—seventh in a class of 114. He was an athlete and stroke the crew in his first class year.

After graduation he joined the USS Ohio and cruised in her to the Far East. In January 1907, after two years' sea duty, then required by law, he was commissioned Ensign and took command of the gunboat USS Panay, which was sunk by the Japanese in China in 1937). He then commanded the USS Decatur and was court-martialed for grounding her, an obstacle in his career which he overcame.

He returned to the United States in 1907 and was ordered to submarine duty, the branch in which he spent a large part of his subsequent sea duty. His first submarine was the USS Plunger, he later commanded the USS Snapper, USS Narwahl and USS Skipjack until 1912.

He had one year in command of the Atlantic Submarine Flotilla before coming ashore in 1913 for duty in connection with building diesel engines and was sent to Germany and Belgium to study engines at their diesel plants. With this experience he served as Executive Officer and Engineering Officer on the USS Maumee until 1917 when he was assigned as Aide and Chief of Staff to COMSUBLANT. He served in that assignment during World War One.

In September 1918 he came ashore to duty in the office of the Chief of Naval Operations and was a member of the Board of Submarine Design. His first sea duty in large ships came in 1919 when he had one year's duty as Executive Officer on the USS South Carolina. After that he continued his duty in submarines in Pearl Harbor as Commanding Officer of the USS Chicago and COMSUBDIV Fourteen. In 1922 he was assigned as a student at the Naval War College, and upon graduation served as Chief of Staff to Commander Battle Forces and later Commander in Chief, U.S. Fleet.

In 1926 he became the first Professor of Naval Sciences and Tactics for the ROTC unit at the University of California at Berkeley. After three years, in 1929 he again had sea duty in the submarine service as Commander Submarine Division Twenty for two years and then went ashore to command the USS Rigel and decommissioned destroyers at the naval base in San Diego. In 1933 he commanded the heavy cruiser USS Augusta, which served mostly as flagship of the Asiatic Fleet. In 1935 he served three years as Assistant Chief of the Bureau of Navigation. His next sea command was in flag rank as Commander Cruiser Division Two and then as Commander Battle Division One in 1939, when he was appointed as Chief of the Bureau of Navigation for four years.

In December 1941 he was designated Commander in Chief, U.S. Pacific Fleet. On October 7, 1943 he was increased to Commander in Chief PacFlt and Pacific Ocean Areas in which he led Allied forces to final victory in 1945. On Dec. 19, 1944, he was advanced to the newly created rank of Fleet Admiral and was one of the Allied signatories to the Japanese surrender.

On Dec. 15, 1945, he became Chief of Naval Operations for two years and for the next few years he was special Assistant to the Secretary of the Navy in the Western Sea Frontier and as a roving ambassador for the United Nations.

In his last years he was an honorary vice president and later honorary president of the Naval Historical Foundation and served eight years as a regent of the University of California. He was involved in raising funds to restore the Japanese battleship Mikasa, Admiral Togo's flagship, which was damaged at the Battle of Tsushima in 1905.

Admiral Nimitz died in 1966.

On the left is Rear Admiral William Furlong, Commandant of the Pearl Harbor Navy Yard; center is Admiral Chester Nimitz, Commander in Chief, Pacific Ocean Fleet; and Captain Homer Wallin, Pearl Harbor Navy Yard's Salvage Division Commander after the attack. Shipyard photographer Tai Sing Loo is filming in the background. May 1942. USN NH 500002

VICE ADMIRAL HOMER NORMAN WALLIN was born in Washburn, North Dakota, on Dec. 6, 1893. Following a brief attendance at the University of North Dakota and a year in the state's National Guard, he was appointed to the U.S. Naval Academy in 1913. He served on the *USS New Jersey* (BB-16). In September 1918 he was transferred to the Navy's Construction Corps and was sent to the Massachusetts Institute of Technology for postgraduate education in Naval Architecture.

After receiving a Master of Science degree in 1921 he served for four years in the New York Navy Yard and was assigned to the Bureau of Construction and Repair in Washington DC in 1925 for four years. Over the following decade he had successive tours at the Mare Island and Philadelphia navy yards and at the Bureau of Construction and Repair (redesignated the Bureau of Ships in 1940).

In 1941, Captain Wallin became Material Officer for the Commander, Battle Force, U.S. Pacific Fleet, and was serving in that position when the Pearl Harbor attack occurred. Early in 1942 he was placed in charge of the Pearl Harbor Navy Yard's Salvage Division. Through most of the year he directed the salvage operation. From November 1942 to August 1943 he was Force Maintenance Officer of the South Pacific Force, and then spent a few months at the Bureau of Ships. Now

a Rear Admiral, Wallin was Supervisor of Shipbuilding and Inspector of Ordnance at Seattle and Commander of the Naval Station in Tacoma, Washington, beginning in October 1943.

Following the war, he commanded the Philadelphia and Norfolk naval shipyards. In February 1951 he became Chief of the Bureau of Ships, a post he held until August 1953, when he took command of the Puget Sound Navy Shipyard. He retired from active service in May 1955 and was simultaneously advanced to rank of Vice Admiral on the basis of his combat awards.

Admiral Wallin died on March 6, 1984 and is buried in Portland, Oregon.

REAR ADMIRAL WILLIAM REA FURLONG, commander of the Pearl Harbor Navy Yard, was born in Allen Township, Pennsylvania in 1881. His paternal grandfather was a coal operator who used his own towboats to ship coal to Pittsburgh and New Orleans. His maternal grandfather was the son of Capt. George Grant, a soldier in the Revolutionary War. George Grant and the grandfather of Ulysses S. Grant were brothers. Furlong's father was a steamboat captain.

Furlong graduated from the Roscoe Public School in 1896 and earned his teaching degree from the Normal School in California, Pennsylvania (now California University of Pennsylvania). He taught for two years and was then recommended for the Naval Academy in 1901. President Theodore Roosevelt handed him his diploma from the academy. After 36 years in the navy, he was appointed Chief of the Bureau of Ordnance with the rank of Rear Admiral by President Franklin D. Roosevelt in August 1937.

His naval career took him to South America, the Philippines, China and Japan. During World War One, he served as a gunnery officer on the battleship *Ramillies*, which patrolled the North Sea and later was stationed in London Admiralty.

At the end of the war and prior to signing the peace agreement, Commander Furlong was sent to Berlin to inspect German ordnance plants.

Besides serving on cruisers and battleships, including the *West Virginia*, he was also commander of a division of destroyers. Furlong served as Chief of the Bureau of Ordnance in Washington DC until his retirement. He died in 1976 at age 95 and is buried in Arlington National Cemetery.

In order to re-supply ships that used coal the huge U.S. Naval Coaling Station at Pearl Harbor was built in 1909. Before World War One, coal was the main fuel for ships. After the war the navy began conversion to oil. Looking West on October 13, 1941, the now obsolete Coaling Station was used only as a mooring and fueling from the near-by oil tanks. Above the docks The Naval Hospital grounds can be seen. In 1942 a large portion of the coal docks close to the Hospital would be dismantled and Dry Dock Four would be built in its place. NA 80G-182284

Kenneth Knutson
A-10-519-14 street
CHA #3
Hon., T.H.

HONOLULU, HAWAII
AUG 3
5-PM
1943

Damaged by Sea Water

VIA AIR MAIL

Miss Margretta Smith
838-8th street apt #1
Bremerton
Washington

Dear Margaret,
Wrote this letter on board
a ship we are building
— details in the next
envelope if you get one.
Love Kenneth

Photograph of incompleted
Ship (Utah on)
Pearl Harbor,
Hawaii

PEARL HARBOR SHIPYARD HISTORY

"His Majesty . . . grants . . . United States the exclusive right to enter the harbor of Pearl Harbor . . . and to establish . . . a coaling and repair station for the use of vessels of the United States, and to that end the United States may improve the entrance of said harbor and do all other things needful to the purpose aforesaid."

This grant, concluded at a convention with King Kalakaua of Hawaii on Dec. 6, 1884, and proclaimed Nov. 9, 1887, probably contained the first mention of Pearl Harbor. From the humble beginning, the harbor, then known as Pearl River, grew into one of the mightiest modern-day naval bases.

Pearl River comes from the Hawaiian name, "wai momi," water of the pearl, or Pearl Harbor, for this was the only place in the Hawaiian Islands where the pearly oyster was found. In the early days, sandalwood gathered from the mountain forests, was brought to Pearl River, where it was measured and shipped to Chinese ports.

A coaling station was established at Honolulu during the Civil War, but was practically abandoned in 1870, due to the policy then of supplying all "men of war" with full sail power, and requiring the use of sail.

Several years later Maj. Gen. J. M. Schofield and Lt. Col. B. S. Alexander, under confidential instructions, visited Honolulu to inspect the defensive capacity of Oahu. They submitted a report recommending that the United States obtain a cession of Pearl Harbor, together with four or five miles back, and suggesting that it might be deeded free of cost to the United States in return for allowing Hawaiian sugar to enter duty free.

The first recorded naval engagement at Pearl Harbor was in 1794, when King Kalanikupule of Oahu, with the aid of Captain Brown of the British ship *Jackall*, gained a decisive victory Kaeo, a would-be usurper. In the final battle, which was fought on the field between Kalauao and Aiea, Kaeo was killed.

At the outbreak of the Spanish-American War in 1898, the United States had but one foreign coal depot, that at Honolulu, which consisted of a dilapidated shed on rented ground with a capacity of 1,000 tons.

It was not until 1905 that Pearl Harbor was finally selected as the site for a large naval base in the Pacific. The California congressional delegation urged that Alameda be chosen as the site, while Hawaii's delegate, Prince Jonah Kuhio Kalanianaole, maintained that Pearl Harbor be selected. The settlement of the controversy was left up to President Theodore Roosevelt, who after being so ably convinced by the Prince, chose Pearl Harbor as the naval outpost in the Pacific.

Four years later an act provided for the construction of a dry dock at Pearl Harbor, with a limit cost of two million dollars. Work on the dock started in September 1909, and it was scheduled to be completed in three years.

The dock, when practically completed, was wrecked by underground pressure (an Hawaiian legend has it that the "shark god" wrecked the dry dock because the necessary sacrifice was not made) on Feb. 17, 1913. The Secretary of the Navy termed it "the naval disaster of the year." No work was done on this dock for the remainder of the year, pending an investigation. A civil engineer of international reputation investigated the disaster and recommended that it be rebuilt. Work on what became Dry Dock #1 began again during the latter part of 1914, and it was completed five years later, with the first ship entering on Oct. 1, 1919.

Just before Christmas in 1911, the channel having been practically completed, the *USS California* entered Pearl Harbor and anchored off of the navy yard. Being the first large vessel to pass through the dredged channel, her trip was made a gala occasion and many local dignitaries took passage.

Realizing little then what a great role Pearl Harbor would later play, but realizing fully the value of the site, a "Special Board of Inspection of Naval Bases on the Pacific Coast" recommended in October 1919, that a first-class naval base, capable of handling the entire United States fleet in time of war, should be immediately developed at Pearl Harbor as a strategic necessity.

Shortly afterward, a navy collier arrived with a cargo of machinery, tools and portable wooden buildings used in France during World War One, from which buildings were erected.

On Sept. 29, 1916, the first official radio message was sent to Washington form the high-power station at Pearl Harbor. A congratulatory reply was received on the same day, just 33 minutes after the first call was made. An increasing number of ships were being overhauled in the yard through the years.

The year of 1940 was marked by the greatest activity in new construction and development ever experienced up to that time. The Pacific fleet had been moved to Pearl Harbor in 1940 from the West Coast. Hundreds of acres of land were purchased for the construction of housing facilities for the increased naval and civilian personnel. In one year from June 1940, the civilian force of the yard was more than doubled. Nearly 40 percent of the increased number were recruited or appointed from the mainland.

Five days after the Japanese attack, Rear Admiral William R. Furlong, who was commander of minecraft, battle force of the U.S. Pacific Fleet was appointed the first commandant of the navy yard.

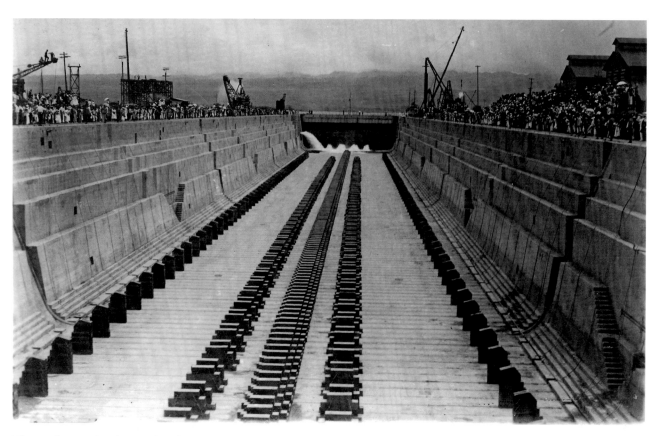

The newly completed 1002-foot long Dry Dock One on opening day, August 21, 1919. This was the second dry dock built in this location. The first one was destroyed in 1913 when underground water pressure caused the walls of the dry dock to collapse into a pile of ruble, destroying two years of work. It was rebuilt with a radical new design and a Hawaiian blessing. The battleship Pennsylvania *and the destroyers* Cassin *and* Downes *were in the dock at the time of the attack.* USN

By an Act of Congress on May 13, 1908 the establishment of the Navy Yard Pearl Harbor, T. H., was authorized. Expenditures of about $6.2 million were allotted for dredging an entrance into Pearl Harbor, construction of machine shops and a 150-ton floating crane, quarters, storehouses a hospital and a dry dock. This photo of the newly constructed Navy Yard and Dry Dock One looking east was taken by Tai Sing Loo in 1919. PHPC

Born in Hawaii of Chinese parents Tai Sing Loo became a well known commercial photographer. In 1919 he climbed a 720-foot radio tower in Pearl Harbor and took panoramic views of the harbor. The photos so impressed the officers of the yard that he was appointed the official photographer of the Pearl Harbor Navy Yard. He always wore his trademark pith helmet and drove his red "Put-Put" three-wheel scooter around the yard on assignments. EA

Seen at the repair basin of the Pearl Harbor Navy Yard are the piers with heavy lift cranes and the dry docks. The large buildings in the industrial section (center) are repair and manufacturing shops, electrical shops, a foundry and other facilities necessary for the refitting and maintenance of ships of the fleet. The Army's air base, Hickam Field is on the left. Note the narrow channel entrance (top) from the Pacific Ocean. NA 80G-182279

View looking South on October13, 1941 at the Submarine Base and the large tank farm for storage of fuel oil for the ships based at Pearl Harbor. Five of the storage tanks have already been painted in camouflage. The Large U-shaped building (center) is Headquarters, for the Commander-in-Chief Pacific Fleet, Admiral Husband E. Kimmel. NA 80G-182880

The new Ten-Ten Dock
as it looked in 1933. After
Dry Dock One had been
completed a wharf was built
adjacent to the dock the following year. The wharf was
originally 1010-feet long and
in 1933, even though it had
been extended another 800
feet, it was still called Ten-
Ten Dock. It also became the
permanent mooring place
for the Flagship of the Fleet,
the USS Pennsylvania. *The
cruiser* Helena *with the old
minelayer* Oglala *alongside,
were docked here on the day
of the attack.* PHPC

*The huge 200-ton capacity
hammerhead crane at 166-
feet high was second only to
the Aloha Tower as the tall-
est structure in the Hawaiian Islands in 1941. It stood
at Berth 12 in the navy yard
and was erected in 1935
at a cost of $423,000. The
mammoth crane's lifting
capabilities were essential
in assisting the salvage and
repair efforts of the heavily
damaged battleships following the attack.* PHPC

Pearl Harbor as it was on May 17, 1938. After six weeks of extensive training exercises ships of the Pacific Fleet anchored in Pearl Harbor for provisions and liberty prior to sailing back to the West Coast. In the fall of 1939 Europe was at war. Following fleet exercises in Pacific waters in the spring of 1940, President Franklin D. Roosevelt ordered the Fleet to be permanently home-ported in Hawaii due to the serious crisis evolving with Japan. NA 80G-184595

Flooding of the nearly completed Dry Dock Two is tested for the first time. The light cruiser USS Raleigh CL-7 is seen in Dry Dock One receiving major upgrades. Just beyond the Raleigh at 1010 dock the training ship USS Utah AG-16 is moored followed by the USS Argonne AG -31 at the end of the dock. PHP

On November 8, 1941 work continues on the nearly completed 1,000-foot long Dry Dock Two. At the right is the battleship Arizona in Dry Dock One for repairs received in a minor collision with the Oklahoma during night maneuvers on October 22. This is the last known photo of Arizona before she was destroyed on December 7, 1941. NA

After a tow of 44 days and 4,771 miles from New Orleans, Louisiana, the Floating Dry Dock YFD-2 arrived at Pearl Harbor on August 23, 1940. The dry dock is surrounded by navy yard tugs that will move it to its permanent area off Hospital Point. The dry dock was capable of docking ships as large as cruisers. NA 80G-411134

In the floating dry dock, YFD-2 on January 6, 1941, are the submarine Stingray *and a repair barge YR-21. The floating dry dock was permanently situated near the navy yard and Hospital Point. On December 7 the destroyer* Shaw *was berthed in the dock. Both would be heavily damaged during the attack.* PHP

Standing out to the open sea two destroyers are seen passing through the open anti-submarine nets that span the main channel entrance. Standing sentinel over the entrance to Pearl Harbor is Fort Kamahamaha. The hangers and runways of the sprawling U.S. Army Air Force Base, Hickam Field is situated above the harbor channel. Ford Island Naval Air Station and Battleship Row is over to the far left with the Pearl Harbor Navy Yard complex near the center of this photograph taken just 6 weeks before the attack. NA 80G-451112

PEARL HARBOR SALVAGE

The pictures on these pages, showing the resurrection of wrecked American warships at Pearl Harbor, represent one of the most remarkable feats of marine engineering ever attempted. They also give evidence that many U. S. battleships, shattered by bomb and torpedo on Dec. 7, 1941 and subsequently refloated and rebuilt, have been sent back to the war as better fighting ships than they were when sunk. Of the 19 ships damaged on that fateful day, 14 have already been repaired and sent to sea under their own power. Three of the remaining five, the *Arizona, Oklahoma* and *Utah,* are at present undergoing salvage operations. The remaining two, the destroyers *Cassin* and *Downes,* were damaged beyond economical repair but more than 50% of their equipment has been utilized in new ship construction. This record has bettered anything the Navy dared hope when it made a preliminary survey of the smoking ruins a few hours after the attack.

The record was achieved by the use of imagination and a good deal of hard work. The *Oklahoma,* for example, lay with about a third of her bottom exposed and sloping at a 30° angle. First a scale model was built and mounted in exactly the same position as the capsized ship. Divers studied this model before going down into the oily muck below-decks to close compartments. When this was done, steel cables anchored to the ship's hull and powered by electric motors set up on nearby Ford Island, slowly drew the 29,000-ton ship over until she was upright (*see opposite page*). Next, salvage men will go to work on her as they have on the already completed *Nevada, West Virginia* and *California*—first removing as much weight as possible, then sealing breaches, refloating the ship and removing it to drydock to be cleaned, rewired and rebuilt with the latest equipment.

The men who made these transformations possible are the divers, burners, pumpers, and other specialists who worked below and above the surface. They struggled in incredible confusion and filth, facing the danger of deadly hydrogen sulfide gas with which most of the compartments were filled, to put the ships back to sea. Their work was as heroic as that performed by seamen of the Pacific Fleet on the terrible Sunday morning when war began.

Oil-covered diver stands on deck of *Arizona.* He has been working down in the inky, cluttered compartments below, where the sense of touch is his only aid to movement.

CONTINUED ON NEXT PAGE

Life magazine did a photo spread featuring the Pearl Harbor salvage operation.

Pearl Harbor Leads Yards In War Bond Sales

Leading all other Navy yards in the U.S. in the purchase of war bonds, Pearl Harbor workmen have bought a total of $26,-795,550.00 since the war bond office was established here in early February, 1942.

Today the war bond office is selling more than a million dollars worth of bonds a month through the payroll deduction plan and cash sales. In twenty-one months of its existence, six successful drives have been conducted, during which Pearl Harbor's men and women have bought bonds.

On Pearl Harbor Day last year, the employees of the Yard remembered Pearl Harbor by storming the war bond office, purchasing $2,777,831 worth of bonds, leading all yards for cash sales on that day. Six months later, June 19, 1943, the Filipino employees rallied to commemorate "Rizal Day" and bought $33,050 worth of bonds. Hardly a month had passed when on July 4 the employees again jammed the war bond booths around the Yard, $1,023,262.50 being the total cash sales for the day. Three months later on Labor Day, September 6, the sales amounted to $93,555. On September 13, the Chinese gathered to uphold the memory of Chinese Full Moon Day and $74,181.25 was placed into these government securities. On September 27 the Yard Negroes staged a Negro Victory Bond Drive with $36,-035 sold in bonds.

A newspaper article from 1943 about the Pearl Harbor workmen leading all navy yards in war bond sales.

COORDINATOR FOR WAR BONDS
90 Church St.
New York, N. Y.

to:

Mr. Harry Sternberg
1830 Prospect Ave.
Bronx, New York.

Greetings

FROM PEARL HARBOR

Congratulations on your great Navy Day record of War Bond sales. Pearl Harbor sends foremost greetings with its best wishes for an equally outstanding record on your "Remember Pearl Harbor Day". Every War Bond purchased in honor of Pearl Harbor Day will carry with it special tribute to the fighting men of the land, sea and air, and do special honor in memory of our heroic defenders here a year ago and *this we dedicate with the blessing of us all at Pearl Harbor.*

December 7, 1942   /s/ W. R. FURLONG
Rear Admiral, U.S.N.
Commandant Navy Yard
Pearl Harbor

IN CASE YOU ARE WONDERING.... Why the attached envelope is "double addressed" - - here's the answer....

WE wanted you to have your Pearl Harbor Envelope dated December 7, 1942 just as quickly as possible....So that your Bond, the Commandant's message and the Envelope would all reach you at the same time.
Postal regulations require an address on every piece of mail actually cancelled and mailed. To save you from waiting, your envelope was mailed December 7, 1942 in Pearl Harbor and air mailed via Clipper to the War Bond Office where it was promptly readdressed to you. Otherwise it would have been delayed. When you stop and realize that the envelope that you are now holding has just been flown 4900 miles from Pearl Harbor to you....That the message attached to your Bond is a Personal Greeting directly from the Commandant of the Pearl Harbor area and that the War Bond itself was purchased as a remembrance of last December...You can sense a Bond between yourself and Pearl Harbor that rings with a personal dedication.

This War Bond purchased on December 7, 1942 will pay higher dividends than the 2.9% interest....The satisfaction you must have thru its timely purchase will make it priceless.

WAR BOND COMMITTEE

11

U.S. NAVY YARD · WE KEEP THEM FIT TO FIGHT · PEARL HARBOR NAVY YARD · PEARL HARBOR HAWAII U.S.A.

A member of your family, as you know, is an employee at Pearl Harbor Navy Yard.

The working force here is busily engaged in the repair of damaged ships to the end that our Navy may never want for ships or material to do battle. The member of your family will assist to make victory sure. We are proud to have your family represented here.

The enclosure is sent to you in order that you may exhibit it as a tribute to the member of your family who is doing duty in promoting the mission of this Navy Yard in support of the Pacific Fleet.

WILLIAM R. FURLONG
Rear Admiral, U. S. N.
Commandant

WORKING at PEARL HARBOR

The PEARL HARBOR BANNER was the weekly newspaper of CHA III covering all events to boost morale of the civilian workers. On the cover of the BANNER is the coveted Army and Navy "E" pennant awarded to the Pearl Harbor Navy Yard for outstanding work and production for the national war effort. It was presented to Rear Admiral William R. Furlong, Commandant of the Yard, by James V. Forrestal, Under Secretary of the Navy on September 6, 1942. The "E" pennant was then raised over the yard and each worker was given a blue and gold "E" lapel pin to wear. Subsequently the Navy yard received a total of five "E" awards during the war. NA

With new defense job opportunities open to the local population, the skilled and unskilled worker among them joined in the common war effort. Defense workers living in Honolulu or other towns on the Island car pooled, took the bus or rode the train to the Main gate to report in for their shift. A half hour later workers of the relieved shift would board the same buses and trains for the ride home. PHP

Residents of Civilian Housing Area III traveled to and from the Navy Yard by foot, bicycle or using special transports nicknamed "Leaping Tuna" that operated on a regular 24-hour schedule. The Leaping Tunas were actually open trailers pulled by a tractor through the yard for workers transportation. It moved at a snail's pace and never stopped. Passengers simply leaped on or off at their destination. PHP

After the attack the most urgent work ahead was to repair the damaged ships and refloat the sunken ships. Huge numbers of civilian engineers, metal workers, carpenters, machinists, electricians and other tradesmen were needed. Thousands of defense workers were recruited from the 48 States to work at the Navy Yard. In 1941 civilian employment at the Navy Yard was 7,500; by June 1943 there were over 26,000 employees working twenty-four hours a day in three eight hour shifts. PHP

With the great influx of workers, housing was a serious problem. In the spring of 1941, Civilian Housing Area III, popularly called CHA-3, began building on 192 acres just outside the Navy Yard's Main Gate. It would become a city of over 10,000 men and bigger than many American towns. It consisted of over 2,000 housing units, a fire station, two post offices, theaters, churches, restaurants, stores, barber shops and numerous recreation facilities. PHP

A work crew of sailor's at the Navy Yard Foundry pour molten brass into molds. The brass was recovered from damaged ships and expended shell casings. The ingots of brass and other reclaimed metals are sorted and stacked for shipment to factories on the Mainland for reuse in the war effort. NA 80G-302458

After the attack, destroyers Cassin and Downes were reported as total losses. Inspection of the two hulks revealed that nearly all machinery, boilers (above) and electrical equipment were in good condition. The Navy decided the hulls to be scrapped and all usable equipment and fittings saved and shipped stateside and installed in new hulls building at Mare Island Navy Yard. The 37-ton stern section of each ship, with their names carefully preserved on them, were also saved. PHP

Each man of the cleaning crew had to wear a tank suit with knee-high rubber boots. After recovery from the ships magazines, all ammunition, projectiles, powder cans and powder bags were washed down with a high pressure steam hose. This was followed with a caustic solution spray to cut the oil and finally fresh water hosing for a clean and finished job. All restored ordnance was sent to Magazine Loch and stored for future use against the enemy. NA

The cleaning detail found that all materials and equipment recovered from the interiors of the sunken ships was covered with fuel oil. Everything that could be saved, from bunks, safes, galley equipment, lockers, mess tables and benches, ladders and even light bulbs, to name some items, went through the same cleaning process as ordnance. All reuseable items salvaged were put into storage for availability when needed by other ships. NA

A serious hazard that was life threatening to men working in partially unwatered compartments was the accumulation of gases formed by the decomposition of various organic materials. After an incident on February 7, 1942, that cost the lives of two men working on the Nevada, it became mandatory for all men working inside the bowels of the sunken ships to wear the special Mark III breathing mask adapted for use in toxic spaces. Ship's crew wore coveralls and rubber boots allowing them to wade in oily water when working in compartments. NA

A competent dive crew is important in assisting a diver in accomplishing difficult tasks in the most trying of conditions. One tender "feels" the diver at his work by signals on the hand line and can tell instantly when he is in trouble. A second diver was always on duty if needed. Other crucial work by the dive team involved communications, handling the lifelines, telephone cable, air hoses and compressors. NA

The life of a diver depends on the proper functioning of his gear and he treats his outfit with the greatest respect. A diving suit weighs about 200 pounds. The helmet tipped the scales at 56 to 64 pounds each, the weight belt is 84 pounds, the dress 19 pounds and the shoes at 35 pounds a pair. The cost of a complete diving outfit including phones and lines in 1943 dollars was about $1,500. NA

Sailors apply a protective coat of grease to preserve one of the 14-inch guns salvaged from the Arizona. The guns were reconditioned and saved for future use in two coastal defense batteries then under construction by the Army to protect Oahu's shores.
NA 80G-302463

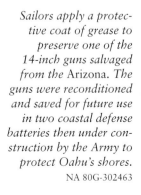

Two Navy Yard workers are preparing a 14-inch gun slide from the sunken USS Arizona for storage. Of Arizona's four main 14-inch turrets; #3 and #4 aft were saved and designated for use as coastal artillery batteries to be built on Oahu. Forward, turret #2 was partially scraped with guns removed. Turret #1 was never recovered and remains on the ship to this day. NA 80G-302456

Heavily laden with barnacles and soon to be scrapped are two of Arizona's 5-inch/51 broadside guns that were underwater for only three months before removal from the wreckage on May 10, 1942. Tied up across the pier is the salvaged hulk of the destroyer Cassin. NA 80G-41625

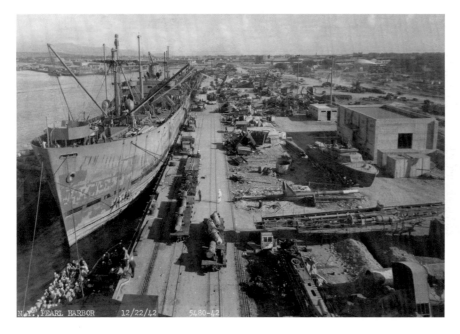

By the end of the first year of war in Hawaii over a million pounds of scrap had been salvaged and shipped to the Mainland. Included were steel scrap, brass and copper, manila rope, rubber scrap and other needed materials. All reusable scrap had to be sorted into separate piles for loading. At Berth 23 in the Pearl Harbor Navy Yard, the SS Malcom Stewart, a new Liberty ship, loads scrap for shipment to the mainland. PHPC

At the Navy Yard women continued to work in important office positions as secretaries, typists, telephone operators and clerical workers. But due to a critical shortage of men in the labor force, local women were hired and trained as mechanics, truck drivers, drill press operators, storekeepers, welders and even as fire fighters, to fill work normally held by men. In 1942 there were over 1,400 local Hawaiian women employed in Federal Civil Service jobs alone. PHP

Under the watchful eye of their Foreman K.T. Soe, far left, as he directs a three-women salvage team using acetylene cutting torches working atop one of the piles of scrap metal recovered from the sunken ships. Cutting up the larger sections of metal for easier handling and transporting are; 2nd from left, Dorothy Waiwaiole, Lilly Arcia and Victoria Yomes. Women in Hawaii continued to join the workforce in unprecedented numbers throughout the war years. PHP

Hard hat divers wearing rubberized suits worked under extreme and often hazardous conditions. Visibility was almost non-existent in the fouled and murky waters where everything was coated with black fuel oil. Floating debris, torn metal wreckage with sharp edges in compartments sometimes upside down, were an added danger. Amazingly in over 5,000 dives adding up to more than 20,000 hours of working under water by Navy and civilian divers throughout the salvage operation there was only one fatality. NA

Hard hat divers in cumbersome dive suits could not work in tight or hard to reach sections. The problem was solved with the introduction of an underwater mask designed for shallow dives. The new dive mask was converted from an Army Mark III field gas mask fitted with an airline and phone lines (above). A diver could only stay underwater for very short periods as he had no insulation against the chilly water and water can be very cold, even in the tropics as any diver will tell you. An oil covered diver (right) after emerging from a powder magazine compartment of the Arizona. NA

December 7, 1942, one year after the Arizona was destroyed, a memorial service was conducted on board led by Rear Adm. William R. Furlong (center), commandant Navy Yard Pearl Harbor, to honor and pay tribute to the ship and her crew lost that fateful day. Six days earlier the Arizona was stricken from the official register of U.S. Navy vessels. There are those today that believe the Arizona is still in commission, but ships sunk in action are not de-commissioned, instead they are stricken from the Navy register. Only ships on the official register are in commission. PHP

In January 1942, at the Oahu Cemetery in Nuuanu Valley, two brothers, James T. Lewis, MM2/c and Robert M. Lewis, MM2/c decorate the grave of their brother John E. Lewis, MM2/c who was killed in action on board the battleship USS California on December 7, 1941. The Navy was over whelmed with the high number of casualties, most of which could not be identified and were buried as unknowns. The Navy buried 328 bodies in its plot at Oahu cemetery, 18 at Kaneohe NAS and 204 in a new naval cemetery which it established at the time at Red Hill near Aiea.
NA 80G-61506

THE PEARL HARBOR FLEET SALVAGE

In less than two hours on December 7, 1941, a vital part of the United States Pacific Fleet lay in a shambles in the waters of Pearl Harbor. The sinking of five of the eight battleships present plus damage to the other three, as well as the sinking and destruction of many other combatants, left the United States Pacific Fleet in a vulnerable position. The immediate problem confronting the Navy was the difficult task of rescue and recovery. Also it may not be able to fully protect Hawaii and the Pearl Harbor Navy Base from further attack and more importantly unable to take offensive action against the powerful Imperial Japanese Navy for months on end. The smoke of battle had hardly cleared away and the enormous job of salvage and harbor clearance began. Despite the disheartening sight of a harbor filled with sunken, beached, burned and damaged ships, there were some positive aspects to the salvage work that lay ahead.

The shops, dry docks, cranes and repair facilities of the navy yard were virtually undamaged.

Key experienced naval officers and their staffs, many already stationed at Pearl Harbor, were assigned to support the salvage operations for the duration.

Naval and civilian engineers currently working on naval construction projects in Hawaii were available, to provide immediate technical support and workforce to assist in the myriad problems of the salvage operations.

Major contractors working for the navy in 1941 were the Hawaiian Dredging Company of Honolulu, the Turner Construction Company and the Pacific Bridge Company whose expertise in the use of underwater concrete would be invaluable.

The first order of work was the immediate repair of the lightly damaged ships, returning them to service as quickly as possible. While this work was in progress, work had also begun on some of the heavily damaged and sunken ships with their more complex salvage problems. The ships that could be returned to service first would receive the utmost priority throughout the salvage work. The Salvage Division studied each ship to determine the order of work to be done, allocated the necessary resources, work crews, divers, etc., and established priorities in acquiring vital equipment, machinery and heavy duty pumps.

Yard craft (left) are fighting fires on the West Virginia *and* Tennessee *at Battleship Row as dark oily smoke rises over the burning and destroyed wreckage of the* Arizona. *It is only a few hours after the attack had ended and already salvage and recovery of the damaged ships had begun.* NA 80G-32732

CONDITIONS WHICH PREVAILED
OR WERE ENCOUNTERED IN SALVAGE
FROM PEARL HARBOR: WHY, HOW, FLEET SALVAGE AND FINAL APPRAISAL

1. LACK OF MATERIAL. Pearl Harbor was noted for shortages. This was a fact of life in a comparatively new fleet base 2000 miles from home. It has already been pointed out that there was a great shortage of oil, of oil tankers, of service craft, and countless other things to support a fleet which was ever growing.

The treacherous Japanese attack on a Sunday morning accentuated these shortages. If adequate pumping facilities had been at hand some of the ships would not have been sunk. If better fire protection had been available many of the fires which caused so much damage could have been extinguished.

The salvage effort would have been made much easier with ample supplies near at hand. The shortage of lumber and fastenings was acute; the shortage of manpower, especially electric welders and carpenters was keenly felt. All civilian mechanics and engineers were in short supply at the Navy Yard and in Honolulu.

The right kind of pumps arrived late. These were the deep-well pumps which were used effectively on the later battleships, especially *West Virginia* and *Oklahoma*. They varied in size up to 10 inches, and for *Oklahoma* as big as 18 inches and even 20 inches. They were driven by electric or diesel power, and were essential in ridding a badly wounded ship of incoming water.

2. FIRE HAZARDS ON THE SHIPS THEMSELVES. The European War taught the fleet much regarding fire hazards and floatability. Before the surprise air attack many fire hazards had been removed from combat ships. There is a tendency on the part of all personnel to be "pack rats," to have at hand anything that may sometime be required. This inclination of human nature resulted in stowing away an excess of rubber sheeting, paints, canvas, oakum, linoleum, and so on. These were removed and greatly reduced the fire hazard and improved the floatability.

During the war all linoleum was taken off the ships and all oil paints were put ashore. Paint was chipped off down to bare metal and later was re-placed with latex or water paints. These have satisfactory preservative qualities and are better than oil paints in resisting fire and high temperature.

3. SALVAGE OF ORDNANCE MATERIAL. Of all shortages, limited ordnance material presented the worst problem. Except for anti-aircraft guns on ships there was little defense of Pearl Harbor and the various airfields. No temporary batteries were installed, and .30 caliber machine guns were the main ones ready at the air bases. The batteries of ships were restricted in their zones of action, and Sunday morning at "colors" was a time of maximum readiness.

Thus it was that one of the prime jobs was to build up the anti-aircraft defense. This was done quickly by transferring the batteries and their ammunition from disabled ships to points of vantage around the Navy Yard and air stations. Much of the removal work from ships was done by divers, and though this slowed up the transfer it was not long before Pearl Harbor had a tolerable anti-aircraft defense.

The Ordnance Section gave attention to other salvage as well as antiaircraft batteries and ammunition. They worked assiduously in saving range finders, directors, small arms, and fine ordnance instruments from various sunken ships. This material required care and preservation in most cases, and the material was soon ready for use against the enemy.

4. ELECTRICAL EQUIPMENT. When it was ascertained from the experience on *Nevada* that total submergence in sea water permitted electrical equipment to be used again, there was much surprise in the fleet. Of course, proper steps for care and preservation had to be taken. Even the most delicate instruments, such as ammeters and wattmeters, were usable if properly cleaned and preserved before exposure to the air. The same pertained to cables and motors. If properly dried out and cleaned thoroughly they were usable. However, vital electric cables and motors were replaced.

It was learned that low humidity helped re-use. The humidity near the ocean meant that the equipment would ultimately fail. To avoid this, some of it was sent as far away as Denver. There it stood every test but proved questionable when returned to the seacoast. It should be clearly understood that here we are dealing with electric gear that has been submerged in sea water only a comparatively short time and has not been subjected to the tidal currents of the sea.

It was realized that no chance should be taken with respect to high potential lines and equipment. Accordingly, all such electrical gear was replaced as work progressed. No difficulty was experienced with either high potential or ordinary electrical equipment later in the war.

5. JAPANESE TORPEDOES AND BOMBS. Salvage experience proved that a fair proportion of Japanese bombs and torpedoes failed to explode. This was especially true of the 800 kilogram bombs dropped from about 10,000 feet. These were made over from armor-piercing shells of 14 or 15-inch size, and were intended to pierce the armored decks of battleships, aircraft carriers, or cruisers. They had an explosive charge of about 430 pounds. On the other hand, the 250 kilogram bombs used by dive-bombers were very effective and were frequently mistaken for incendiary bombs by our forces. The explosive charge of these bombs was about 135 pounds.

The torpedoes used by the Japanese seem to cover a variety of explosive charges. According to the Japanese story given after the surrender, they all were of the "Long Tom" variety which were so effective in the Guadalcanal Campaign. These use oxygen in lieu of air. which is safer, and carry an explosive charge of about 1,000 to 1,200 pounds. The American counterpart has an explosive charge of only 500 to 600 pounds.

It is worth noting that American torpedoes fired by our submarines early in the war sometimes failed to explode although they could be heard making contact with enemy ships. This deficiency was rectified after we developed a more reliable exploder.

Likewise, our close range anti-aircraft batteries had limitations. The American 1.1 inch in quadruple mounts seemed to be effective but frequent jamming curtailed efficiency. Our Bureau of Ordnance was in the process of getting from Sweden the 40-millimeter Bofors gun which could be mounted in twos or fours, and the 20-millimeter Oerlikon gun from Switzerland. These were used in great numbers on our ships from 1942 on.

There was much strafing by Japanese airplanes. Aside from causing a few casualties, this was ineffective. It has a value when it deters personnel from doing what should be done, but the evidence is clear that such things were done despite the strafing. So far as the ships were concerned, it is evident that strafing causes no real damage. At times, however, strafing is highly effective against personnel.

6. DIVING EXPERIENCE. Without competent divers the salvage work would have been impossible. Credit has been given to the various divers in each operation, but their outstanding efficiency deserves mention again. The supervision of the divers was excellent. Lieutenant Haynes was a stickler for safety, as were his assistants. The divers from the Salvage Division, the Navy Yard, *Ortolan*, *Widgeon*, and elsewhere made about 4,000 dives totaling some 16,000 hours underwater without a single serious casualty. The contractor had one casualty. The total of the contractor and the Navy was about 5,000 dives with about 20,000 hours underwater. Considering the difficulty, hazard, and importance of the work, this is a remarkable record.

7. DEADLY GAS ENCOUNTERED ON MOST SHIPS. The prevalence of hydrogen sulfide in *Nevada* and other ships was indeed a new phenomenon. While we usually think this gas has the smell of rotten eggs; the gas when absorbed in water at high pressure has no smell at all. At higher concentrations it is undetectable because it tends to paralyze the sense of smell. There were other gases encountered but none so deadly and widespread. Lack of oxygen in the spaces unwatered was commonplace.

Hydrogen sulfide is formed by polluted water working on paper products. It was found in compartments of every large ship, sometimes in lethal doses. After the *Nevada* incident, in which two men were lost, great care was taken with regard to sending men into spaces recently unwatered. Tests were taken of the air and frequent inspections made by experts of this industrial hazard. Each man wore some litmus paper on his tank suit to reveal the presence of gas.

ROBERT TRUMBULL'S CENSORED COVERAGE OF THE PEARL HARBOR SALVAGE OPERATION

ROBERT TRUMBULL was a correspondent for the *New York Times* at the time of the attack on Pearl Harbor. He wrote a lengthy series on the salvage operation two years after the attack with Keith Wheeler of the *Chicago Times*. The series went unpublished due to wartime censorship until December 2006 when the *New York Times* released an edited version of the dispatches.

He saw the war in the Pacific from the beginning to the end, witnessing amphibious landings including Iwo Jima. He was on the battleship *Missouri* at the surrender ceremonies. After the war he continued as a *Times* correspondent in Southeast Asia and India. In 1948 he was at the scene of the assassination of Gandhi in India. He retired in 1979 as the senior *Times* correspondent.

Trumbull was born in Chicago in 1912 and died at age 80 in Honolulu.

WESTERN UNION TELEGRAM
December 24, 1942

Krock
Washington

I have been asked to request you to intervene on this one. On December 19 Robert Trumbull our Honolulu correspondent submitted to the Navy Censor there a series of six stories totalling 15,000 words which had to get approval in Washington. The stories had to do with the good job of salvage work done in Pearl Harbor and were worked on by Mr. Trumbull and Kieth [sic] Wheeler of the Chicago Times.

Today we have a wire from Mr. Trumbull saying the series has been impounded by Fleet Public Releations Officer pending release of the story to all correspondents through a mass interview. You are requested to tell the Navy people that when a story is held up because it might give information to the enemy we have no complaint, but when an exclusive story is held up until it can be handed out to everybody we register a most distinct complaint and ask what the hell is the use of having special correspondents everywhere.

Hoping we can get a prompt reply.

Honolulu
December 23, 1942

Mr. Edwin L. James
The New York Times
New York City

Dear Mr. James:

This letter is to explain in more detail what happened to the stories Keith Wheeler of the Chicago Times and I had, exclusive, on the salvage operations at Pearl Harbor. I told you in my letter of December 18 that my series of six articles would be sent to the Navy Department in Washington for final censorship and release.

The stories, both mine and Wheeler's, have now been impounded by the Pacific Fleet public relations officer, Cmdr. Waldo Drake—contrary to fleet public relations policy to release an exclusive story on material desired by all the correspondents. I was told today by Capt. Wiltse, Admiral Nimitz's assistant chief of staff, that this policy amounts to a regulation here. I pointed out that, while every correspondent has asked for this story, Wheeler and I through our own enterprise *got* it. Nevertheless, our copy will be released only after the essential facts have been given to all correspondents at a mass interview some time in the future with an officer of the fleet service force.

I protested vigorously to Capt. Wiltse and Cmdr. Drake the unfairness of this, and requested to see Admiral Nimitz. I was informed that Admiral Nimitz had already made his decision on the matter, and that I would be given a copy of his letter stating his action to the commandant of the Pearl Harbor Navy Yard, Admiral Furlong, who had supplied to Wheeler and me—at our request—most of the information in our articles.

The stories were checked by Admiral Furlong and by the public relations officer of the fourteenth naval district, who thought then that this matter was under their jurisdiction. Lt. Cmdr. Charles Duffy, chief public relations officer of the district, had even notified the navy department at Washington that the stories were coming.

You will note that the question of security involved in release of the articles appears to occupy a minor place in my discussions with the fleet public relations officer and Capt. Wiltse. They did not dispute my contention that any statements jeopardizing security could be edited out without impairing the general story.

As matter stand now, a clean cut scoop for the New York Times lies in the icebox. Wheeler and I feel that the story of the salvage and repair work on the battleships damaged December 7, 1941, will be of great value to the national morales, and reflect high credit on the Pearl Harbor Navy Yard. We ourselves did a great deal of work on the story, and checked all facts thoroughly with Admiral Furlong, who was in direct charge of the work. In the course of our research we put on divers' suits and explored inside the hull of the capsized battleship "*Oklahoma*"—a mere sidelight on the story, but a stunt that no other laymen have ever done.

As your correspondent I believe that any pressure you can bring to rescue the stories from the icebox will be well worth the effort. I trust, also, that this letter will throw some light on the conditions under which I cover Pearl Harbor. It has been made clear to me that any personal enterprise I may show in running down any major story concerning the fleet will be wasted if it conflicts with the fleet policy of making all releasable news available to all correspondents. Enterprise must be restricted to magaziners and features not of smash front page importance.

Best regards,
Robert Trumbull

TO THE NEW YORK TIMES, NEW YORK
VIA THE NEW YORK TIMES\
WASHINGTON BUREAU
FROM ROBERT TRUMBULL

REPAIR:

PEARL HARBOR. December 13 (Passed by naval censor)—Two of the great stories of world naval history concern Pearl Harbor. First is the stunning blow dealt the United States Pacific Fleet in the Japanese sneak attack here December 7, 1941. The second, which may well be the more significant story when the world returns to the ways of peace, deals with the miracle of reclamation and repair accomplished here to undo the incredibly complex destruction wrought by the Japanese bombers.

Undoing of the Pearl Harbor damage is a story that continues today; as this is written its climax is still in the future. Its first full telling in this series of articles reveals the greatness of American industrial ingenuity, which has reached at Pearl Harbor a historic flowering.

What has been done here to put back into fighting trim the once proud warships that were unmercifully rent and shattered by bomb and torpedo, the ships pounded and broken into an unholy mess and then jammed by their own great weight into the muck of the harbor bottom, could scarcely be grasped by anyone who has not seen it.

Two newspaper men, the writer and Keith Wheeler of the Chicago Times, have seen it in detail. We tell now for the first time how the Pearl Harbor naval constructors accomplished a job of such magnitude as no engineers had ever faced before. To get the story, we interviewed Rear Admiral William R. Furlong, Commandant of the Yard, who has been directly responsible from the outset for getting the vast job done. We talked to other officers who head various divisions of this complicated project, and as the last step we inspected personally some of the ships under repair.

We saw a completely reconditioned auxiliary ship that had been on the bottom a year ago, and will sail soon to join the fleet. Another, a battleship, was in the intermediate stage, the immediate and most baffling problems behind but the really dirty work just beginning. Then we boarded the still remaining hulk which represents the very gen-

esis of the total project involved in undoing December 7, and surpasses them all.

Guided by Commander F. H. Whitaker, Admiral Furlong's Chief Salvage Officer, we put on compressed-air masks and spent a half hour in the fantastic labyrinth inside the capsized hull of the battleship *Oklahoma*, where we had to orient ourselves, as the professional divers do, to a dark and slime-covered world where everything was upside down except us.

To understand adequately the staggering problem that faced the naval engineers December 7, 1941, one must go back and survey Pearl Harbor as she lay in the silence of death and ruin after the attack.

The battleship *Nevada*, staggered by a number of heavy bomb hits and punctured by a torpedo that struck near the bow, was able to get under way and leave the hell that was Battleship Row. She beached herself in the channel and sank back to rest with water lapping her quarter deck.

The *California*, her bow burned and her insides horribly scrambled by torpedoes amidships, sank at her moorings, settling in the mud with a list of five to seven degrees. Only her high turrets poked above the water, which swirled over her stern and quarterdeck, and rushed inside the torn hole to add its own vast weight to the mass pressing into the soft harbor bottom.

Also sunk at her moorings in Battleship Row was the *West Virginia*, terribly wounded by both bombs and torpedoes. Like the *California*, she remained in an upright position. This circumstance made reclamation more readily workable, although discouragingly complicated problems remained.

The *Arizona*, the only battleship listed as lost—and rightfully so, as will be seen—rested on the bottom near Ford Island, devastated by fire within as well as wrecked by bombs and torpedoes.

The one-time battleship *Utah*, long used as a target ship and as an experimental vessel, was turned over like the *Oklahoma*, her bottom facing the sky. Her loss was not then and is not considered serious. She still lies along Ford Island, embalmed in salt water and her own oil until the appropriate time arrives to salvage such of her skin and vital organs as can be grafted onto a living vessel. The *Utah*, like the *Arizona*, has been abandoned only as a ship of war; she will, like the *Arizona*, yet serve her country well as a reservoir of valuable scrap metal and still usable machinery.

On the opposite side of Ford Island from the *Utah*, and in the same unseemly attitude, the *Oklahoma* lay capsized, 150 degrees from the vertical, her ravaged port side turned under. She was anchored to the bottom by her own masts and super-structure, which were pushed down through layers of harbor mud that closed over the masts with uncounted tons of downward pressure.

Sunk by a heavy bomb hit was the big floating drydock, which contained the destroyer *Shaw* at the time. The minelayer *Oglala* was sunk on her side at her dock, and the two destroyers *Cassin* and *Downes* were lost in the drydock. The *Downes* was literally blown in two by the explosion of her magazine. The *Cassin*, which lay alongside of her to starboard in the drydock, also caught fire and, her hull mottled like wetted paper, fell off her blocks and leaned over wearily against the *Downes*.

It might be said here parenthetically that the *Nevada*, *California* and *West Virginia*, though horribly mangled and actually not afloat, were left unmentioned in the navy's first report of sunken ships because it was believed that they could be raised and put under way. And they were.

If to the lay mind the navy's first estimate appears optimistic, it must be admitted now that this optimism was justified. The early navy reports were sketchy through military necessity; it would have been the sheerest folly to tell the enemy how badly crippled the Pacific Fleet actually was. Such a course could easily have been suicide.

But now it can be told, for the ships that were on the bottom December 7, 1941, but were not mentioned as such by the navy, are actually afloat today; indeed, many of them are fighting.

The story of the destroyer *Shaw* has already been widely publicised, because the Japanese made much of her sinking. With a false bow replacing the one that was completely burned away in the drydock, she returned to the Pacific Coast under her own power. Today she is once more a combat ship with the Pacific Fleet.

The floating drydock, badly need by the Yard, was raised quickly by attaching to her open wound a patch lowered in an arrangement like a gigantic window-frame. Admiral Furlong showed Wheeler and me this drydock, doing admirably the work for which she was built.

Another sunken ship raised early was the minelayer *Oglala*, beaten down at her dock by a torpedo after merciless bombing and strafing. She was raised by immense, specially constructed buoys, submarine rescue pontoons, was patched, and has now rejoined the fleet.

The two destroyers *Cassin* and *Downes* were unequivocally lost, and were admitted as such by the navy from the first. However, they were patched and floated for the purpose of getting them out of the drydock. Then they yielded 50 per cent of their value back to the fleet. Their main and auxiliary machinery will power the two new destroyers that are their namesakes.

Three cruisers were damaged, the *Helena* by a torpedo that passed under the lighter-draft *Oglala*, which was outboard of the *Helena* at their dock. The *Honolulu* and *Raleigh* suffered only bomb damage. The *Helena* and the *Honolulu* have since hit back at the Japs in the South Pacific.

The repair ship *Vestal* and the seaplane tender *Curtis* also suffered only bomb damage, about which navy reconstructors are by now rather casual. The *Curtis* was additionally injured by the crash on her deck of a Japanese plane. Both of these vessels have returned to the fleet. Months ago I stood aboard the *Vestal* with other correspondents while Admiral Chester W. Nimitz, Commander in Chief of the Pacific Fleet, presented a Congressional Medal of Honor to Captain *Cassin* Young, her commander of December 7.

Captain Young, since killed aboard the cruiser *San Francisco* in the Solomons, was one of the great heroes of Pearl Harbor. The *Vestal* was set ablaze by the fires from the adjacent *Arizona*. The explosion of the *Arizona*'s magazines blew Captain Young (then a commander) from his bridge. His crew then prepared to abandon ship, but Captain Young swam back and clambered aboard. He summarily stopped the abandon-ship operations, got his vessel under way and off from the dangerous position she was in beside the *Arizona*. Then he grounded her in comparative safety. The day Captain Young got the Congressional Medal for this, there were no scars showing on the *Vestal*, at least to my unpracticed eyes.

Somewhat in the same class as the *Cassin* and *Downes* in value to the fleet after December 7 was the battleship *Arizona*. Wheeler and I boarded her to watch the Salvage crew unload scrap metal and machinery which will go into other ships. Some of her guns, mounted on a Liberty Ship, spoke against Axis marauders in the Mediterranean. Her heavier armament was removed, covered with barnacles like snow, and after reconditioning it was disposed to strategic gun position about the Island of Oahu.

The *Arizona* today lies in about 40 feet of water, with only her upperworks showing. She is no longer a ship, for her back was broken, but she flies the flag, for she is still a commissioned battleship.

A curious and little-known fact about Pearl Harbor is that the *Arizona*, the *Oklahoma* and the *Utah* are still carried on the naval rolls as warships in commission, with commanding officers who must attend to numberless details attendant to the disposal of a floating city, even one that is no longer inhabited.

Three other battleships in Pearl Harbor December 7 suffered damage which was comparatively minor and has been repaired. They were the *Pennsylvania*, hit forward by one heavy bomb while in drydock where the Japanese thought a carrier would be on that morning. The *Maryland* and the *Tennessee* were also bombed, but were repaired in a matter of days. The *Tennessee* was tied up starboard of the *West Virginia*. The *West Virginia*, her port side torn away by eight torpedoes, wallowed over and her starboard bilge hooked against the *Tennessee*. The contact put an unimportant wrinkle in the *Tennessee*'s hull, but it kept the *West Virginia* upright. Incidentally, it became necessary to blast away the great quay blocks to which the *Tennessee* was moored, before she could be gotten away from her stricken companion.

Admiral Furlong, grey, stocky Pennsylvanian, was commander of the Fleet mine force on December 7, 1941. He rose early, as is his custom, that Sunday morning. He was on the deck of his flagship, the ungainly *Oglala,* which was nestled against the *Helena* at the dock where the Japs thought the *Pennsylvania* lay.

Admiral Furlong's amazed blue eyes saw the first Japanese bomb dropped in the Pearl Harbor phase of the attack strike a seaplane ramp on Ford Island. He saw the second bomb hit a Ford Island hangar, setting it afire. This plane, having done its

share in the Japs' primary objective of nullifying the Fleet's air power, circled, turned and flew back by the *Oglala* at eye-level to the admiral. "I could have hit the plane with a potato," Admiral Furlong said.

Then came the deadly torpedo plans and the high-level bombers over Battleship Row, a wave over the *Pennsylvania* in drydock (thinking she was a carrier, as captured Japanese maps showed) with the *Cassin* and *Downes* side by side ahead of her. Admiral Furlong saw the Japanese bombs whizzing down toward the *Pennsylvania*, saw them go beyond and blast the two destroyers.

A Japanese bomb struck a torpedo aboard the *Downes*, and the explosion that resulted blew out her side and started ravaging fires which spread to the *Cassin*.

Then the *Pennsy* got a bomb in her forward end. The missile wiped out a five-inch gun crew which included four men whom Admiral Furlong had sent over to aid the battleship's hard-worked company.

Meanwhile, the Admiral was having trouble at home. The *Oglala* was under continuous strafing and bombing. "I could see three torpedoes coming at us," the Admiral recalled. "Only one hit, though, but that one sank us."

Thus Admiral Furlong saw the terrible damage done. Shortly, as Commandant of the Pearl Harbor Navy Yard, he was assigned to get it undone. He had the entire Pearl Harbor establishment at his call for a job that was heroic in its broad proportions, and which in detail was often seemingly impossible, frequently discouraging, and always, out on the ships where office planning, was being put into effect, was physically arduous, filthy, stinking and dangerous.

Every man from the Admiral down knew that each new phase of the task was to present unforeseeable difficulties. The obstacles that arose were met as they came. They were hurdled in some cases by improvement of known devices, in others by sheer invention in which American engineering genius shown at its best.

The smaller jobs, the repair of the ships damaged least and therefore most quickly convertible from yard liability to battle fleet asset, were tackled first; but behind them like a mountain yet to be crossed after the plodding foothills, lay the dead battlewagons. The enormity of the battleship project can be realized by comparing that salvage job with the righting and re-conditioning of the *Normandie*, lying on her side in New York harbor.

Each of the sunken battleships far surpassed the *Normandie* as a salvage problem. Nothing has happened to the *Normandie* that was not done by clean-cutting fire, and easily removable water. Her bottom has no enormous, ragged punctures. Her superstructures has not been twisted and reduced to ash which fouls the deck below, through gaping apertures made by bombs. Her side is whole. Tremendous explosions within her hull have not made her innards, stem to stern, a fetid brew of every conceivable animal, vegetable and mineral material that goes into the construction and manning of a skyscraper.

If all these things were true of the *Normandie*, and if the nightmare hulk were then squirted thoroughly with stinking black oil and pumped full of deadly gas and noisome odors theretofore unknown to man—then the fitting of the *Normandie* would be comparable to the job done and still being done at Pearl Harbor.

Admiral Furlong gathered his crew of naval constructors, engineers, and yard workmen—artisans and machinists of every variety—into a compact though vast reconstruction unit. The naval constructors did the fundamental planning, since these were military ships and up their alley. Civilian contractors were assigned specific tasks and they can legitimately claim their share in the amazing success of the project as a whole.

It was a civilian engineer, Fred W. Crocker of the Pacific Bridge Company, who designed the wooden patches which fitted onto the steel hull of a battleship over a torpedo slash and enabled the wound to be permanently healed.

Among the navy men, there was the succession of salvage officers, head men under Admiral Furlong, Captain J. M. Steeler was the first. Then came Captain Homer N. Wallin, who was awarded a Distinguished Service Medal for his work. Now Commander F. H. Whitaker is the salvage officer.

More than a thousand men organized as a salvage and repair unit in the States for duty elsewhere (not in Hawaii) were brought to Pearl Harbor immediately after the disaster December 7. They were used principally on the *Cassin*, *Downes*, *Oglala* and the floating drydock, where some of the groundwork techniques were tested for the later projects of greater magnitude. This expert corps also supplied many of the divers who played a vital role in the reclamation of the capital ships.

Nowhere in the world, according to navy officers here, have navy and civilian workers toiled together in such close coordination and harmony on a monumental task. Their joint achievement has never been equalled, either as a feat in mechanics or as an example of cooperation between military and non-military men.

The credit goes down through the ranks, and it would be impossible to mention anyone by name. There was Lt. Bill Painter, the field officer in charge of the scene for the raising of the *California* and the *West Virginia*, while Commander Lebius Curtis, and old sailing ship expert, was invaluable in the salvage of the *West Virginia*. Jack Graham, Hawaii manager for the Pacific Bridge Company, was an important civilian executive. Two of Graham's men Les Freeman, Superintendent of Salvage, and Bert Rice, Rigger Foreman, who designed the tackle to flop the *Oklahoma* over, must be in any list of credits. Then there was T. C. Suggs, Chief Diver.

But this is only a cross-section. Admiral Furlong named many others who gave long and strenuous months to the work.

Salvage and repair of the damage done December 7, 1941, is by no means the only function administered from Admiral Furlong's office. The Navy Yard has three functions: salvage and repair, servicing of the battle fleet, and defense of the Yard itself.

Any one of the three is a complex job. Servicing of the battle fleet is a function that requires little elaboration. Pearl Harbor is the heart of American naval operations throughout the broad Pacific area. The motto of the Pearl Harbor workers who take over the ships returning from battle is, "We Keep 'Em Fit to Fight." On that basis they won the Navy "E".

Security of the naval establishment is a continuing responsibility in which the sunken ships of December 7 played a part. Some of their guns now mounted ashore will hurl hot steel back at the Japs if the chance ever comes.

The two functions of service and defense are routine. The salvage job was unprecedented, and may never be approached again. It is with this aspect of Pearl Harbor during the past year that this series will deal in detail.

U.S.S. RIGEL

ARb-1/A9-8/(016)

Pearl Harbor, T.H.
December 9, 1941.

From: Commanding Officer.
To: Commander Train Squadron SIX.

Subject: Report of particulars after battle of Sunday, December 7, 1941.

Reference: (a) Articles 712 and 874 U.S.N.R., 1920.

Enclosure: (A) List of wounded.

1. This vessel was moored in berth 13, U.S. Navy Yard, Pearl Harbor, T.H. on December 7, 1941, undergoing major repairs and conversion. No motive power or other power available from own plant due to work in progress of replacing power units, boilers, generators, etc. All essential services of steam, electricity, fresh and salt water and compressed air were being supplied from the Navy Yard. Approximately half the officers, including the Captain and Executive Officer and one third of the crew were on shore on authorized leave or liberty.

2. At about 0815, December 7, 1941 an air attack by Japanese aircraft began on ships moored in Pearl Harbor and other military objectives on the Island of Oahu. This vessel has no armament installed hence could take no offensive or defensive action. The attack developed rapidly and due to existing conditions heavy damage was inflicted by the attackers with little loss to themselves or opposition.

3. This command concerned itself with rescue efforts with ship's boats available. Ensign Charles R. Hake, U.S.N.R. volunteered as a boat officer and was put in charge of *Rigel's* #1 motor launch with a volunteer crew consisting of MILLER, Keith M., S1c., USN, Coxswain, WINEBARGER, Eugene, F1c., USN Engineer, SHEPHERD, Robert H., S2c., USN Bow Hook and BLAIR, William E., S2c USN Stern hook. This boat proceeded to rescue survivors from the *U.S.S. West Virginia* and succeeded in saving between 50 and 100 men who were injured or blown overboard and were in imminent danger of drowning or death from suffocation or burning due to flaming oil which covered the surface of the surrounding water. The work of this boat was stopped by a fouled screw in such a position that it was in imminent danger of destruction by burning. Ensign Hake and the crew succeeded in saving the boat. The attack on the West Virginia consisting of torpedo, bomb and machine gun assaults by waves of planes was at its height during the rescue operations above mentioned. it is considered that Ensign Hake and the crew of #1 motor launch as enumerated above are deserving of special commendation for the initiative, resourcefulness, devotion to duty and personal bravery displayed on this occasion.

4. Ensign James P. Bieniak U.S.N.R. was detailed as boat officer of #2 motor whaleboat, the crew of which consisting of DZINBUCH, Stanley J., S1c. USN, coxswain, STOCKER, Robert F., F1c., USN engineer and ROGERS, Robert E., S2c., USN bow hook, and directed to proceed and assist in rescue work. This boat was manned and in the act of getting underway from its berth under the starboard bow of this ship when an enemy plane dropped light bomb which struck the port quarter of the boat and cut all planking from capping to keel in two. This bomb exploded after passing through the boat and underwater, throwing Ensign Bienia and his crew into the water. STOCKER, Robert F. F1c., USN and ROGERS, Robert E., S2c., USN sustained serious injuries and have been hospitalized. From the above it is believed this was an armor piercing bomb with a delayed fuse setting.

5. The captain returned on board about 0830 when the attack was at its height.

6. Shortly after the bomb referred to in paragraph 4 fell another bomb dropped near *USS Rigel* stern and approximately midway between piers 13 and 14, this bomb exploded on contact with water and fragmentation appears to have been most complete. Approximately one hundred fifty holes, varying from 21/2 to 1/4 inch in diameter, were blown in port quarter of *Rigel* between frames 12 and the stern. All above the waterline. This damage is being repaired by ship's force. Flying splinters and fragments injured WIGGAM, Richard E., SK3c, USN, CRAWFORD, Lawrence E., F3c., USN, TALEVICK, William D., F3c., USN, JOHNSON, Henry E., MM2c., USN and GOODMAN, Eldon W. Bmkr1c., USN, who have been hospitalized.

7. The Executive Officer returned to the ship about 0900 and other officers and crew members returned as soon as possible, all being more or less delayed due to traffic congestion on main highways. There is one exception to the above, viz: Lieutenant Harry E. Morgan, U.S. Navy, who resides at 3239 Oahu Ave., Honolulu, T.H. did not return on board until about 0800, December 8, 1941. When questioned as to why he had not returned as soon as possible after the hostile air raid began he stated in effect, to the executive Officer, Commander William E. McClendon, U.S. Navy that he was unaware that a hostile raid had been made on Pearl Harbor and other military objectives, or that any material damage or personnel casualties had been inflicted on United States forces. He appeared at that time to have been drinking but was not considered intoxicated or drunk.

8. Two officers from this vessel -- Ch. Elect. W.H. Moore, U.S. Navy and Machinist H.H. Vanaman, U.S. Navy left the ship about 0615 for a hike through the hills back of the town of Aiea. At about 0800 they had reached a point at such elevation that they were able to witness the attack on the ships and Hickam Field which were apparently the initial objectives. They stated that three separate flights of planes at three levels, viz: low, medium and high passed over them from the north heading in for the attack. The attack on ships appeared to them to be made only by torpedo planes and dive bombers. The attack on Hickam Field was made by high level bombers according to these officers and the bombs were dropped in rows similar to planting potatoes. Three different plantings were observed and it appeared that the attack was well planned, coordinated and executed.

9. Lieutenant Commander Loar Mansbach, U.S. Navy, was acting commanding officer at the beginning of the attack and until the captain (Roy Dudly) returned on board. This officer had taken immediate action to assist in fire fighting and rescue on damaged vessels and had assembled repair parties, tools and equipment ready for dispatch to any point where they could be of service. his prompt action in this and his general conduct of this command period are considered deserving of special mention.

10. Chief Boatswain Ashley D. Holland, U.S. Navy was officer-of-the-deck at the beginning of and during the attack. he performed all of his duties in a highly satisfactory manner and deserves special mention for his zeal and efficient performance of duty.

11. The commanding officer has no complaint to make concerning the conduct of any officer or man who was on board during and immediately following this action, but on the contrary feels that every one of these officers and men conducted themselves in a highly creditable manner.

[signed]
R. DUDLEY

The USS Rigel *(AR-11) a repair ship was moored in Berth 13 at the Navy Yard Repair Basin for an extensive refit and conversion. The ship's superstructure was incomplete and no armament had yet been installed on board. Her crew, unable to fire at the attackers, assisted other ships in rescue and salvage work.* Rigel *received minor damage and returned to service on April 7, 1942.* EA

U.S.S. ARGONNE

AG1/A16-3/A(-8.(011)

Pearl Harbor,
T.H.
January 28, 1942

CONFIDENTIAL

From: Commanding Officer.
To: Commander-in-Chief, U.S. Pacific Fleet.

Subject: *U.S.S. Argonne* (AG31) -- Enemy attack, December 7, 1941; Detailed report of.

Reference: (c) CinCPAC desp. 102102 of December, 1941.

1. In compliance with reference (a), the following detailed report is submitted:

1. Offensive Measures During Raid:

Manned guns as quickly as possible (about 0758). Total rounds fired: 3" .23 Cal., 196; .50 Cal. Machine Gun, 3885.

2. Damage to Enemy:

One enemy bomber plane was shot down by .50 Cal. machine gun fire from this vessel. (Corporal Alfred Schlag, U.S.M.C.), as bomber came along "1010" dock and turned toward Ford Island.

3. Own Losses and Damage:

No losses to personnel. Minor damage.

4. Distinguished Conduct of Personnel:

The entire crew of this vessel performed their duties in accordance with the best traditions of the service, assisting to get wounded from damaged ships, taking bodies from water and assisting with repair facilities to full capacity.

5. Items of Interest:

a. During the bombing and torpedo attack a large winged and apparently slow plane was seen by one observer coming from the vicinity of Barber's Point, approaching Pearl Harbor at an altitude of about 4000 feet. This plane, after reaching a point approximately over West Loch, turned and reversed its direction and was not seen again.

b. At 2116 a .50 caliber machine gun bullet passed through port side of *Argonne* at frame 70, second deck, killing BROWN,, . . Sea.1.c., *U.S.S.* Utah, and wounding PRICE, W.A., Sea.1c., *U.S.S.* Utah, in the left arm.

c. At exactly ten minutes to eight, Sunday morning, December 7, 1941, M.F. POSTON, M.M.2c., U.S. Navy, attached to *Argonne*, was engaged in flying a light training plane, the property of KT Flying Service, Honolulu, from Halewia to the KT landing field. He was accompanied by another plane piloted by Bob Tice, owner of KT Service. They were passing over the Pali at 6000 feet when attacked by two enemy planes. The attacking planes shot away the propeller and engine from POSTON's plane and he parachuted to safety from an altitude of 4000 feet. The accompanying plane was also shot down. POSTON definitely observed the markings of the attackers, claiming them to be German Messerschmitt 109's with distinguishing Japanese "Red Suns" on their wing tips. POSTON landed beyond the Pali and was taken into custody by two deputized civilian police who returned him to the Honolulu Shore Patrol Station where he was questioned then returned to his ship.

[signed]
F.W. CONNOR.

On the morning of December 7, 1941 USS Argonne (AG-31) flagship of Rear Admiral William L, Calhoun, Commander Base Force, Pacific Fleet, was moored port side to berth B-4 at Ten-Ten Dock. At the sound of General Quarters at 0758 the ship's crew manned the antiaircraft batteries and immediately commenced firing at the attacking planes. During the raid Argonne dispatched fire and rescue crews to Battleship Row to help with the wounded and recovery of bodies. NA

The USS Tern, a "Bird" Class minesweeper, was commissioned in 1919. She was assigned to Hawaii in June 1941 with Train Squadron 2. On December 7th Tern was tied up at the end of Ten-Ten Dock undergoing upkeep. As the attack began, all hands immediately made preparations to get underway. Tern moved to BB Row where she picked up 47 survivors. She was then ordered to assist in fighting fires on the West Virginia and Arizona (above). She was not damaged in the attack and continued fighting fires on the battleships for two more days till all fires were out. NA 80G-32610

BATTLESHIPS AT PEARL HARBOR
DECEMBER 7, 1941

USS Nevada (BB-36)
Keel Laid - Nov. 4, 1912
Launched - July 11, 1914
Commissioned - March 11, 1914
Displacement Full Load - 28,400 tons
Built - New York Shipbuilding Corp.
Decommissioned - Aug. 29, 1946

USS Oklahoma (BB-37)
Keel Laid - Oct. 26, 1912
Launched - March 23, 1914
Commissioned - May 2, 1916
Displacement Full Load - 28,400 tons
Built - New York Shipbuilding Corp.
Decommissioned - Sept. 1, 1944

USS Pennsylvania (BB-38)
Keel Laid - Oct. 27, 1913
Launched - March 16, 1915
Commissioned - June 12, 1916
Displacement Full Load - 32,657 tons
Built - Newport News Shipbuilding Co.
Decommissioned - Aug. 29, 1946

USS Arizona (BB-39)
Keel Laid - March 16, 1914
Launched - June 19, 1915
Commissioned - Oct. 17, 1917
Displacement Full Load - 32,567 tons
Built - New York Navy Yard
Decommissioned (stricken from Navy list Dec. 1, 19??

USS Tennessee (BB-43)
Keel Laid - May 14, 1917
Launched - April 30, 1919
Commissioned - June 3, 1920
Displacement Full Load - 33,190 tons
Built - New York Navy Yard
Decommissioned - Feb. 14, 1947

USS California (BB-44)
Keel Laid - Oct. 25, 1916
Launched - Nov. 20, 1919
Commissioned - Aug. 10, 1921
Displacement Full Load - 33,190 tons
Built - Mare Island Navy Shipyard
Decommissioned - Feb. 14, 1947

USS Maryland (BB-46)
Keel Laid - April 24, 1917
Launched - March 20, 1920
Commissioned - July 21, 1921
Displacement Full Load - 33,590 tons
Built - Newport News Shipbuilding Co.
Decommissioned - April 3, 1947

USS West Virginia (BB-48)
Keel Laid - April 12, 1920
Launched - Nov. 17, 1921
Commissioned - Dec. 1, 1923
Displacement Full Load - 33,590 tons
Built - Newport News Shipbuilding Co.
Decommissioned - Jan 9, 1947

USS Utah (AG-16)
Keel Laid - March, 1909
Launched - Dec. 23, 1909
Commissioned - Aug. 31, 1909
Displacement Full Load - 23,033 tons
Built - New York Shipbuilding Corp.
Decommissioned as battleship.
Converted to a training ship (AG-16)
in 1930

GETTING THE LESS DAMAGED SHIPS READY FOR ACTION

The first aim of the high command was to get the less damaged ships ready as soon as possible for action. This work engrossed "all hands" around the clock. The crews themselves did considerable work in getting their ships ready. They were assisted by repair ships, tenders, tugs, and by the Navy Yard.

As yet there was a dire shortage of pumping equipment, lumber, and other materials necessary for efficient salvage work. However, the spirit of the times was "to do our best with what we had." Each echelon of command did everything possible to overcome obstacles which were encountered.

U.S.S. PENNSYLVANIA (BB-38), BATTLESHIP

The lightly damaged *Pennsylvania* gave promise of being one of the first ships to be ready for action. The Navy Yard expedited the lining up of her shafts and propellers. One of the 5-inch anti-aircraft guns was put out of commission temporarily and one 5-inch 51 caliber gun was seriously damaged by the same 250 kilogram bomb which exploded two decks below. The latter was replaced by a gun from the *West Virginia*. The fragmentation and explosion damage was quickly overcome. The splinter protection, wooden deck, electrical gear, water mains, and structural steel were soon repaired and the ship was ready to leave the dry

dock by 12 December and the Navy Yard by 20 December.

Pennsylvania's dry dock was flooded to within one foot of floatation when it was expected that the enemy planes might return. This flooding was precautionary in case a bomb explosion should take out the caisson. When *Pennsylvania* was removed from the Dry-Dock #1 on 12 December, *Downes* was righted and set down on permanent blocks while *Cassin* was left in a toppled state until later.

The hits by bombs on the ship and the dry dock sidewall resulted in the death of two officers and 18 enlisted men and the wounding of 31 more.

With a warm Hawaiian sun beaming down on the quarterdeck of the USS Pennsylvania (BB-38) *on 1 February 1941 at Pearl Harbor, Admiral Husband E. Kimmel broke his flag at the main truck of the Fleet Flagship and relieved Admiral James O. Richardson as Commander-in-Chief of the U.S. Pacific Fleet. For the remainder of the year the battleship continued operations and training exercises in Hawaiian waters. On 1 December 1941* Pennsylvania *was moved into dry dock for needed repairs.* USN NH 67585

The above image of the destruction in Dry Dock One is one the most memorable photographs of that fateful Sunday morning in December 1941 and was taken by a navy photographer a few hours after the attack had ended. Earlier that morning of the 7th the Pennsylvania *and the two destroyers were still resting on blocks in the dry dock. Three of the* Pennsylvania's *propellers and shafts had been removed and were resting on the floor of the dock. The ships were receiving all steam, power and water from Yard facilities. Shortly after 0900 the ships in the dock came under attack. In the attack 18 men were killed on the* Pennsylvania *and another 27 were wounded.* NA 80G-19943

At the start of the second wave shortly after 0900 a flight of three dive bombers from the Japanese carrier Soryu *dropped three 550-lb. bombs. Two were near misses on* Pennsylvania *that detonated on either side of the dock cutting off all Navy Yard electrical and water services. The third bomb crashed through the boat deck near the starboard boat crane of* Pennsylvania *and detonated below in the casemate of 5"/51 gun No.9 causing extensive damage.* NARA

The explosion started fires in the casemate that spread to the main and second decks and were difficult to extinguish due to the lack of pressure on the fire mains. The blast also blew plating upward on the boat deck, a large hole downward through the upper deck, dished in the main deck, wrecked a part of the galley and nearby compartments and caused fuel oil to run into the decks below. NA

Flames onboard the two stricken destroyers set off approximately 40-50 rounds of 5-inch ammunition and a torpedo warhead showering the area with debris. A section of a torpedo mount from the Downes weighing about a thousand pounds landed on the forecastle of the Pennsylvania causing minor damage. The dry dock was flooded in an attempt to extinguish the fires. Before the fires were brought under control burning oil on the water had blistered the paint on the battleship's bow for about 80 feet. NA 80G-32509

1114-42   U.S.S. PENNSYLVANIA
STERN VIEW
MARE ISLAND, CALIF.   3/2/42

In less than two weeks yard workers had reinstalled the shafts and propellers and working with ship's forces made temporary repairs to the bomb damage. On 20 December 1941 Pennsylvania was ready for sea and sailed for San Francisco arriving 29 December. On New Year's Day the ship entered the dry dock at Hunter's Point for permanent repairs and upgrades. The Pennsylvania would go on to serve gallantly in the Pacific Theater for the duration of World War Two earning eight battle stars and a Navy Unit Citation. NARA II

U.S.S. HONOLULU (CL-48), CRUISER

Honolulu was at the Navy Yard and suffered severe flooding forward. The ship was not hit, but a near-miss of a 250 kilogram bomb passed through the concrete surface of the pier and exploded about 20 feet from the hull. This resulted in an in-buckle five or six feet deep at about frame 40 and extending fore and aft about 40 feet. Although the shell of the vessel was not completely opened, the flooding was extreme and could not be stopped. Due to the rupture of a magazine sea-flood, the flooding included the handling room of turret II and several storerooms and compartments.

Honolulu followed *Pennsylvania* in Dry dock Number One and remained there for permanent repairs from 13 December until 2 January 1942. By 12 January the Yard completed permanent work to the structure, electric wiring, etc.

With the ship's crew manning the rails one bright Sunday morning on July 14, 1939 the Aloha Tower and a traditional Hawaiian canoe welcomed the new light cruiser USS Honolulu *as she arrives for the first time to the city whose name she proudly bears. A few years later on that fateful Sunday morning December 7, 1941,* Honolulu *was moored portside to at Berth 21 in the Pearl Harbor Navy Yard. About 0755 some men on the ship's bridge saw planes bombing nearby Hickam Field. General Quarters was sounded and word passed "Enemy Air Raid"* NA 80G-451205

About 0920 during the second wave a group of Val dive bombers attacked the Navy Yard. A bomb barely missed the Honolulu *and crashed through the concrete pier exploding underwater near the ship's bow. The force of the explosion crushed in 40 feet of hull plating, ruptured a number of forward oil tanks, and ammunition magazines. The ship moved into Dry Dock One on 13 December to repair her damaged hull. Work was completed on 2 January 1942. On the twelfth* Honolulu *departed Pearl for San Francisco and a major overhaul at Mare Island.* PHPC

U.S.S. HELENA (CL-50), CRUISER

Helena was struck on the starboard side by the aerial torpedo which passed under *Oglala* at the 10-10 Navy Yard pier. The starboard side was opened up below the armor belt. Number 1 engine room and Number 2 boiler room flooded and the water percolated slowly into other spaces.

Dry dock Number Two was in an unfinished state at the time but the contractor, the Pacific Bridge Company, arranged to use part of the dry dock for *Helena* after obtaining suitable bilge blocks from the Navy Yard. The vessel entered dry dock on 10 December, the first vessel to occupy Dry dock Number Two.

Temporary repairs were made to the ship, including various piping systems, electric wiring, etc. On 21 December she was undocked and on 5 January 1942 she sailed on half power for the Mare Island Navy Yard where permanent repairs were completed.

The light cruiser Helena *was docked at Ten Ten Pier in the Navy Yard with the old minelayer* Oglala *tied up outboard. By chance* Helena *was in the berth normally assigned to the Fleet Flagship* Pennsylvania. *Within 3 minutes after the first bomb exploded on Ford Island, as the crew raced to battle stations, a torpedo plane launched its lethal weapon that passed under* Oglala *and struck* Helena *below the armor belt amidships that resulted in the immediate flooding of her forward engine and boiler rooms.* USN

Outstanding damage control by the ship's crew with the prompt closing of watertight hatches and compartments throughout the ship kept Helena *afloat. The torpedoed cruiser was moved into the nearly completed Dry Dock Two on December 10, 1941 for emergency repairs. The damaged* Pennsylvania *(right) is seen in Dry Dock One.* PHP

U.S.S. HELENA

CL50/A16-3/(0149)

December 14, 1941.

From: The Commanding Officer.
To: The Commander-in-Chief, U.S. Pacific Fleet..

Subject: Brief Report of the Japanese Attack of December 7, 1941.

Reference: (a) Your restricted dispatch 102102 of December.

Enclosure: (A) Copy of C.O. announcement to officers and crew by general announcing system, dated December 11, 1941.
(B) *Helena* Mailgram 140115 of December 1941.
(C) Medical Officer's Casualty List.

1.The following brief report of the Japanese attack on Pearl Harbor on December 7, 1941, is submitted in compliance with reference (a). Considerable study has been made of this attack in an endeavor to eliminate conflicting impressions, and arrive at concrete conclusions, particularly with reference to times, numbers and types of planes, damage inflicted to the enemy, punishment received, etc. Statements have been collected from all key men and officers. Heads of Departments have surveyed these reports, and, from these and their own observations, have submitted a correlated report representing their own department conclusions to the Commanding Officer. This report is based on the Commanding Officer's own observations and conclusions after a review of the reports submitted by Department Heads. Evidently any report submitted at this time will have to be augmented as a further and more complete study is made.

2. Offensive Measures Taken.
a. Planes were observed over Ford Island at about 0757. These were recognized as Japanese planes when at an altitude of about 4000 feet. The Officer of the Deck as promptly notified by C.A. FLOOD, S.M.1c, on watch on the signal bridge. This man has had recent duty on the Asiatic Station, and identified the character of the planes immediately. Ensign W.W. Jones, U.S.N., Officer of the Deck, without delay, turned on the general alarm and passed word over the general announcing system, "Japanese planes bombing Ford Island, Man all battle stations, break out service ammunition". (This time is fairly accurately fixed by the signalman in charge of watch, C.A. Flood, who was standing by the "Prep" signal for 0800 colors. It is confirmed by the Engineering log and also by H.F. Korloch, C.T.C., U.S.N., who had just relieved as gangway Security Watch; also by Ensign J.J. Armstrong, U.S.N.R., and Ensign W.W. Jones, U.S.N., who were in the process of relieving as O.O.D.). *Helena* guns were in action about 0801.

b. Ammunition was expended approximately as follows: Five inch 375 rounds; 1.1"/75 3000 rounds; .50 caliber 5000 rounds.

c. Enclosure B outlines attacks, phases, and results.

3. Damage inflicted on the enemy. As outlined in enclosure B.

4. Own losses and damage.
a. Direct Hit. One torpedo observed to be fired by a torpedo plane flying low over the southern tip of Ford Island was fired at the *Helena* at a range of about 500 yards. This torpedo was fired about one minute after general quarters had been sounded, and about one and one-half minutes after the Japanese planes

were sighted over Ford Island. Our crew were running for their general quarters stations. This accounted for a large loss of personnel by flash burns from the explosion and from concussion in passageways. No guns were yet in action and therefore no opposition to the Japanese plane. The torpedo struck with a violent explosion on the starboard side at approximately frame 75 about 18 feet below the water line.

b. Near Hits by bombs. About four near misses from bombs received from which there were a few fatal casualties and many minor injuries to personnel.

c. One strafing attack from which little damage was received. This was due to the very early period of the engagement in which the attack occurred. This attack was delivered just prior to the torpedo hit noted above, and was about the time general quarters were being sounded (0757), and for this reason the men had not reached their exposed machine gun stations on the top side.

d. The damage received, and measures taken to meet it is listed by departments as follows:

GUNNERY DEPARTMENT

1. The major damage affecting the Gunnery installations were to fire control and power wiring to both main battery and 5" anti-aircraft battery. The major portion of wiring passing through the engineering spaces flooded as a result of torpedo hit are now unserviceable. Auxiliary power sources are available, and in general only auxiliary fire control circuits are available. minor material damage was inflicted by bomb splinters and machine gun bullets.

2. The initial torpedo hit put out of commission the turbo generator then in use. Prompt action by the Engineers in starting and cutting in the forward Diesel generator made power available to all gun mounts within one or two minutes. Considerable difficulty was experienced in attempts to maintain fire control circuits during and subsequent to the action. On four occasions electrical fires resulted in the Plotting Room and on another occasion in the forward distribution room. These fires were quickly and efficiently put out. During periods of actual firing power was always available at the mounts.

3. Most casualties to personnel were caused by flash burns from the torpedo explosion. Other casualties inflicted during the attack included:

Two men (trainer and number one loader) on mount I of the 1.1"/75 suffered powder burns from the blasts of the 5" Mount I.

Two men (the pointer and one loader) of Mount I of the 1.1"/75 suffered injuries, the pointer from powder burns from the blast of No. II 5" Mount, the loader, a flesh wound in the arm by bomb splinter.

On Mount III of the 1.1"/75 the trainer was killed by bomb splinter. The second loader suffered wound in shoulder from machine gun bullet, the gunner's mate suffered minor wound on face under left eye from glancing machine gun bullet.

On Mount IV of the 1.1"/75, the gunner's mate received minor wounds upon arm, nose, and chest from bomb splinters.

Bomb splinters from near miss on starboard quarter inflicted casualties as follows to men in vicinity of .50 caliber machine guns aft: One gunners' mate second class killed, two seaman first class wounded, one officer (Ensign P.V. Thompson, USN) wounded.

DAMAGE CONTROL

1. Damage sustained:

Major:

    a. Compartments flooded due to torpedo hit at approximately frame 75 starboard side below the armor belt.

        Boiler room Boiler room B-1-1
        Boiler operating space B-2
        Boiler room B-3-1
        Boiler room B-4
        Port shaft alley

    b. Fuel tanks flooded by torpedo hit at approximately frame 75 starboard side below armor belt.

B-921-F	B-935-F
B-929-F	B-936-F
B-931-F	B-939-F
B-932-F	B-940-F
B-933-F	B-941-F
B-934-F	B-942-F
Diesel Fuel Tank	B-625-F

Reserve Feed Tanks
B-944-W	B-945-W

Minor:

    a. Fuel oil seepage and fire hazard on third deck causing securing of compartments frames 61-82

Areas:

B-301-L	Optical Workshop.
B-301-L	Ice Machine Room.
B-302-L	Machine Ship
B-1	Uptake
B-3	Uptake
B-305-L	Engineers' Office
B-303-2L	Electrical Workshop.
B-306-L	Ship Store.
B-306-L	Provision Issue Room.
B-306-L	Barber Shop.

    b.Paint Locker A-203-1A -- Shock ruptured many cans of paint causing fire hazard. Paint locker is secured until adequate cleaning has been completed.

    Smoke Screen Generator -- frame 150 -- Shock weakened foundation and carried away air supply lines.

Sick Bay Area -- frames 39-49 third deck -- Flooded to depth of about 6 inches with water due to open drains and settling of the ship and lack of sufficient firemain pressure on eductors of forward drains. This was corrected after the action.

c. Drafts:

Before Action:	Forward	24'8"
	Aft	24'6"
	Mean	24'7"
After Action:	Forward	29'6"
	Aft	25'2"
	Mean	27'4"

d. Distortion of midsection of the ship.

1. Indications show force of explosion forced third deck up in the vicinity of frame 75.

When docking, indications show keel forced down one foot in vicinity of frame 75.

e. Services to forward part of the ship (bow to frame 61) ruptured in forward fire room:

1. Fire main.

2. High pressure air.

3. Drainage main.

4. Ventilation power.

f. Bulkheads:

Frame 61 -- Plotting Room -- leakage via armored cables.

Frame 61 -- Distribution Forward -- leakage via armored cables.

Frame 82 -- Boiler room B-5-1 -- Starboard lower corner showed buckled plates but not ruptured. only leakage through #1 shaft gland and one pipe flange.

g. Numerous shrapnel and missile holes throughout the structure above the water line on the starboard side.

Shock and blast carried away many fittings, light bulkheads and deck lockers.

2. Action taken:

a. Flooded compartments, boiler rooms and fire rooms -- bulkhead 81 in the Plotting Room was shored.
    -- bulkhead 82 in boiler room B-5-1 was shored.
All hatches and watertight doors closed to flooded areas.

b. Services forward:

   1. Jumper hose connection over flooded spaces provided fire main pressure forward.

   2. Jumper power leads over flooded spaces provided ventilation forward.

   3. Sick Bay Area -- drains closed and plugged -- flooded area closed. Battle Dressing Station Forward moved to Wardroom.

c. Isolated third deck area -- frames 61 to 82 -- because of fire hazard. Oil seepage extended throughout third deck in this area to about 4 inches. This was relieved by removal from the ship of fuel oil forward and aft, and by removing ammunition, thus decreasing the draft.

d. Damage Control -- General Comment:

   a. The personnel of the C&R Department report that upon hearing of the bombing of Ford Island they proceeded to their general quarters stations and set condition afirm as soon as possible. The time required for setting condition afirm was 8 minutes, approximately.

   The torpedo hit placed out of commission power and fire main pressure. Also apparently started fires on the third deck. The fire was the explosion blast venting from the engine room via engine room hatch, passage B-306-L, and hatches 31 port and starboard to the second deck. The remainder of the blast was vented via the boiler rooms and stack uptakes.

   Repair parties entered passage B-306-L putting out small burning particles. There was no general fire. The flooded compartments were isolated and bulkheads were shored.

   Repair parties assisted the wounded and the battle dressing stations in whatever manner requested.

   The men attempted to hook up the fire main to the dock but were stopped because of the second attack. later, they were unable to locate plugs on the dock.

   Gas Masks and protective clothing were issued to the crew as soon as possible.

   Power and fire main jumpers were placed. Compartments were patrolled and void soundings taken continuously. The fire main was out of use about 17 minutes.

   Repair I assisted in sending 1.1" and .50 caliber ammunition to forward guns from forward whip hoist.

   In general the personnel of the repair parties conducted themselves in an exemplary manner, being extremely versatile in carrying out their own duties and assisting in whatever manner they could other activities. The highest praise belongs to each and every one for a duty well done.

ENGINEERING

1. <u>Damage repaired during and after action</u>.

    a. <u>Fire main</u> forward of after boiler rooms. This was partially restored by Repairs III and I running jumpers between risers 3 and 6. Firemain pressure was restored to ice machines on Monday, December 8, by running a jumper direct to this machine.

    b. <u>Main Drain</u>: The after section from #3 Fireroom throughout the after part of the ship was restored by closing the after out-out-valve in the forward engineroom by its remote control from the 2nd deck. unfortunately, while the forward room was flooding, and before the cutout valve was closed, the bilge suction in the port shaft alley, being either partially or fully open -- this cannot be determined -- allowed this room to flood. later, however, when the situation in #3 fireroom (flooding, through the gland of #1 shaft) was brought under control, the port shaft alley was pumped and restored. it was necessary throughout the period the Forward engine-room was flooded to keep #3 Fire and Bilge pump on the bilges of #3 Fireroom.

    c. <u>Electric Power and Lighting served by #2 Distribution Board</u>: As #2 Distribution Board was blown out by the torpedo explosion all its power and lighting outlets went dead. jumpers were run by the Electrical Division to restore essential circuits.

2. <u>Damage that can and must be repaired to make vessel seaworthy</u>

    a. Remove propellers from #1 and #4 shafts. (To enable vessel to proceed with 32 and #3 shafts without drag.) Propellers are not damaged.

    b. Restore evaporator plant. This requires supply of auxiliary steam for air ejectors and exhaust steam for heat. The electric power has been temporarily restored by cutting in on #1 Distribution Board.

    c. Restore main drain throughout ship. Damaged in #1 engine room.

    d. Restore fire main. Damaged in 31 engine room and possibly in #2 boiler room.

    e. Port auxiliary steam line. (This may not be damaged, however.)

    f. Auxiliary exhaust line through forward engine room.

    g. High pressure air line through forward engine room.

    h. Leads from #2 Distribution Board and all electric leads running on starboard side of 31 engine room are destroyed. it is essential that as many as possible be restored to enable 5" and 6" battery to be fired in the designed manner.

    i. Sound-power telephone circuits 2JZ, 2JV, 3JV. Temporary leads may be used to restore these circuits.

3. <u>Damage that will require an extended period to repair</u>.

      a. All machinery in #1 engine room.

      b. All machinery in #1 Boiler Operating space. (Salt water immersion damage.)

      c. All boilers in #1 and #2 Boiler Rooms. (Salt water immersion damage). The extent of damage to 33 boiler may be larger than merely salt water immersion damage due to its position relative to the torpedo hit.

      d. #2 Distribution Board and #2 generator, and electrical leads to and therefrom.

      e. Main steam and other steam and fresh water drain piping.

      f. All reserve feed bottoms and fuel-oil tanks on starboard side and bottom. Some port side tanks may be damaged, the exact status unknown at this time.

e. <u>Distinguished Conduct of Personnel</u>.

a. Every man and officer observed on this ship conducted himself in a meritorious and exemplary manner. All were cool, determined, resourceful, vigorous and individually and collectively conducted themselves with no hint of confusion or hysteria and with no thought of danger to themselves. To point out distinguished conduct would require naming every person I observed. The following quoted report of one Gunnery Division Officer is indicative of all:

"Subject: Distinguished action, report of.

1. Because every man of the 5th Division did his duty I feel it impossible to mention or commend any single person without a resulting injustice to the others. But in fairness it seems nothing but proper to commend GREENWALD, R.D., Sea1c, U.S. Navy who died at his station as trainer during the action. other commendations must include the entire roll call of the crew for the 5th Division.

                            Respect, submitted,
                            [signed]
                            D.L.G. KING"

U.S.S. MARYLAND (BB-46), BATTLESHIP

Maryland was berthed inboard of *Oklahoma*. She was struck by two 15-inch armor-piercing bombs. Fortunately both bombs had a low level of detonation. The first struck the forecastle awning and tore a hole about 12 feet by 20 feet and caused some damage in the compartments below. The second entered the hull at the 22 foot water level at frame 10. It exploded within the ship and caused considerable flooding. The bow was down about five feet.

Since a dry dock was not available, the Navy Yard assisted, by the forces afloat, made repairs without docking. A small caisson was fitted over the hole on the port side. When sufficient pumping facilities were available to control the flooding, temporary repairs were easy to complete. *Maryland* was fully repaired and ready for action by 20 December.

From 1923 to 1941 the USS Maryland *served with the Battle Fleet along the western seaboard and the Hawaiian Islands. Throughout those years the ship was kept busy in training operations, Fleet exercises and good will visits to foreign ports. This Sunday morning was no different from any other. Many of the officers had gone ashore for the weekend, mess tables were being cleared away, some of the crew were getting ready for Liberty, while others lounged in their bunks writing letters to family and loved ones back home in the States.* EA

That morning, "Old Mary" as her crew called her, was moored at "Battleship Row" inboard of the Oklahoma *along the eastern shore of Ford Island at Berth Fox-5. When a large flight of planes were spotted at 0755 and identified as Japanese, the ship's bugler immediately blew General Quarters over the PA system.* Maryland *managed quickly to bring her anti-aircraft batteries into action. The ship was protected from the torpedo onslaught suffered by* Oklahoma *who bore the brunt of the attack.*
NA 80G-32703

During the second wave high level bombers hit Maryland *with two 16-inch converted artillery shells fitted with fins. One smashed into the port bow about 17-feet below the water line causing extensive flooding. The second bomb struck the forecastle opening a hole approximately 10x20 feet in the deck but did not explode. Battleship Row (above) as seen on Wednesday morning three days after the attack. To the left is the capsized* Oklahoma *with* Maryland *inboard. At the right with her decks awash is the sunken* West Virginia. *Above her is the trapped* Tennessee. NA AN-42-861

The moderately damaged Maryland's *casualties were light having lost only two officers and two enlisted men with thirteen wounded. During the aftermath of the attack flooding was brought under control. The ship's crew quickly formed fire-fighting and rescue parties to assist some of the more critically damaged ships and to rescue men from the oil covered waters. At noon on December 10 two yard tugs eased the* Maryland *away from beyond the hull of* Oklahoma *and over to the Navy Yard repair basin.* NA 80G-32488

After temporary repairs by the navy yard work force to make the ship seaworthy, Maryland *departed Pearl Harbor in convoy with battleships* Pennsylvania *and* Tennessee *plus four escorting destroyers for Bremerton, Washington on 20 December 1941.* Maryland *is seen here at the Puget Sound Navy Yard in January 1942 as work progresses on her overhaul. Note the nearly completed installation of new hull plating at the ship's port bow.* EA

After a complete overhaul and permanent repairs, installing radar plus upgrades to her anti-aircraft weapons, the Maryland *was ready for action by February 26, 1942. During the historic Battle of Midway in June 1942, the older battleships* Maryland *and* Colorado, *not fast enough to keep up with the fast carrier Task Forces, operated in a rear area as a backup force about 1,200 miles northeast of Hawaii.* Maryland *received seven battle stars for her World War Two service.* NA 80G-13059

ACTION REPORT

USS MARYLAND   BB-46

SERIAL 0234   19 DECEMBER 1941

ATTACK OF DECEMBER 7, 1941.

       REPORT OF CAPT. D.C. GODWIN, USN, TO COMMANDER IN CHIEF PACIFIC, COVERING DAMAGE SUSTAINED AT PEARL HARBOR FROM TWO HITS BY JAPANESE PLANES AT 0908.

                  UNITED STATES PACIFIC FLEET

BB48/A16-3/Of10/   BATTLESHIPS, DIVISION FOUR

                  U.S.S. MARYLAND

                                      December 19, 1941.

From: Commanding Officer.

To: The Commander-in-Chief, U.S. Pacific Fleet.

Via: (1) Commander Battleships, Battle forces.

         (2) Commander Battle Force.

Subject: Damage sustained in action December 7, 1941.

1. In accordance with the requirement of Article 840, U.S. Navy Regulations, 1920, the following known damages sustained in action on December 7, 1941, and the corrective action taken to date to make the ship seaworthy and to restore it to its previous battle efficiency is submitted.

2. Summary of damages and losses sustained by departments:

   A. HULL DEPARTMENT

      1. Structural damage.

         a. From hit or hits on forecastle:

           General wreckage of deck, fittings, topside gear including anchor and paravane chains, piping and electrical circuits between frames 9 and 20 on Upper and Main Decks. Trunk A-404-T badly holed and W.T. doors and hatches bulged; hatches in trunks A-407-T and A-507-T also bulged; ladders in trunks wrecked; Bulkhead 9 wrecked on main Deck level.

         b. From hit through shell into A-103-A:

           Shell holed at frame 10 about 22 foot waterline, 18" by 22". This missile apparently penetrated deck of A-201-A and detonated in A-103-A, the blast being principally aft, to starboard, up and down. Much canvas and 530 lifejackets in this compartment absorbed many fragments and splinters and possibly saved further holing of the shell. Five fairly large (about 3") holes in bottom A-1-V, several loose and missing rivets and many gouges and splinter holes in shell plating of A-1-V, principally in vicinity of frame 14. Seam badly bulged at frame 14, starboard, about 14 foot waterline, leaky. Some floors and frames (beams) in A-1-V completely wrecked. Bulkhead 15 badly wrecked with whole panels blown through into A-104-A from A-103=A. Much of deck and overhead plating of A-103-A wrecked, holed and torn. This hit apparently accounted for all underwater body damage and damage to stores from resultant flooding of fore part of ship. Bulkhead 9 leaky at bounding angles. Blast damage upward wrecked deck and hatches in A-201-A. Structural damage in A-104-A apparently limited to vicinity frame 15 includes deck and longitudinal bulkheads. W.T. Hatch from A-204-T to A-104-AA and W.T. Door to A-205-E buckled from blast.

    c. <u>Superstructure</u>:

    Minor damage to foremast structure, holes in secondary forward and shield around forward .50 cal. machine gun station.

  2. <u>Damage from flooding</u>.

    a. No structural damage is known to have occurred from flooding, but due to above described damage and intentional flooding of magazines forward of frame 24, paint stowage and gasoline stowage, there was about 1000 tons of water in the forward part of the ship and most stores therein were ruined by flooding, which also caused further damage to electrical circuits.

  3. <u>Corrective Action</u>.

    a. <u>Boundaries of damaged area being made watertight</u>:

    From Keel up bulkhead 90, First Platform Deck to bulkhead 15, Second Platform Deck to bulkhead 20, thence to keel.

    b. This will leave compartments A-1-V, A-2-V, A-103-A, A-104-A and A-201-A as one large open compartment capable of being isolated from the rest of the ship at the above boundaries by watertight bulkheads, decks, hatches and doors.

    c. Repair work is on a basis of making the shell tight with patches, replacing major structural strength members which were damaged, principally in A-1-V and A-103-A, and obtaining the watertight envelope described in subparagraph A(3)(a) above. Much other structural work beyond the capacity of the ship's force is required to place that section of the ship in condition for its designated use. It is considered that, barring additional damage to the shell, what water the ship may take on completion of repair work this date can be controlled by the secondary drainage pumps forward.

    d. In the event that the 5 compartments listed in subparagraph A(3)(b) above become flooded there will be introduced into the ship about 530 tons of water, resulting in increased mean draft of about 5 inches, trimming the head down about 28 inches and the stern up about 15 inches.

B. <u>ENGINEERING DEPARTMENT</u>

<u>ITEM</u>	<u>DAMAGE</u>	<u>STATUS OF REPAIRS</u>
No. 1 and No. 2 Torpedo Air Compressor	Electric motor and starting panel wiring insulation damaged. Bearing journals and cylinders walls corroded. H.P. air gauges inoperative.	Motors and panels are in Navy Yard. Mechanical end is being repaired in place. Gauges are in Navy Yard.
Degaussing Cable "A" Coil	Cut on port side. Damaged on Stbd. side.	Port side due for replacement 18 December 1941. Stbd. side 19 December 1941.
Light and power wiring in vicinity of bomb hits.	Wiring broken, insulation damaged.	Main and second deck wiring restored.
Eight submersible pumps	Burnt out during pumping operations.	Approximately 2 to 3 days to complete repairs.
Twelve spare armatures.	Insulation damaged.	
No. 1 and No. 2 Diesel oil pump motor and starting panel.	Insulation damaged.	Seven have been repaired to date. Navy Yard taking out. Six completed.
Diesel Oil Purifier motor.	Insulation damaged.	Navy Yard is repairing.
RADAR	- - - - -	Navy Yard is repairing. Estimated completion four (4) more days.

C. GUNNERY DEPARTMENT

    a. Turret I

    Six inch piece knocked out of coaming of gun port, starboard side. Hole gouged out of third hoop, left gun (gouge 2 inches by 1 inch).

    b. No. 8, 5"/25 cal. A.A. Gun.

    Bomb fragment hit rammer cylinder just forward of slide and dented cylinder to such extent that rammer piston could not slide through. (Rebored by Navy Yard and replaced).

    c. Right lens of Spot I glass shattered by machine gun bullet or bomb fragment. (Repaired by *Medusa*).

D. SUPPLY DEPARTMENT

    a. Total cost of stores and provisions lost - $8778.92.

E. COMMUNICATION DEPARTMENT

ITEM	DAMAGE	STATUS OF REPAIRS
Antennae	Forestay antenna feeding into 2 antenna trunks destroyed.	Being replaced by ship's forces.
Windows (Flag Bridge)	Broken by gunfire.	Being replaced as expeditiously as possible.

F. NAVIGATION DEPARTMENT

    a. Four (4) windows broken in Pilot House (believed by own gunfire due to not being housed).

G. MEDICAL DEPARTMENT

    a. Although no actual loss was sustained during the action, the following were expended as a result of furnishing to survivors from damaged ships:

Sheets	103
Blankets	64
Pajama coats	62
Pajama trousers	65

[signed] [Capt.] D.C. GODWIN. [USN]

U.S.S. *TENNESSEE* (BB-43), BATTLESHIP

Tennessee was moored inboard of the *West Virginia* and became wedged hard against the forward quay as the latter ship settled and finally sank to the bottom. *Arizona's* oil fire engulfed the stern of the vessel and caused serious fires aft, especially in the officers' quarters on the second deck.

The explosion of the magazines aboard *Arizona* showered *Tennessee* with burning powder and debris. The forward magazines were purposely flooded as a precaution against the many fires on the ship. These fires were ominous for a long period and were so intense as to warp the stern plates and cause some pulling out of hull rivets.

In order to minimize fires the vessel played several water hoses over the stern to keep the burning oil on the water at a distance. Also the engines were turned over to make five knots and the wake was effective in keeping the oil clear of the ship. There was no movement of the ship even when the engines were run at 10 knots. This shows how securely the ship was wedged between *West Virginia* and the quay.

The vessel was struck by two bombs of the 15 or 16-inch armor-piercing type from high-level bombers. Both bombs had a low order of detonation or perhaps did not explode at all.

The first bomb hit the centerline gun of turret II, causing the barrel to crack. All three guns were rendered inoperable. The second bomb passed through the roof plate of turret III and damaged the structure and the rammer of the left gun.

Several attempts were made to free the ship. About 650,000 gallons of oil were removed by pumping while work progressed on the quay and its buffer. The work proved more onerous than expected and was finished by dynamite blasting about 16 December. In the meantime, repair ship *Medusa* and the Navy Yard patched the warped plates by welding, and blanked off a number of air ports. When *Tennessee* was finally freed she was moved to the Navy Yard where all inside damage was repaired. The ship was ready for service by 20 December.

The day began with the usual Sunday morning routine aboard the twenty year old battleship Tennessee. *She was moored inboard of the* West Virginia *along Battleship row at Berth Fox-6. Many of the crew were looking forward to shore leave and a day in Honolulu. The marine color guide was forming on the fantail for morning colors. On deck a cleaning detachment was preparing for an upcoming Admiral's inspection when some of the men on duty noticed a number of planes off in the distance.* NA 80G-414594

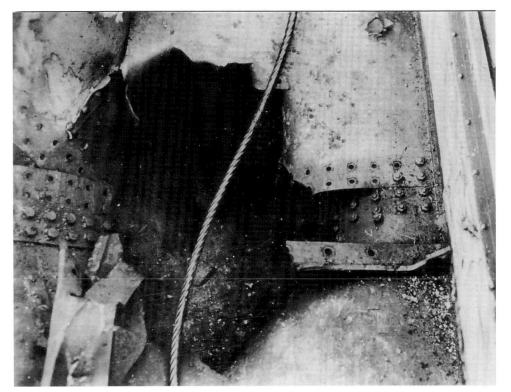

Tennessee *was struck by two 16-inch armor piercing bombs dropped from high-level bombers. One crashed through the catapult and into Turret Three (above) but burned rather than explode killing two men and wounding others. The second bomb struck the centerline gun of Turret Two but did not penetrate the turret or any part of the ship. Shrapnel from the explosion sprayed the ships superstructure and the nearby* West Virginia *wounding a number of men on both ships.* USN NH 64479

The immense explosion of Arizona's *magazines ignited the ship's leaking fuel oil drifting down onto the stern of* Tennessee *that started fires on her quarterdeck and ignited the many layers of paint accumulated over the years. The intense heat from the flames warped* Tennessee's *hull plating, loosened rivets, and burned out electrical wiring. The after magazines were flooded as a safety precaution. The crew fought the fires valiantly while the ship's propellers were kept turning over at 5-10 knots trying to wash away the burning oil from the ship.* NA 80G-32426

U. S. S. *TENNESSEE*

BOMB DAMAGE

December 7, 1941
Pearl Harbor

List of Photos

List of Plates

Class. . . . . .Battleship (BB43)		Length(W. L.). . . 600'	
Launched . . . . .Nov. 20, 1919		Beam. . . . . . 97'6"	
Displ. (Std.) . . . . . . 32,600 tons		Draft (on Dec. 7) .. 35'1"	

References:
(a)   C.O. *TENNESSEE* conf. ltr. to Buships BB43/A16-3/Lll-1 (020), dated Feb. 11, 1942.
(b)   C.O. *TENNESSEE* conf. ltr. to Cincpac BB43/A16-3/(0157), of Dec. 11, 1941.
(c)   Comdt. P.H. conf. ltr. to Buships C-L11-1/BB43/NY10(Y-0224), dated Feb. 4. 1942.
(d)   NYPS to NYPH QS15/L9-3(M-3A) of Feb. 6. 1942.
(e)   O.N.I. Serial 23-42, dated Feb. 16, 1942.

Section I - Narrative

1.   On the morning of Sunday, December 7, 1941, *U.S.S. TENNESSEE* was moored with her starboard side to the quay at berth F-6, Pearl Harbor. *U.S.S. WEST VIRGINIA* was moored alongside, *ARIZONA* astern, and *MARYLAND* and *OKLAHOMA* ahead as shown on Plate I. The wind was force 2 on the port quarter, about 080°T. The average depth of water at berth F-6 was about 40 feet. Boiler No. 1 was steaming for auxiliary purposes.

2.   About 0755, planes, determined to be Japanese by their markings, were observed dive bombing on Ford Island. General Quarters was sounded at once and the ship started setting Condition Zed and preparing to get underway. Almost immediately about 15 torpedo planes came in low over the repair basin and docks on the other side of the channel and delivered a torpedo attack on the battleships. Several torpedoes hit WEST VIRGINIA and she started to list rapidly to port. Quick counterflooding stopped her at about 28° and she came nearly upright and settled to the bottom. *OKLAHOMA* was torpedoed and capsized outboard of *MARYLAND* in about ten minutes.

3.   Simultaneously with and following the torpedo attack planes were bombing from high altitude, dive bombing, and strafing the battleships. Several bombs hit *ARIZONA* and her forward magazines blew up about 0830, showering *TENNESSEE*'S quarter deck with burning powder, oil, and debris. About this time *TENNESSEE* herself received two bomb hits, apparently from high level bombers at about 10,000 feet. One hit and exploded on the center gun of No. 2 turret and the other penetrated the top of No. 3 turret, broke up and did not explode. *WEST VIRGINIA* was also hit by bombs, both of which failed to detonate, and was on fire from her numerous torpedo hits. *TENNESSEE* was ready to get underway on 6 boilers by 0900, but she was blocked in her berth by the events described above.

4.   Large surface oil fires were raging around *TENNESSEE*'S stern and port quarter, fed from both *ARIZONA* and *WEST VIRGINIA*. This started numerous fires on the main deck and in the wardroom country on the second deck, but these were under control by about 1030. Port side magazines D-306-M, D-310-M, and D-312-M were deliberately flooded when they became hot from the surrounding fires. The projectile room, D-316-M and 4 magazines on the starboard side vere apparently not considered in any immediate danger and were not flooded. This left turret IV with over half the ammunition available. Hoses were led out to fight the fires on *WEST VIRGINIA* also and this continued throughout Sunday and Sunday night.

5.   About 1030 it was decided to move *TENNESSEE* forward to escape the fires around the stern and the engines were turned over for five knots with no results, *WEST VIRGINIA* having wedged *TENNESSEE* tightly against the quays. The engines were kept turning for from five to ten knots and fire hoses played over the stern to wash the burning oil away throughout Sunday and Sunday night.

6.   *TENNESSEE* was finally freed on December 16 by cutting away the concrete tops of the quays sufficiently to clear her and allow her to get out by going inside *OKLAHOMA*. She then moved into the Navy Yard for limited repairs.

Section II - Bomb Hit - Turret III

7.   Both bombs which hit *TENNESSEE* were dropped about the same time. The bomb which hit Turret III penetrated the turret top, but it broke up and did not detonate. It was apparently dropped from about 10,000 feet by a plane coming in from about 50° on the starboard bow. The angle of fall was about 75°. The bomb probably struck the after starboard yard of the main mast, which was carried away, and then passed through the catapult on turret III, striking the turret top about five feet from the back plate and three feet in from the left side plate, the turret being trained 180°.

8.   The turret structure in the vicinity is shown on plate II. The roof is made up of 5-inch STS plates with seams extending transversely across the turret. These plates are fitted together by scarf joints; the rear plate marked "A" on plates and photos, being bolted to the underside of the next plate, marked "B". As shown on plate II there is a heavy built up transverse girder supporting plate "B" about a foot and a half from this seam. The bolts used

in the seam were originally bronze, but were partly replaced by steel. Complete replacement had not been made owing to the presence of the catapult foundation.

9.   The bomb apparently struck the left edge of the catapult and bent the sides outward, shearing the bolted seam as shown in plate II and photo 3. It tore a hole about 3 feet by 4 feet in the 10-lb. plating Photos 3 and 4 and then hit 5-inch plate "A". A few pieces were knocked off and projected upward through the catapult plating and the bomb started to punch a hole through the turret top. It made about a two-inch dish in plate "A" and the armor bolts gave way by breaking or pulling through, allowing the front edge of the plate to drop, and creasing the plate in line with the impact of the bomb. The plate then tore along this crease as shown on plate II and in photos 3, 5, and 6. The bomb was deflected forward and broken up. Fragments and filler passed through the hole opened up by failure of the seam connections and fell onto the shell table and rammer in the left gun chamber. These fragments consisted of the nose intact and weighing about 300 lbs., and various other pieces, each about 200 lbs. in weight. Damage inside the turret was primarily due to these large fragments.

10.   The rangefinder tube was cut in two by the sag in plate "A" and by the bomb fragments. It is clearly visible in photo 5. Optical parts which were not actually hit were uninjured and were salvaged. Pieces of the rangefinder constituted a missile hazard, but are not known to have injured anyone.

11.   The transverse girder in the left gun chamber, mentioned in paragraph 8 and shown in the sketches, had a considerable portion carried away and was bent downward about two inches in the middle of its arch. Rivets holding the girder to the roof plate and to the outboard vertical structure were broken, but welded 1/4-inch mild steel mantlet plates over them remained intact and prevented missile hazard.

12.   The flame proof bulkhead between the turret booth and left gun chamber was torn down and in this case also, mantlet plates were effective in preventing missile hazard. Damage to this bulkhead and some fragment damage carried away the following:

(a) Sprinkler control piping

(b) Turret double train indicator (this grounded the turret target indicator and put it out of commission temporarily)

(c) Sound powered telephones to the booth from pointers, ammunition supply, and plot.

(d) Firing circuits.

The flameproof door between the left and center gun chambers was slightly warped, but the dogs remained operable.

13.   Heavy bomb fragments, falling to the shell table of the left gun chamber, broke the rammer head and chain and bent the turret deck down, causing all rammers to run heavily. This was corrected by shimming up the foundation.

14.   There was an intense fire in the left gun chamber due to fiercely burning bomb filler, but this was quickly put out by a 002 extinguisher which was brought up from the electric deck in about three minutes. After the fire was put out the gun chamber was filled with heavy fumes and a considerable amount of unburned filler was scattered about the after end. Inhaling these fumes resulted in serious lung trouble in several cases and considerable discomfort in many others. Contact with the unburned ammonium picrate caused severe inflammation and skin trouble. This danger was removed by cleaning and painting the turret bulkheads.

Section III - Bomb Hit - Turret II

15.   Turret II was trained 000° with guns elevated 90 minutes above horizontal at the time of the attack and while in this position the center gun was hit by a bomb about 40 ft. from the muzzle and about 10 inches to the right of the center-line of the gun. The bomb apparently bit into the C hoop, was turned aft and to starboard, and

gouged out a cylindrical groove extending about two inches into the B hoop. The axis of this groove extended struck the face plate about 4 inches from the outer surface at a point where it was slightly dented. It is difficult to tell exactly how the bomb was falling. Judging from the position of the gouge in the gun and from the fact that the bomb hit at the same time as the one which hit No. 3 turret, it seems probable that it was travelling slightly aft and to port, having been dropped from about 10,000 feet.

16.   When this bomb struck it detonated with a brief, intense flash and fragmentation was apparently good, no fragments over 2 pounds in weight being recovered. Fragment damage was widely distributed but not serious, largely because there was nothing in the immediate vicinity to be damaged.

(1) Turret and guns - The center gun and face plate only had the paint scratched but the right and left guns were quite heavily pitted and gouged from 36 ft. to 40 ft. from the muzzles, the deepest pits being 1/2 inch deep about 38 feet from the muzzles. The slides of the right and left guns had small craters in them with the edges raised about 1/8 inch. These would probably have jammed the guns in the slides if they had been fired while in this condition. These raised areas were filed off smooth.

(2) Air Defense Platform - This is above the pilot house and about 75 feet from the explosion. Two fragments struck the 25 lb. STS bulwark here and made small dents. One fragment struck the 5-lb. windscreen, made a one-inch dent and caused a 4-inch tear in a butt welded joint.

(3) Pilot house, also about 75 ft. from the explosion - Two fragments, each about 2 lbs. in weight passed through the pilot house overhead. One went through the 10-lb. web of an I beam, a 5-lb. bulkhead, and was stopped by a 10-lb. bulkhead faced with an inch of cork insulation. The other bounced off several fittings and was stopped by the same cork covered bulkhead. Several electric cables were cut by these fragments.

(4) Conning tower platform about 40 ft. from the explosion - About twelve fragments-struck the 5-lb. windscreen of the platform around the conning tower where two 50 cal. machine guns were mounted. Eight of these fragments penetrated the screen, making holes from 2 inches to 5 inches in diameter. The other 4 fragments only dented the screen. Those which penetrated severed a few telephone cables, carried away a gyro compass repeater, broke a piece off one machine gun mount, and caused two casualties.

(5) Upper deck, 40-45 feet from explosion - There were about ten holes through the 3" wood and 10-lb. plating on the port side of the upper deck between frames 37 and 40 and a few holes in the wood. A chock at frame 7 (port) and a stanchion at frame 10 (port) were broken, probably by fragments. No fragment effect was observed on the starboard side.

(6) It is also probable that fragments from this bomb caused one casualty on the starboard wing of *WEST VIRGINIA'S* bridge.

17.   The impact of the bomb on the center gun caused considerable damage to the gun and slide. The gouge in C and B hoops has been described in paragraph 15. The C hoop was cracked from this gouge to the forward end as shown on plate II and photos 7 and 8. Several large pieces of C hoop were almost knocked free and there was a constriction of about 1 inch in the bore under the gouge. The slide was cracked completely through on each side, the cracks extending axially through the gun port shield and aft under the trunnions, where they were about 3/4 of an inch wide, to a point about 3 ft. abaft the trunnions, then upward to within about a foot of the top of the slide. These cracks allowed the lower forward part of the slide to sag under the weight of the gun until the gun port shield rested on the face plate at the gun port. This sagging spread the upper part of the slide outward, forcing the center slide trunnions outboard and pushing the wing guns outboard against the deck lugs. There was apparently no damage to elevating gear or gun telescopes and the wing guns appeared to be fully operable. It is interesting to note that the impact of the bomb apparently forced the gun and turret sharply to the left causing the wing guns to "whip". This was apparent at the forward end of the C hoops as cracked paint on the right sides of the B hoops but in no other way.

18.   There was little damage from blast, primarily because there was no light structure in the immediate vicinity to be damaged. Four inch coamings around the gun ports, visible in photo 8, were torn loose and jammed

between the guns and the face plate, thus putting the guns out of action temporarily. These coamings were bolted on the face plate for securing turret bloomers. Flames were reported to have entered the turret through the center gun telescope ports for several feet but these did no damage. The pointer and trainer in the center pit received no injury other than temporary shock. Bridge windows were blown in with a shower of glass splinters. These windows were apparently the original plate glass and have since been replaced by shatterproof glass.

Section IV - Fire and Other Damage

19.   The most extensive damage on the ship was caused by the fires in and around the stern. These fires were started and kept burning by fragments and burning debris which fell on the stern from *ARIZONA*, and oil fires blown down on the water. Although, as stated in paragraph 3, these fires were under control by 1030 Sunday and hoses were continually played over the stern with the engines going ahead, the heat was sufficient to start a fire in the after crane room about 1800 Sunday. This fire was brought under control by 1930 but the danger from oil fires on the water still existed on Monday and Tuesday.

20.   Considerable hull damage was done by the fires on the water from frame 104 to the stern on both sides. All plating above the waterline was warped and buckled, seams opened, and rivets loosened. When the ship obtained temporary repairs approximately 500 ft. of open seams and the points of 700 rivets were welded. Considerable recaulking was necessary. Regular ports in this area had the lenses fused, and gaskets burned out. The welding of one of the blanked ports pulled apart due to distortion of the shell. The main deck was buckled on the port side between frames 127 and 130, and deck planking was charred and burned from frame 136 to the stern. The stern crane electrical system was put out of operation by these fires. One interpole was grounded by flooding, the remote control system burned out, and the power lead burned out on the second deck. The Q coil and quarter deck section of the M coil of the degaussing circuit were destroyed.

21.   Inside the ship the second deck was gutted by fire aft of frame 112. Electrical circuits, including lighting and I.C. circuits were burned out and telephones and equipment burned. What was undamaged by fire was water-soaked by the fire fighting and had to be replaced. In magazines D-306-M, 310-M, and 312-M cable was soaked and cork insulation loosened by the water incident to flooding these spaces.

22.   When the ship was docked for final repairs a dent was uncovered on the port side amidships. This dent was about 40 feet long and 14 feet wide. The deepest point was about 5 feet below the armor belt at frame 64 and was about 6 inches deep. This dent was probably caused by *WEST VIRGINIA* when she heeled over to port. When *WEST VIRGINIA* was docked a long crease was found in her hull just above the turn of the starboard bilge where she had apparently come up against the bottom edge of the armor belt on *TENNESSEE'S* port side. The turn of the bilge beneath this crease probably made the dent in *TENNESSEE'S* hull.

Discussion

23.   The design of the seam between turret plates "A" and "B" is of interest. The stress of impact on top of plate "A" was carried in tension through the armor bolts to plate "B" and to the supporting transverse beam. Had the flange of plate "A" been on top of plate "B" the stress would have been transmitted directly to plate "B" and the bolts would not have failed. The bomb would probably have broken through anyway, but the performance of the armor would undoubtedly have been better.

24.   Fragments collected from this bomb indicated that it was similar to one which was recovered from turret III on WEST VIRGINIA and reconstructed and also to one which was recovered intact on that ship. These bombs were apparently 16-inch projectiles converted for use as bombs by tapering the after portion about 3 inches and by fitting two base fuses and a tail. They were 16.1 inches in diameter, 5 calibers long, and weighed 1575 lbs. without the tail. The charge weight was 66.5 lbs. The penetrating action of the bomb which hit turret II indicates that it was probably of the same type.

25.   It is interesting to compare the fragment effect of the bomb which hit turret II with the one which hit *CHESTER* on February 1, 1942, (See BuShips War Damage Report No. 10, dated April 10, 1942, USS *CHESTER*). The bomb which hit *CHESTER* was apparently a light bomb with an instantaneous fuse and fragment effect was severe, 17-1/2 lb. plating 60 feet from the explosion being penetrated in numerous places and 10 lb. plating 84 feet away being punctured. It has been determined from tests that most of the fragments from a shell or bomb explosion are projected forward in a cone and outward in a belt roughly 90° to the bomb axis. *CHESTER* afforded a good example of this, the major portion of the fragments being projected horizontally and fairly close to the deck. It is this performance and the location of the hit on turret II which explains the distribution and relatively small amount of fragment damage on *TENNESSEE*. The only structure in the immediate vicinity was heavy armor plate and this was only marked by fragments in concentrated areas.

It is probable that most of the fragments went overboard, particularly the large pieces which generally result when a bomb or shell of the armor piercing type explodes. It also appears that some pieces may have been heaved overboard by the repair parties.

26.   An interesting point brought out in reference (a) is the fact that except in small isolated cases the linoleum on decks aft did not burn; even in the areas exposed to greatest heat.

27.   The cases of lung trouble encountered in dealing with the damage in turret III give a graphic illustration of the care needed in dealing with damage caused by an explosion in a confined space where the gases cannot be dissipated. In all such cases rescue breathing apparatus should be used until the space is thoroughly ventilated and cleared.

28.   At the end of the day *TENNESSEE* was immobilized by being pinned against the quays. The high catapult and after airplane crane were out of commission, and the three planes attached to the ship had been destroyed on Ford Island. Damage had been done to the bridge and forward machine gun platform but this in no way affected the fighting condition of the ship. The ship's main propulsion machinery, power and light, secondary battery and anti-aircraft armament were intact and ready and the main battery was ready for action except for the center gun of turret II and the left gun of turret III.

Prompt counter flooding of the heavily damaged West Virginia *(right) during the attack prevented her from capsizing, but as the sinking ship slowly settled on the shallow harbor bottom she wedged* Tennessee *(left) tightly against the mooring quay. Tennessee was finally freed on December 16 after 650,000 thousand gallons of fuel oil was removed to lighten the ship and a large section of the mooring quay was removed by carefully dynamiting it.* NA 80G-41615

After temporary repairs by the Navy Yard, Tennessee *with the battleships* Maryland, Pennsylvania *and a destroyer escort, departed Pearl on December 20 and set course for Bremerton, Washington. At the Puget Sound Navy Yard the "Big T" underwent extensive repairs and major upgrades and was ready for duty in eight weeks. She then steamed to San Francisco in early March 1942 where she joined Task Force One for convoy and patrol operations in the waters between Hawaii and the West Coast.*
NA 80G-395008

USS VESTAL (AR-4), REPAIR SHIP

Vestal was berthed outboard of the ill-fated *Arizona*. The first torpedo which hit the latter ship probably passed under *Vestal*. That vessel saw many of the torpedoes which hit *Arizona* and some which missed both ships.

Vestal was struck with two bombs which were dropped by dive-bombers early in the attack. They were, from Japanese surrender accounts, the 250 kilogram type although the ship assumed that they were the 15 or 16-inch armor-piercing variety. The first bomb hit the forecastle about 0805 and passed through several decks at about frame 43. This bomb exploded in the metal storeroom where the prevalence of metal products deadened the explosion and prevented the bomb from passing through other decks or the shell. Consequently there was no flooding, but the lower platform deck and other structures were badly ruptured.

The second bomb was dropped between the two ships from an elevation of about 1000 feet and struck the ship aft. It passed entirely through the vessel before exploding, and caused serious flooding. It lowered the stern about 10 feet and produced a port list of about seven degrees.

When the fuel oil between the two ships became ignited the captain of *Vestal* decided to move. The vessel got underway about 0830, aided by two tugs as the ship's steering gear was inoperative. After coming to anchor it was decided that the damage was so extensive as to warrant beaching. Accordingly she got underway again at 0950 and grounded herself on Aiea Shoal.

Vestal was a repair ship, and her own artisans undertook the repair work. The temporary work was quite satisfactory but *Vestal's* experience is that water-tight integrity cannot be counted on in the case of older vessels. This ship was about 33 years old at the time, and it was found that flooding was progressive through the bulkhead and deck boundaries which supposedly were watertight.

The repair ship USS Vestal *(AR-4), was moored alongside of* Arizona *at Battleship Row. About 0806 the ship was struck by two 16-inch armor piercing bombs meant for nearby* Arizona. *Taking on water and badly damaged, a yard tug moved her away from the dying* Arizona. *To prevent the ship from sinking* Vestal *was run aground in shallow waters off Aiea Shoals. After the attack yard facilities were at a minimum. In the following six weeks the repair ship's own crew made the hull watertight, cleared damaged and twisted bulkheads, pumped out water and oil keeping the ship afloat till a dry dock was available.* USN NH 50273

U.S.S. VESTAL

From: The Commanding Officer.
To: The Commander-in-Chief, U.S. Pacific Fleet.

Subject: Report of action on December 7, 1941, in accordance with references (a) and (b).

Reference: (a) Art. 840 Navy Regs.
            (b) Cincpac conf. desp. 102102 of Dec. 1941.

a. The *USS Vestal* was struck by two bombs at about 0804 December 7, 1941, while moored port side to port side of the *USS Arizona* berthed at Fox 7, Pearl harbor, T.H. One bomb struck the starboard side at frame 44 penetrating three decks, passing through the upper crew space, GSK stores A-161/2, A-141/2, and exploding in GSK stores lower hold A-9. The fire main and electric cables in crew space were cut. W.T. hatch to A-141/2 buckled and stores in GSK stores and lower hold set on fire and wrecked. As far as can be ascertained there are no indications that this bomb or fragments caused any rupture in the hull.

2. The second bomb struck at frame 110 port side, passed through the carpenter shop, shipfitter ship, shipfitters locker room (D-11/2), fuel oil tanks D-80-P-F and D-82-P-F and left an irregular hole in the hull about 5 feet in diameter just inboard of the bilge keel. The above spaces (D-11/2) flooded up to the level of the carpenter shop with fuel and water.

3. Due to the bomb explosion forward and fire and water in GSK stores, practically all stores are damaged, the extent cannot be ascertained until completion of removal. Heat from this fire necessitated the flooding of the forward magazine containing 100 rounds of target and approximately 580 rounds of service 5" ammunition.

4. Damage as a result of the magazine explosion on the *Arizona* and the resultant fires on the *Vestal* were three life rafts, 6 mooring lines, 1 gangway, rigging and blocks and paintwork burned, stanchions bent, port lenses and windows broken.

1. At about 0820 a torpedo was seen to pass astern of the *Vestal* and it apparently hit the *Arizona* whose bow extended about 100 feet beyond the *Vestal*. The *Arizona's* forward magazine exploded. This explosion started fires aft and amidships on the *Vestal*. Shortly after the *Arizona* was observed to be settling and the fuel oil between *Vestal* and *Arizona* was ignited.

2. At 0830 orders were given to make preparations for getting underway -- this had been anticipated by the Engineer Officer. At 0845 the forward lines were cut, the *Arizona's* quarterdeck was awash, and *Vestal* got underway on both engines, no steering gear. Tug pulled *Vestal's* bow away from the *Arizona*. The *Vestal* started to list to starboard and was taking water aft. She was maneuvered to position with south end of McGrew's Point bearing 30°, distance 910 yards and at 0910 anchored in 35 feet of water.

3. Soundings and draft readings were taken continuously; these showed the ship was settling aft and continuing to list to starboard. Draft aft increased to 27 feet and the list to 6 1/2°. Because of the unstable condition of the ship due to large amount of free surface, the knowledge that we had two holes in the hull -- subsequent inspections showed only one - ship being on fire in several places and the possibility of further attacks, it was decided to ground the ship. At 0950 got underway and maneuvered to position with Old Aiea Railroad Station bearing 73° true and West Tangent of McGrew's Point bearing 320° true; ship grounded. Number 2 white spar buoy close aboard on starboard side amidships. Ship's head 092° true. Depth of water forward 11 feet, amidships 18 feet, aft 27 feet. Draft forward 15 feet, aft 29 feet.

4. Offensive measures.

    a. At 0755 sounded general quarters. Manned the 3" anti-aircraft and 4 - 5" broadside and 2 - 30 caliber machine guns. At about 0805 opened fire with 3" anti-aircraft gun and both machine guns. After firing three rounds, 3" anti-aircraft gun breech jammed; breech was cleared and one additional round was fired when blast from *Arizona* magazine cleared gun station killing one man. Machine guns continued firing on enemy planes until they withdrew.

    2. 3" anti-aircraft and after machine gun both fired at plane which released torpedo at *Arizona* and turned toward *Vestal*. This plane was seen by crew of the machine gun to burst into flame and disappear over Ford Island, this was substantiated by others in the vicinity. Whether the plane was hit by gun fire from *Vestal* or adjacent ships is not known.

5. **Identified dead** - Six

    Unidentified dead - Three, one from 3" anti-aircraft gun platform and two from stern of *Vestal*. These men may have been either *Arizona* personnel blown over by magazine blast or members of *Vestal* after gun crews; they were burned beyond recognition.

    Missing - Seven.

    Hospitalized - Nineteen. About twenty per cent of those hospitalized are seriously injured suffering primarily from burns and fractures.

6. The conduct of all officers and enlisted personnel was exemplary and of such high order that I would especially desire to have them with me in future engagements.

                [signed]
                C. YOUNG.

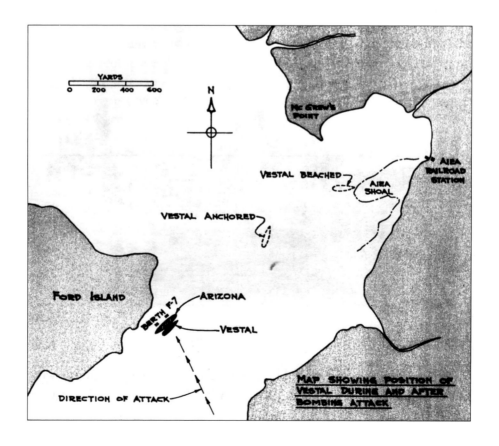

MAP SHOWING POSITION OF VESTAL DURING AND AFTER BOMBING ATTACK

U.S.S. RALEIGH (CL-7), CRUISER

Raleigh was struck by a torpedo early in the attack. Like *Utah*, she occupied a berth usually used by an aircraft carrier. At 0756 the two torpedoes were dropped about 300 yards from the ship. One hit the ship below the 80 pound armor belt and another passed about 235 yards ahead of the ship. The one which hit the ship caused immediate flooding of the two forward boiler rooms and the forward engine room.

General Quarters was sounded at once, and the anti-aircraft battery went into action promptly. Men not at the guns were ordered to jettison weights on the port side, especially those high on the ship.

About 0900 the ship received a bomb hit from a dive-bomber. This was dropped from about 800 feet and passed through three decks and out the side of the ship. It exploded clear of the vessel at frame 112 and caused damage typical of a near-miss. Luckily the compartment, which held 3500 gallons of aviation gasoline, was left intact.

The ship counter flooded, but the construction of the ship was not favorable to a great deal of counter flooding as loss of buoyancy was more important than list. Due to defective hatches the main deck had some free water surface, which, added to that produced by the damage, was almost fatal. The jettisoning of topside weights and the reduction of free surface by pumping water from the main deck saved the ship. It certainly would have been lost in a seaway, as it developed negative stability. This was gradually overcome, partly by lashing an available barge alongside.

Raleigh is an unusual case. The ship was almost lost even with moderate damage. The Commander Battleships commended the captain and crew for saving the ship by remedial actions.

The ship's force and repair ships repaired most of the inside damage to the ship, after removing almost all the fuel, oil, and water which were aboard. It was not until 3 January that the Navy Yard had Dry dock Number One available. Then the yard completed permanent repairs to the hull and bulkheads until undocking on 14 February. Soon she departed on one engine for Mare Island where new engine parts were provided and electrical repairs made.

After training exercises at sea in late November 1941, the light cruiser, Raleigh returned to Pearl Harbor and moored on the northwest side of Ford Island at berth F-12, a berth normally used by carriers. Sunday morning of December 7th a motor launch was alongside waiting to take the Church party to services. The officer-of-the-deck, Ens. Donald L. Korn noticed some low flying planes in the direction of Pearl City. Thinking that they were Marine planes on maneuvers he called out the antiaircraft crew for some practice.
USN NH 64621

About 0755 as the ship's crew prepared for Morning Colors some men noticed the incoming planes had dropped something into the water. Suddenly a violent explosion shook the ship, a torpedo had slammed into the ship's portside raising a huge geyser of water amidships. The inrushing waters quickly flooded the forward engine room and Nos 1 and 2 firerooms causing the ship to lose power and list to port. The Commanding Officer Capt. R. B. Simons, immediately ordered counter-flooding in an effort to prevent the ship from capsizing. NA 80G-32654

The list continued to increase and the ship still was in danger of capsizing. Capt. Simmons gave orders for the crew to jettison all topside weight trying to save the ship. Over the side went the anchors and chains, booms, metal lockers, boat skids, ladders, torpedoes and torpedo tubes, aircraft catapults and anything that could be pried loose, over 60 tons in all. An officer wisely recorded the position of where each item was thrown into the water for recovery later. Fortunately, casualties were light, no one was killed and only a five men were reported wounded during the engagement. NA 80G-32488

USN NH 50769

Shortly after 0900 three Val's of the second wave dove on the Raleigh. *Two bombs missed the ship, but the third, a 500-lb bomb, struck the ship on the port side aft crashing on through three decks, barely missing an aviation gasoline storage tank and on out through the bottom of the hull exploding in the mud about 50-feet from the ship. The list continued to endanger the ship. Capt. Simmons signaled the Navy Yard to send over a lighter. The tug* Sunnadin *came alongside with the barge YPK-2, with four huge salvage pontoons aboard and lashed the barge to* Raleigh, *assisting the cruiser in her valiant struggle to stay afloat.*

NA 80G-32742

December 13, 1941

From: Commanding Officer.
To: Commander in Chief, U.S. Pacific Fleet.
Subject: Report of *U.S.S. Raleigh*'s participation in the battle of Pearl Harbor, December 7, 1941.
Reference: (a) Article 712, Navy Regulations.
Enclosure: (A) Executive Officer's Report

1. About 0755 on the morning of December 7, 1941, I was in my cabin drinking a cup of coffee when I heard and felt a dull explosion in the ship. Looking out my airport I saw the water boiling amidships. I started up to the bridge and was met by Lieutenant Taylor who reported that the Japanese were attacking the Fleet. All hands were called to general quarters and about five minutes later this ship opened fire with the anti-aircraft battery of 3"/50 caliber, 1/1" and .50 cal. guns.

2. Ensign J.W. Werth, USN, was controlling the starboard battery and Ensign J.R. Beardall, Jr., USN, the port battery, both doing a splendid job. The guns were magnificently handled; all hands from chief petty officers to mess boys volunteering to fill out the regular gun crews and keep ammunition supplied.

3. The ship started to heel over to port and it was reported that an airplane torpedo had struck #2 fireroom, flooding it, and that #1 fireroom and the forward engineroom were completely flooded. #3 fireroom was the steaming fireroom, but all fires went out due to water and oil. The damage control party under Ensign H.S. Cohn, D-V(G), USNR and Carpenter R.C. Tellin, USN, was directed to counterflood to bring the ship on an even keel, and they handled their jobs to perfection.

4. It appeared, however, that the ship would capsize. Orders were given for all men not at the guns to jettison all topside weights and to put both airplanes in the water first. Both planes were successfully hoisted out by hand power alone, and were directed to taxi over to Ford Island and report for duty, along with all the aviation detail on board. The senior doctor was directed to report to the *U.S.S. Solace*, to aid in caring for the injured and wounded from other ships (we had no dead and only a few wounded on this ship). An oxy-acetylene outfit and crew were sent over to the capsized *U.S.S. Utah* to cut out any men in the hull. One man was rescued and this man, as soon as he took a deep breath, insisted on going back to see if he could rescue any of his shipmates. A signal was sent to send pontoons and a lighter from alongside the Baltimore to this ship, and they were delivered expeditiously and secured to our port quarter with steel hawsers under the ship and acted as an outrigger. Extra manila and wire lines were run to the quays to help keep the ship from capsizing.

5. Our torpedoes, minus their warheads, were pushed overboard by hand and beached at Ford Island. Both torpedo tubes, both catapults, the steel cargo boom, were all disconnected and jettisoned by hand power. Also, all stanchions, boat skids and life rafts and booms were jettisoned. Both anchors were let go.

6. Shortly after 0900 a glide-bombing attack came in which met with a warm reception. Many near misses fell about the ship. Only one bomb hit. This bomb hit #7 - 3" ready ammunition box a glancing blow and went through the carpenter shop, then through an oil tank, piercing the skin on the port quarter below the water line, and finally detonating on the bottom of the harbor about fifty feet from the ship. In its flight this bomb went over the heads of the gun crew of #7 - 3" gun and also passed very close to

our two large tanks containing 3000 gallons of high-test aviation gasoline. This plane machine-gunned the ship also.

7. Apparently the enemy planes had expected to find the Lexington and Enterprise near our berth and fired at the *Utah* and *Raleigh*, as the carriers were fortunately not in. When it appeared that the ship might not capsize or sink (the water was 45' deep at our berth) Ensign J.H. COYLE, USN, of the *Raleigh*, was told to see if he could find an oil bottom that was free from water and to raise steam in either #3 or #4 fireroom, as water was getting in to the after engine room and #3 and #4 firerooms, and if they were flooded there would be little hope of keeping the ship afloat. This was done and the pumps started.

8. Meanwhile the gun crews on the top side kept up a heavy and accurate fire. Five bombing planes which this ship had under fire and on which hits were observed, were seen to crash close aboard, either in flames or in fragments.

9. It would be difficult to single out all individuals who acted above and beyond the call of duty, as the conduct of every one was magnificent. The commanding officer, however, was particularly pleased to note that the junior officers and non-rated men acted like veterans and their spirit and morale was only heightened by the surprise attack.

10. As this ship has been in the Hawaiian Detachment for over two years, many of the married officers and men live ashore when not in the duty section. When the attack opened, the acting gunnery officer, chief engineer, and damage control officers were all Ensigns. Those officers and men who were ashore reported back to the ship most expeditiously and participated valiantly in the last plane attack. After the attack and during the night of December 7th, the ship would vary in list from 11 degrees port to 8 degrees starboard without any apparent reason and was very tender.

11. The tugs Sunnadin and Avocet came alongside during the afternoon and furnished light, steam and food as fast as practical and their services were very helpful.

12. Damage to enemy: The following ammunition was expended on this vessel during the day:

3"/50 caliber	266 rounds
.50 caliber	9990 rounds
1.1"	3270 rounds

Many planes were taken under fire from time to time without apparent results. However, there were five planes destroyed which this vessel registered hits on and assisted in their destruction, namely:

#1 - Bomber flew over stern from starboard to port, burst into flames over *Raleigh* and crashed on deck of *U.S.S. Curtiss*.

#2 - Plane flew over bow from starboard to port and crashed near Pearl City.

#3 - Plane flying north on our starboard beam crashed in water between Dobbin and Baltimore.

#4 - Plane off our stern flying over air station towards Curtiss was hit by a 3" shell and was blown to pieces in the air.

#5 - A plane flying across our stern had its tail blown off and fell over by Pearl City without burning or great damage. The pilot may have escaped.

13. One torpedo ran between the bow of the *Raleigh* and the stern of the *Detroit* and apparently sank in shoal water at Ford Island without exploding and is still there.

14. The end of the bomb that went through the port quarter of this ship was recovered from the damaged fuel tank and was forwarded to Commander in Chief, Pacific Fleet.

15. Damage control and salvage efforts are being continued successfully at the time of this report.

[signed]
R.B. SIMONS

Within a week following the attack Raleigh's *own repair party had temporarily patched the bomb hole aft and Yard workers installed a concrete patch over the underwater torpedo damage. The ship was moved into Dry Dock One on 3 January 1942 for permanent repairs to the hull. Once declared seaworthy* Raleigh *cleared Pearl Harbor in a convoy on 21 February 1942 bound for San Francisco and the Mare Island Navy Yard to repair her machinery, misc. interior spaces and for weapon system upgrades.* Raleigh *returned to active duty in early July 1942.* USN NH 54563

U.S.S. *CURTISS* (AV-4), SEAPLANE TENDER

The seaplane tender *Curtiss* was moored near the Ford Island Air Station. General Quarters was immediately sounded and all guns were in action within five minutes. By 0825 the enemy planes were repulsed. At 0840 the ship sighted a submarine periscope at 700 yards and promptly opened fire when the sub partly surfaced. Two hits were made by 5-inch projectiles from number 3 gun.

Damage to the ship resulted from an enemy aircraft colliding with the forward crane. The enemy plane burned on the boat deck. This occurred at 0905. Another bombing attack occurred at 0912. One bomb fell on the mooring buoy aft and two bombs fell alongside. Fragment damage from these three bombs was considerable. Another bomb struck the starboard side of the boat deck, passed through three decks and exploded on the main deck causing considerable damage.

These bombs were about 250 kilograms, measured about 12 inches in diameter, and carried about 130 pounds of TNT. They were released by dive-bombers from a height of about 300 to 400 feet.

The widespread damage caused by fragments to the piping, electric wires, steam lines, and ammunition supply, etc. overshadowed entirely the structure damage which they caused. Even the after engine room was affected by fragments from the bomb hit. Many fires were started and these were difficult to extinguish due to smoldering cork insulation and poor lighting.

Much of the fragment damage could have been prevented by use of some armor, which was forbidden in auxiliary vessels under the arms limitation treaties. Later designs provided two-inch splinter protection for 60 percent of the length, as well as splinter protection for gun, fire control, and ship control stations.

The Navy Yard undertook repairs to *Curtiss* on two separate availabilities: the first was from 19 to 27 December. When replacements parts were received, *Curtiss* was in the yard from 26 April to 28 May 1942. At that time final repairs were made.

The large seaplane tender, USS Curtiss *having returned from a voyage transporting needed supplies and several hundred civilian workers to Wake Island, entered Pearl on the evening of 5 December 1941. The* Curtiss *tied up at the mooring buoys at berth X-22 near the mouth of Middle Loch opposite Ford Island. About 0750 on the morning of the 7th the deck watch heard a loud explosion from the hanger area on Ford Island and immediately sounded General Quarters.* NA 80G-266628

During the second wave of the attack a Val dive-bomber piloted by Lt. Mitsumori Suzuki was pulling out from a dive over Ford Island when his plane was hit by AA fire from Curtiss *and other nearby ships setting it aflame. The crippled plane crashed into* Curtiss's *starboard boat crane amidships disintegrating upon impact. The planes gas tank exploded spraying the ship's decks with burning gasoline. The tender was in serious danger from the resulting fires.* USN NH 96660

The burning gasoline had set the ships nearby starboard boats aflame forcing the crew of #3 anti-aircraft gun to abandon their battle station. They returned to duty once all fires were extinguished. Several voids were flooded to correct the list to starboard and bring the Curtiss *to an even keel. Casualties were heavy with 21 men killed in action and another 58 wounded. Some of the seriously wounded were transferred over to the hospital ship* Solace. USN

At 0912, few minutes after the crash of the Japanese plane, the tender came under attack by four Val dive bombers. One bomb hit the stern mooring buoy, another fell short while a third overshot the ship. A fourth bomb did not miss and smashed into the ship's top deck on the starboard side of the boat deck. The bomb penetrated through three decks and exploded on the main deck inside the hanger causing heavy damage and raging fires in the upper deck compartments, the hanger and the second deck below. AM PH358-41

The detonation from the bomb that crashed through the ship's upper decks demolished several shops in its path starting many fires and destroyed a 5-inch ammunition handling room. The blast also made a shambles of the radio room's electronic equipment trapping two enlisted men under the heavy radio transmitters. Valiant rescue efforts saved one man but flames and smoke forced the rescuers back and they could not save the last man. NA

By early afternoon all fires were brought under control. The crew then turned to for emergency repairs, pumping out of flooded compartments and clean-up. View of the main and hanger deck looking forward, showing the wrecked hanger doors and interior damage from the bomb that exploded inside the hanger. In the foreground is the wreckage of a Navy OS2U-2 "Kingfisher" scout plane that was set afire and destroyed by the explosion. AM PH358-41

It was nearly two weeks before the ship was put in yard hands. Working round the clock for eight days the temporary repair work was finish by December 27. The next day Curtiss was underway for San Diego and permanent repairs and upgrades. The damaged crane was removed a replaced with 20mm guns. The work was completed in only four days. The seaplane tender was back in Pearl Harbor by 13 January 1942 begin operations in the South Pacific. Curtiss received seven battle stars for World War II service. EA

U.S.S. HELM (DD-388), DESTROYER

The *Helm* was attacked by a dive-bomber at 0915 when about five miles southwest of Aloha Tower. She reported that the enemy fighter dropped two bombs from a height of about 1000 feet. The first fell about 100 to 150 feet off the port bow, and the other about 30 feet to starboard abreast frame 10.

The second bomb deluged with water the forecastle and the gun director. No fragments were observed. The forward part of the ship suffered considerable damage from the near-miss. The foundation of the gun director steadily grew worse, and the flooding forward was severe in the peak tanks and forward compartments. Some damage occurred due to short circuiting and kicking out of circuit breakers in the forward part of the ship.

Helm was dry docked in the Yard's marine railway on 15 January 1942. Here permanent repairs were made to the shell plating, structure forward, gun directors, and electrical lines. The shell plating showed the effects of the near-miss. Shear lines were seen forward of bulkhead 14. The practical effects of the near-miss were in accordance with the naval architectural theory.

On the morning of 7 December the destroyer Helm was underway for the deperming buoys in West Loch. General Quarters was sound immediately upon sighting planes attacking the hangers on Ford Island. Helm turned into the main channel toward the harbor entrance and began patrolling off shore. At 0915 a lone dive bomber attacked the ship. The concussion from two close near misses off the bow split seams flooding some forward interior compartments. Luckily, there were no injuries. The damage was brought quickly under control and the ship resumed patrolling. NA 19N-18036

DD388/A1603 (483)

U.S.S. *HELM*,
December 11, 1941.

From: The Commanding Officer.
To: The Commander in Chief, U.S. PACIFIC FLEET.

Subject: Action during air raid on December 7 -- Report on.

Reference: (a) CinCPAC desp., 102102 December 1941.

1. In compliance with reference (a) the following report is submitted:

a. **NARRATIVE**

0726   Underway from berth X-7 for deperming buoys at West Loch. All hands at special sea detail stations. Both boats manned and in the water with instructions to follow the ship to West Loch. All magnetic compasses and chronometers had been left in the Blue preparatory to deperming.

0755   Turned into West Loch channel and headed up toward deperming buoys.

0759   First enemy plane sighted in shallow dive over Ford Island, headed northwest. Observed first bomb hit on hanger at southwest end of Ford Island. Called crew to General Quarters. Executive Officer went below to assist in opening magazines and getting ammunition to guns.

0800   Torpedo planes sighted approaching from direction of Barber's Point. They passed over West Loch channel and dropped torpedoes either in North Channel or across the island. Targets for these planes appeared to be ships in berths F-9 to F-13. The planes came in low, and several strafed the ship. All bullets missed the ship by a few feet. no fire was opened, since the forward machine guns which could bear were coated with preservative grease and had to be cleaned before they could fire.

0800   Backed engines and commenced maneuvering ship out of West Loch channel to head for entrance.

0805   Opened fire with after machine guns at planes over the main channel, followed shortly by the forward machine guns firing at passing torpedo planes.

0807   Opened fire with 5" battery. No hits observed.

0810   In main channel steaming toward entrance. Fire from port after machine gun, manned by HUFF, W.C., GM.2c, 337 00 90, hit plane approaching from south. Plane veered sharply, caught fire, and crashed behind trees near Hickam Field. Ordered al boilers lighted off.

0813   Passed gate vessel.

0817   Sighted conning tower of submarine to right of channel, northward of buoy #1. Gave orders to open fire, pointer fire, but submarine submerged before guns could get on.

0818   Increased speed to 25 knots, cleared entrance buoys, turned right.

0819   Submarine conning tower surfaced.

0820   Opened fire on submarine off Tripod Reef, bearing 290 distance 1200 yards from buoy #1. No hits observed, but there were several close splashes. Submarine appeared to be touching bottom on ledge of reef, and in line of breakers. While still firing at submarine it apparently slipped off ledge and submerged.

0820   Main contact relay on power panel of steering motor short circuited due to loose pigtails. Bridge lost steering control. Orders were given to shift to hand steering, commenced maneuvering ship by engines. Main circuit breakers opened, taking all light and power off ship for about one minute.

0820   Made plain language contact report of Submarine to CinCPAC on 2562 Kc.

0821   Men on after guns and amidships observed torpedo pass close under the stern on a northwesterly course. Report of this did not reach the bridge.

0824   The shift to hand steering was completed.

0830   Steaming on various courses and speeds off Harbor entrance, steering by hand, firing intermittently at enemy planes, and searching for submarines, numerous large splashes being observed close at hand. One plane under fire from forward machine guns was observed to veer sharply away and may have been hit.

0900   Destroyers commenced sortie.

0915   Small enemy fighter plane approached ship from astern (northwest), in medium glide and dropped two bombs, which exploded in water 50 yards off port bow and 20 yards off starboard bow. Plane was sighted by after machine gun crews while close in on dive. They opened fire, but apparently did not hit plane. Ship was swinging rapidly to port, which probably caused bombs to miss. Ship shook violently and all forward part was deluged with water. Steering casualty had just been repaired, but shock shorted relay again and hand steering was continued. Cyro rotor tumbles; all repeaters out. Choke coils tubs and resistors in sound gear burned out; echo rang-

0920   ing inoperative.

0930   (about) Received orders by TBS to patrol sector 3.

1000   Shifted steering motor power to diesel generator; regained bridge control of steering.

       Reported to ComDesRon Four that ship was patrolling sector 3. Continued patrol until orders

1100   were received at 1215 to rendezvous on Detroit.

       Sound listening watch heard screws on starboard quarter. Ship circled for attack but lost contact.

1215   No depth charges dropped.

       Received orders to join Detroit. Ceased patrolling.

2. SPECIAL REPORTS

1. Offensive measures taken:5" and .50 caliber fire at all enemy aircraft within range, after 0805. Fire was slow due to necessity of breaking ammunition out of magazines and belting all but a small amount of .50 caliber ammunition. Total of 90 rounds 5" and 350 rounds .50 caliber was expended.

5" fire at enemy submarine off Tripod Reef at 0820.

2. Damage to enemy:

One plane shot down by machine gun fire at 0810. One plane possibly hit by machine gun fire at 0830.

Possible fragment hits on conning tower of submarine at 0820.

3. Own losses and damage:

Losses:

There were no losses or injuries to personnel.

Damage:

1. Steering casualty at 0820. This was not the result of enemy action, and was probably caused by vibration incident to heavy backing while clearing West Loch channel and shock of gun fire.

2. Damage as result of bomb near-misses at 0915:

    a. Seams below water line on starboard side forward sprung. A-15, A-301, A-401, and A-402 flooded. These compartments were closed off and pumped out during the afternoon.

    2. Steering gear inoperative due to phase relay breaking loose on panel and short circuiting main contact relay which had just been repaired from previous casualty.

    3. Cyro rotor tumbled; all repeaters inoperative. This casualty rendered impossible effective director control of AA fire, due to absence of own course component. All magnetic compasses had been landed preparatory to deperming.

    4.Welded seams around director pedestal on director platform cracked on three sides where pedestal is secured to top of director tube. At the time, this damage did not render director inoperative. On the following day, these seams cracked open further due to high speeds and heavy seas, until director was in imminent danger of going overboard. Shored up director on all sides, reported situation to ComDesRon Four, and was directed return Pearl.

    5. Choke coils, tubes, and resistors in QCB power unit in sound room burned out, rendering echo ranging inoperative. Listening facilities not affected.

    6. Sheared rivets and burned out tubes in rectifiers in main radio room. Temporary repairs effected immediately.

    7. TBS contactor relay on motor generator knocked out of adjustment.

    8. FS smoke generators jumped tracks, breading air line connection.

4.Conduct of personnel:

Throughout the attack the conduct of personnel was of the highest order. Men of the engineer force and torpedomen turned to without orders belting Machine gun ammunition and breaking out powder and projectiles. The spirit evidenced by all hands was a true "fighting spirit"; the Commanding Officer knows of no instance where this was not the case.

Helm was dry docked in the Yard's marine railway on 15 January 1942. Here permanent repairs were made to the shell plating, structure forward, gun directors, and electrical liens. The shell plating showed the effects of the near-miss. Shear lines were seen forward of bulkhead 14. The practical effects of the near-miss were in accordance with the naval architectural theory.

[signed] C.E. CARROLL.

SHIPS SUNK

U.S.S. SHAW (DD-373), DESTROYER

Shaw was in Floating Drydock Number Two when hit by three bombs from the same dive-bombers that attacked *Nevada* about 0850. The first two bombs came from port to starboard and apparently hit just aft of 5-inch gun number 1. They penetrated the forecastle and main decks and exploded with a low order of detonation in the crew's mess on the first platform deck. These bombs, according to Japanese records, were the 250 kilogram type, and were in part responsible for severing the bow forward of the bridge.

The third bomb was of the same type and passed through the bridge. It exploded in the wardroom pantry, and ruptured the fuel oil tanks, scattering burning oil throughout that portion of the ship. The heat from this oil fire caused the forward magazines to blow up. This wrecked the forward part of the ship as far back as frame 65.

When the floating drydock sank, the forward section of the ship went down with it, but the area from frame 60 aft was buoyant and remained afloat. There was considerable flooding of the forward boiler rooms, and the after boiler rooms had 10-15 inches of water. This entered through leaks in the periphery of bulkhead 106 but was controlled by the portable gasoline pump procured next day from the Navy Yard.

Shaw was originally reported as a total loss but its machinery was in good condition. It was only from frame 65 forward that the vessel was severely injured. Accordingly, the forward part was entirely cut off and the portion abaft frame 60 was docked on the Yard's marine railway on 19 December. At that time the Navy Yard took measurements for the fabrication of a false bow. This was installed on Shaw on 26 January 1942 when the ship subsequently was docked on Floating Drydock Number Two.

The Navy Yard scrapped the bridge area of Shaw and installed a temporary mast and. ship control station. The vessel was undocked on 4 February, and after a few trials departed for Mare Island on 9 February. She was the first severely damaged vessel to put to sea, and there was great jubilation at Pearl Harbor to see her leave under her own power only two months after she was given up for lost. She was under command of Commander W. G. Jones.

In the last week of November 1941, the USS Shaw (DD-373) *and the yard tug,* Sotoyomo (YT-9), *were moved into the floating dry dock, YFD-2 for overhaul and repairs. They were still in the dry dock on the morning of December 7. Fortunately while work was in progress most of the crews of both vessels were ashore.* NA 19N-17929

At 0910 three 250-kilogram bombs smashed through the Shaw, two went through the forward machine gun platform and one hit the portside of the bridge. The explosions started uncontrolled raging fires and within twenty minutes the forward 5-inch ammunition magazine blew up destroying the bow forward of frame 65. In an instant twenty-five of the ship's crew were lost. The fiery blast hurled shells and flaming debris hundreds of feet into the air with some landing as far away as Ford Island. A moment in time caught on film by a navy photographer, the spectacular explosion of the Shaw, remains as one of the most memorable images of the attack on Pearl Harbor. NA 80G-16871

The explosion of the ammunition magazine destroyed the bridge superstructure and nearly tore the bow completely off just aft of the second 5-inch mount. When the dry dock, already badly holed, was flooded to prevent further damage from the fires, the Shaw's bow, barely holding on by a few shreds of torn metal, broke off and rolled over into the water. Despite the loss of her bow the remaining two-thirds of the ship though seriously damaged remained afloat. NA 80G-19939

By late afternoon most fires were extinguished but the remains of Shaw's bridge super-structure, now reduced to a mass of molten and twisted steel, still smolders from the explosion that destroyed the ship's forward section. When the badly holed floating dry dock, YFD-2, finally sank the bow of the Shaw went with it but the aft section from frame 60 remained buoyant.
NA 80G-32516

A few days after the attack Salvage personnel did a survey of the damaged Shaw. At first thought to be a total loss, they found that damage to the ship's engine spaces and everything aft of the shattered bridge was minor and could be saved. They recommended the removal of as much topside weight as possible and use pumps to reduce the water level so the ship can be moved onto the Navy Yard's marine railway where yard workers could cut away the wreckage forward and measure the ship for a temporary bow.
PHPC

To get the Shaw *ready for the journey to the West Coast everything forward of the stack was removed down to the main deck. A temporary bow was fabricated in the yard shops and attached to the hull. A tri-pod mast with an observation platform was built in place of the bridge and a single 5-inch gun was mounted just forward of the aft deckhouse. Following sea trials the* Shaw *left Pearl Harbor on 9 February 1942 still capable of steaming at 25-knots.* PHPC

When the Shaw *(right) arrived at the Mare Island Navy Yard, California for permanent repairs, a new bow, surrounded by scaffolding (left), had already been built in the dry dock awaiting the ship's arrival. After the* Shaw *was moved into the dock the water level was lowered so the ship would come to rest on keel blocks before starting work to remove the temporary bow.* NA 80G-21336

The temporary bow has been removed and placed forward in the dock where yard cranes will lift it out to be cut up later into scrap metal and melted down and re-used for the war effort. The dock will then be flooded enough to carefully shift Shaw's *surviving hull (right) into place to have the new forward section permanently installed and the first step in the work to restore the ship back to fighting trim.* NA

After two months of round-the-clock work, the new forward section including a completely new bridge, pole mast, and gun platforms firmly installed, the Shaw is now ready to be launched. The ship will then move to a fitting out dock where she will receive the latest in guns, anti-aircraft weapons, radar and other upgrades. A brand new Shaw steamed to Pearl Harbor in mid-July 1942 to rejoin the Pacific Fleet. Shaw would earn eleven battle stars for her service in World War Two. NA

On December 7, 1941 the yard tug Sotoyomo YT-9 built in 1903, was the oldest active duty ship at Pearl Harbor. After the attack she appeared to be a total loss having been severely damaged and set afire when the Shaw blew up and then completely submerged when the dock sank. But the Pearl Harbor Salvage Unit thought otherwise, the tug was raised and repaired and by late summer 1942, a new Sotoyomo again assumed full time tug duties at Pearl Harbor. PHP

DD373/A8
Serial (026)

U.S.S. SHAW (373)
Pearl Harbor, T.H.
January 29, 1942.

From: The Commanding Officer.
To: The Chief of the Bureau of Ships.

Subject: War Damage Reports.

Reference: (a) BuShips conf, ltr. C-EF 13/A9(374); C-S81-3; C-EN28/A2-11 of October 28, 1941.

1. In compliance reference (a), the following report is submitted. The paragraph nomenclature of reference (a) is ued throughout, using only those captions where applicable to this vessel or where information known.

    A.   [1] *U.S.S. Shaw* (373)
           {2} 0755-0915, December 7, 1941.
           [3] In Floating Drydock No. 2 at Navy Yard, Pearl Harbor, T.H.

      1. Three (3) aircraft bombs. Apparently liquid incendiary -- estimated 200-300 lb.
      2. (b) Dive release; 1,000 feet; steep.
      3. Two through forward Machine Gun platform between frames 50-55; one through port wing of bridge structure at frame 60.
      4. Inclined sightly from the vertical from port to starboard.
      5. (a) First two penetrated following decks: Machine Gun platform, gun shelter platform, forecastle and main decks, exploding, it is believed in the crew's mess room.
        (b) The third apparently passed through the bridge platform, chart house deck and forecastle deck, exploding in the wardroom pantry.
        All decks are 10-12 lb. plate except main deck which is 15-18 lbs.
      6. (a) 30 feet, approximately.
        (b) 24 feet, approximately.
      7. Due to the tremendous fire that ensued after the explosion of the bombs, no estimate of damage to machinery can be made. While it was thought that liquid-filled incendiary bombs were used, it may well be that the explosion ruptured the forward fuel tanks, igniting the oil and throwing blazing oil all through that section of the ship and down into the dock. Twenty minutes later the forward magazines blew up, totally wrecking the area between frames 35-65.

      1. The magazine explosion separated the bow from the rest of the ship with the exception of the keel structure. While the dock was sinking, the bow slowly toppled over to starboard and was submerged in the rising water. The forward fireroom filled with water due, as was ascertained days later, to a leaking forward starboard bulkhead and to empty rivet holes along the top edge of plating at the main deck, starboard side, between frames 68-75. Frames 70-75 had been under repair, necessitating removal of the rivets.

       ,li> Some water was present -- 10"-15" -- in No. 2 fireroom due to leaks around edges of bulkhead between the two firerooms. A portable gasoline pump obtained from the yard on the morning of 8 December was effectual in preventing further flooding of No. 2 fireroom.

2. It is believed that had there been water available to immediately fight the fire caused by the bombs, the magazines might have been kept from blowing up. Furthermore, it is believed that the magazines blew up as a result of the external fire and heat coming from the burning fuel oil and wooden blocks in the dock.

3. All machinery from the forward fireroom bulkhead forward was destroyed or rendered beyond economical repair with the possible exception of the anchor windlass which is now undergoing inspection in Navy Yard, Pearl Harbor, T.H., having been salvaged from the bow portion. One anchor and two chains plus miscellaneous chocks and bitts have also been salvaged.

4. It is believed, in connection with the above, that two or more bombs exploded in the dock between the ship and the starboard side of the dock which enhanced the oil fire within the ship. As the dock slowly sank, its tanks, which had been just refueled on the previous day, were ruptured covering the water around the ship with sheets of blazing oil. It was only due to a strong wind from the stern aided by the strenuous efforts of the remaining personnel, that the after portion of the ship was saved from the same catastrophe as overtook the *Cassin* and *Downes*, both being gutted by fire after the bomb explosions.

5. Practically all the records and files of the ship were completely destroyed. Those saved intact were all those engineering blue prints in the log room, one typewriter, and the medical records in the ship's sick bay.

/signed/
W. GLENN JONES.

Copy to:
OPNAV
CINCPAC
COMBATFOR
COMDESBATFOR
COMDESRON THREE
COMDESDIV SIX
CMDT, NYMI
CMDT, NYPH

PRELIMINARY REPORT

U.S.S. *SHAW*

BOMB DAMAGE

Dec. 7, 1941

Pearl Harbor

Class	Destroyer (DD373)	Length (L.W.L.)	334'
Launched	October, 1935	Beam	35'-5"
Displacement		Draft	
(standard)	1500 tons	(designed)	10'-7-1/2"

References:
(a) Navy Yard, Pearl Harbor, conf. plan DD370-11/1-5,
    Alt. O (Damage Investigation).
(b) C.O. SHAW conf. ltr. to Buships, DD373/A8, Serial
    026, of January 29, 1942. (War Damage Report).

Narrative

1. *U.S.S. Shaw* was in the old New Orleans floating drydock (YFD2) at the Navy Yard, Pearl Harbor, on the morning of December 7, 1941. The weather was clear, with scattered clouds.

2. Three bombs struck the ship between 0755 and 0915. These were released from steep dives at about 1000 feet. Reference (b) reports that the bombs were liquid-filled incendiaries weighing from 200 to 300 lbs. There is no positive evidence that incendiaries were used elsewhere in the attacks on ships at Pearl Harbor, and it is believed that none were dropped on *Shaw*. The subsequent fire can be ascribed to ruptured oil tanks.

3. The first two bomb paths were inclined from port to starboard. These bombs apparently struck the machine gun platform just abaft 5-inch gun No. 2, and penetrated the gun shelter platform, forecastle and main decks. They perhaps exploded in the crew's mess room on the first platform deck.

4. The third bomb seems to have come in at an angle of about 30 degrees with the horizontal and inclined slightly forward. It appears from the photographic evidence that this bomb struck the port side of the superstructure deck (Photo 10), passed through the corner formed by the after side of the radio room and the port side of the stores office (Photo 11), entered the supply office, went out through the starboard after corner of that office (Photo 12), and thence went overboard through the starboard rail just above the main deck. This path is sketched on Plate I. It may have penetrated the main deck and gone out through the starboard sheer strake. But in any case, it appears impossible that the hole shown on Plate I at frame 64 and in Photo 15 could have been the exit point of this bomb, nor is it likely that it exploded within the ship.

5. It appears that all three hits were made at about the same time. Fire broke out at once. Twenty minutes later the forward magazines blew up. This explosion severed the bow at about frame 65 with the exception of some bottom structure. The dock was deliberately flooded to prevent more damage to it. As it sank, the bow of *Shaw* toppled over to starboard and went down with the dock. This is shown by Photos 1 and 2. The Yard tug Sotoyomo was also in the dock and sank with it.

6. Two or more bombs may have exploded in the dock between the ship and the starboard side of the dock, according to reference (b).

7. As the dock sank, oil from its ruptured tanks burned on the water surrounding the ship. A strong wind from the stern aided the personnel in saving the after portion of the ship from the flames.

8. The after portion was later docked on the marine railway. Photos 10 to 13 show the underbottom damage.

9. A temporary bow was built on the as shown on Plate II and Photo 17, and the voyage to the mainland for permanent repairs was safely made under her own power. The remains of the original bow are shown by Photo 18.

10. Evidence from the *Cassin* and *Downes* attack suggests that the 12-inch, 250-kilogram general purpose bomb was used, such as the sample recovered near Schofield Barracks. It is probable that at least the first two hits on *Shaw* were from this type of bomb. The holes made by the third bomb in *Shaw* indicate either the above-mentioned bomb, or possibly a 16-inch A.P. bomb. Blast effects are greater and fragment sizes are smaller for relatively light-case general purpose bombs than for A.P. bombs of the same or somewhat greater sizes. There have been no reports of any discoveries of large fragments from A.P. bombs in or near *Downes*, *Cassin* or *Shaw*, so the general purpose bomb is the more probable.

Structural Damage

11. No information is available other than that given by the attached photographs and the notes on Plate I, which were entered by the Navy Yard, Pearl harbor. Some points of interest are:

a. The director and its foundation held up remarkably well; see Photos 4, 7 and 8.

b. Aluminum construction disintegrates in a bad fire and has practically zero salvage value.

c. The wrinkling of the bilge keels and dimpling of the hull shown by Photos 13, 14 and 15 appear more like near-miss damage to a waterborne ship than like blast damage from a ship high and dry in dock.

d. Indentations made by the bilge blocks in the floating dock are seen on Photo 14. These may have been caused by the ship lifting bodily and dropping back on the blocks while the after portion was only partly waterborne.

12. In connection with (c) above, a somewhat similar case was the bomb damage to H.M.S. Cameron. This ex-U.S. destroyer was knocked off the bilge blocks while in drydock at Portsmouth, England, on December 5, 1940, by a bomb which struck a dock altar alongside the ship. It does not appear from the British report that Cameron's hull was nearly as badly wrinkled as Photos 13 to 15 show for *Shaw*. Both ships were surrounded by burning oil. Perhaps the bombs mentioned in paragraph 6 fell after the magazine explosion, while the dock was sinking, and caused the "near-miss" type of damage seen on *Shaw*'s hull. But this, as other aspects of the damage, is in the realm of conjecture and will probably remain so.

Flooding

14. As the dock sank, the forward fireroom filled with water. There were leaks in the forward bulkhead on the starboard side. There were also some rivets out of the shell at the main deck between frames 68 and 75, where repairs were being made to frames.

15. About 10 or 15 inches of water entered the after fireroom due to leaks around the periphery of bulkhead 106. This was controlled by a portable gasoline pump obtained from the Yard the next day.

FLOATING DRY DOCK NUMBER TWO YFD-2

This floating drydock was subjected to a heavy blitz about 0850. The Japanese planes were dive-bombers dropping 250 kilogram bombs, five of which fell near the floating drydock. She was submerged for protection.

Four of the bombs impaired her watertight integrity. At least 155 holes were welded or plugged by divers before she was raised on 9 January 1942.

She had rested on the bottom of Pearl Harbor for over a month at an angle of over fifteen degrees. Besides the damage from fragments she suffered from the fires which occurred on *Shaw*.

This floating dock was restored to service on 25 January 1942, and the next day she docked *Shaw* as her first customer since the morning of 7 December. For some time she operated on a limited basis because of a large hole which had not yet been repaired. It was not until 15 May that she was considered as good as new.

The 525-foot long floating dry dock was lowered by letting water into port and starboard side ballast tanks to allow a ship to enter for maintenance or repairs. The water in the ballast tanks was then pumped out to raise the dock and bring the ship out of the water. After the attack the sunken dock was raised and restored for temporary service by 25 January 1942. It was fitting that the next day the first ship to enter the floating dry dock was the Shaw *to have her newly fabricated false bow installed for the journey to the West Coast.* PHP

Bridge structure of the USS Shaw *showing the damage caused by the explosion of her forward magazines. The super-structure of the half-sunken flotation drydock is in the foreground.* NA 80G-32771

U.S.S. CASSIN (DD-372) AND *U.S.S. DOWNES* (DD-375)

These two vessels were a sorry spectacle indeed, as can be seen from the illustration on page 207. They were docked forward of Pennsylvania, and were the victims of serious fires, much fragmentation, and precautionary flooding of the drydock. After the attack *Cassin* and *Downes* were reported as total losses. The big question seemed to be how to get them clear of the drydock. They had gone through every kind of ordeal which ships could be subjected to, from bomb hits to severe fires, to explosions, to fragmentation damage, etc. These vessels were the only ones of the Pearl Harbor group that suffered all the kinds of damage enumerated, for which reason they are given special attention.

The bombs which struck or exploded near *Cassin* and *Downes* were the 250 kilogram type and were dropped by both high-level and dive-bombers. Incendiary bombs were not dropped as was reported originally by ship crews.

High-level planes were active in the area at about 0815, but it was not until 0850 that ten or fifteen dive-bombers approached. About ten of these attacked *Nevada* while the remainder covered the ships in Drydock Number One and in the floating drydock. At this time a hit was scored on *Cassin*. It went out through the bottom of the ship at frame 140 and struck the drydock floor between *Cassin* and *Downes*, starting a fire immediately. A few minutes later a bomb struck the edge of the dock on the starboard side, and another on the port side. These hits cut off the water supply of the Yard and also the electric power. A second bomb struck *Cassin* and passed through the ship in the vicinity of frame 60. The fragments from this bomb penetrated both ships and their fuel oil tanks. By this time the oil fires extended the full length of both ships, and both were being abandoned when the second bomb landed. The third bomb hit *Downes* and demolished the director platform, the bridge, and the charthouse.

The fuel oil fires eventually reached the depth charges and the torpedoes. Without adequate water the fires raged on both ships and in the drydock. The Yard desired to flood the drydock as early as 0815 but no action was taken for an hour. At that time *Cassin* came afloat astern and pivoted

on her forefoot. This, together with the free surface, caused *Cassin* to become unstable. She fell over on *Downes*. The fuel oil fires caused havoc before the water level was high enough to protect the hulls of the two ships. The fragments from the first bomb penetrated the oil tanks of both vessels and loose oil fed the fires which were started. The thick black smoke, which is characteristic of burning fuel oil, prevented the crews from fighting the fires which engulfed both ships.

Explosions on *Downes* were the cause of much of the damage. The bomb hits were not in themselves of real account. The explosions were caused by fuel oil tanks becoming overheated, by 5-inch ammunition in ready boxes, by the powder in the forward magazine, and either by torpedo air flasks or torpedo warheads. Regardless of which part of the torpedoes was the real culprit, one of the assemblies was found in the yard seventy-five feet from its starting point. The force of the explosions was sufficient to wreck everything in its path. The most severe damage on *Downes* was caused by a torpedo explosion near the after stack. Here a large hole in the deck and side resulted.

The damage to the hulls of the two destroyers from oil fires, the toppling of *Cassin*, and explosions, etc. was extensive. Both vessels were pocked with holes. As for *Cassin*, the flat keel was warped and was about 18 inches above the baseline, the hull was hogged (raised in the middle) from 10 to 17 inches, the bow was about two feet high, and both struts were out of position. The shell plating of *Cassin* was badly wrinkled especially on the starboard side.

Downes was in worse shape as regards longitudinal strength. The bow was nearly 40 inches high, the stern 40 inches low, and the hull twisted and hogged. The plating was badly wrinkled from fire and strain, and damaged by many fragments.

Both vessels, on later examination, showed that their main propulsive machinery was in relatively good shape, as were the hull fittings and machinery throughout. However, the aluminum plating of *Downes'* deckhouse was completely destroyed and the corrosion-resisting steel panels of the deckhouses of both ships were badly wrinkled.

Lessons learned included the following for vessels in drydock in a war zone:

a. Portable pumps should be available.

b. Means should be provided by the Yard to fight oil fires.

c. Rescue breathing apparatus and flame proof clothing should be near at hand.

d. Torpedoes, depth charges, and warheads should be removed.

e. If circumstances dictate that the dock should be flooded, care must be exercised in maintaining correct blocking under the ships.

The newly named Pearl Harbor Repair and Salvage Unit went to work to restore the float-ability of these ships. They patched up hundreds of fragment holes on both vessels and on *Downes* they put in place some large sections of deck and side which had been blown out by the explosions. They used electric welding after fitting steel patches to suit the contour. At the same time the unit removed much of the machinery and put some in a state of preservation in suitable Navy Yard storage.

When *Pennsylvania* was taken out of the dry-dock on 12 December *Downes* was set on correct blocking, but *Cassin* was left in a toppled state until holes could be patched on the port side. *Cassin* was righted on 5 February, at which time patches were electric welded on the starboard side. She was floated and removed to the Navy Yard on 18 February. In the meantime *Downes* was floated and removed from the drydock on 6 February.

There was wide diversity of opinion as to the proper disposition of these ships. The Salvage Of-ficer felt that in view of the dire scarcity of ships *Cassin* and *Downes* could be used for limited escort or patrol duties. Some felt that the machinery and suitable hull fittings should be preserved and installed in new hulls. Eventually the forces afloat agreed with the opinion of the Navy Yard that the hulls be scrapped and the machinery and usable fittings and parts of the vessels be sent to Mare Island. To this the Bureau of Ships and the Navy Department agreed.

It was ordered that both ships be scrapped after removing from them all the machinery and parts that would be helpful to Mare Island. It was important that these be properly labelled before the parts were sent in various ships to the building yard. The scrapping of *Downes* was completed in drydock in August 1942 and of *Cassin* in October 1942. Mare Island Navy Yard completed the ships in November 1943 and February 1944 respectively. They then left the West Coast to look for Japanese ships.

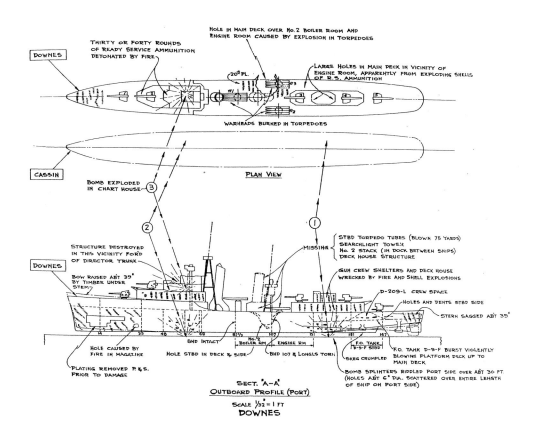

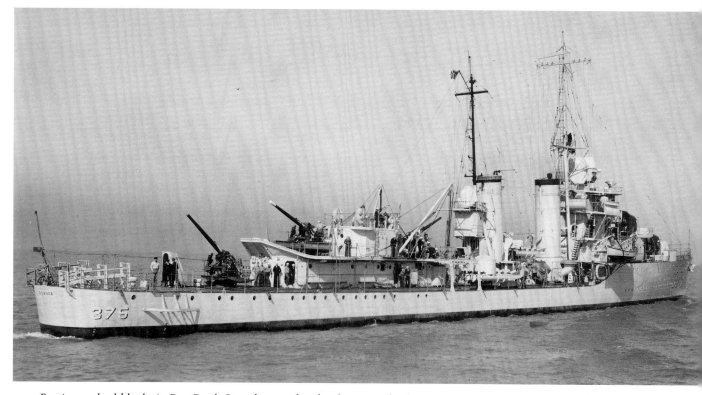

Resting on keel blocks in Dry Dock One abreast of each other were the destroyers USS Cassin DD-372 and her sister-ship USS Downes DD-375. Sharing the dock with them was the battleship USS Pennsylvania BB-38, Flagship of the Pacific Fleet. The destroyers were docked for major upgrades and maintenance. The ships were wide open with large sections of old hull plating forward having been removed along with propellers and shafts. Neither ship was prepared for what came at them that Sunday morning. USN

About 0850 in the opening moments of the second wave dive-bombers from the carriers Hiryu and Soryu scored three hits and two near misses on the destroyers that blew out water-tight hatches, severely punctured the hulls and ruptured fuel tanks. The explosions started raging oil fires in the dry dock and throughout both ships forcing the crews to abandon ship and fight the fires from dockside. The intense heat set off munitions and torpedo warheads, further devastating the two destroyers. NA

The dry dock was flooded several times in an attempt to put out fires consuming the two destroyers and prevent further damage to the Pennsylvania. The burning oil merely floated on top of the water and rose and fell with the futile attempts to flood the dock. Later that morning the rising waters finally caused the battered Cassin to float free of her keel blocks stern first, resulting in the destroyer becoming unstable and to topple over onto the Downes. NA

The next day, Monday December 8, the dock was finally pumped out. Both vessels were in a sorry state and at first were considered to be beyond any hope of salvaging. Their burnt and shattered hulls were badly holed, twisted and distorted from the searing heat and explosions. The torpedoes on mount number three of the Downes (left) had exploded demolishing the after stack leaving a huge hole in the main deck. PHP

Adding to the distress of the battered Cassin *was her bridge being hopelessly crushed when it fell over against her already dev-astated sister ship. First priority was to get them afloat and moved out of the badly needed dock. Topsides of both ships was a shambles. Numerous fragment holes on both destroyers had to be patched up and whole sections of deck and sides of the hull, blown out by explosions, would have to be cut away and replaced to make the ships watertight. The only real hope of saving the ships arose from the unexpectedly good condition of their machinery.* USN NH 54562

On February 6 the patched up hulk of the Downes (above) was removed from the dry dock and towed over to the repair basin. Cassin *was ready on February 18 and moved out to join her sister-ship. The Bureau of Ships in Washington agreed with Pearl Harbor Navy Yard that the two battered hulls could not be saved and would be scrapped by the navy yard. It was further decided that all useable equipment, machinery and ship fittings that could be salvaged would be saved and installed in new hulls to be built at Mare Island Navy Yard.* PHP

The first load of materials left Pearl Harbor for the West Coast on June 5, 1942 aboard the USS Jupiter AK-49 *and ending with the last shipment arriving in mid-December. There were some 564 huge crates weighing over 1,000 tons shipped stateside in over two dozen individual cargo ships. Included in these shipments were the 37-ton stern sections of each destroyer for the new hulls on which the names* Cassin *and* Downes *were carefully preserved.* PHP

With little fanfare, no band, no sponsor and no ceremony, the "new" Downes was launched on 20 May 1943. The "new" Cassin (above) slipped down the ways a month later. The shipyard completed the new hulls and final fitting out of the destroyers by November 1943 and February 1944 respectively. In the months following the destroyers completed shakedown and training with all new crews. After they had been given up for lost on December 7, 1941 and given a new life, both Cassin and Downes were ready to serve their country again for the remainder of World War Two. PHP

UNITED STATES FLEET
DESTROYERS, BATTLE FORCE, PACIFIC FLEET
U.S.S. CASSIN (372)

Pearl Harbor, T.H.,
December 13, 1941.

From: The Commanding Officer.
To: Commander-in-Chief, United States Pacific Fleet.

Subject: Air Attack on Pearl Harbor, T.H., December 7, 1941.

Reference: (a) Art. 712, U.S. Navy Regulations.

1. At approximately 0750 Sunday morning, December 7, 1941, as I stepped from my cabin to go below to breakfast, my Chief Gunner's Mate, E.L. JAMES, dashed into the passageway and said, "Captain they are here, bombing Hickam Field".

2. I stepped aft and out the starboard passageway door and about 100 feet away from the starboard side of #1 drydock facing inboard, and at an altitude of approximately 100 feet I saw an airplane with large red discs on bottom wings. I ordered JAMES, E.L., C.G.M., to sound general quarters and started for the bridge. JAMES had the word passed as there was no power on the general alarm.

3. The *Cassin* had no 5"/38 caliber guns ready for service as ordnance alterations being accomplished rendered them inoperative. Men were despatched to the Navy Yard to see if parts could be obtained. The .50 caliber guns were prepared at once.

4. About 0800 I saw another plane come down in a glide to about 75 feet on a course paralleling drydock #1 on port side facing outboard. It turned slightly in the channel and dropped a torpedo definitely aimed at the California from a distance of not over 200 yards. The plane kept going and disappeared from sight.

5. A few moments later the *Helena* opened fire, followed by the *Pennsylvania*. The *Cassin* and *Downes* opened up with .50 caliber machine guns.

6. The Executive Officer, Gunnery Officer and Communication Officer were ashore, as was the JA talker. By voice I called down to gun #2 to expedite obtaining breech plugs at the yard if possible and ordered men to seek protection of gun shelters, as I had no guns to fire. Many of them stayed well out to see what was going on. Others assisted repair party who led out hoses and stood by for handling damage.

7. About 0810 a Japanese plane crashed over the trees near the hospital, passing low (parallel to the *Pennsylvania* and *Downes*) with a tail of flame 50 feet long.

8. A few minutes later five high altitude (12,000 feet) bombers passed overhead from forward aft and let go large bombs. These were let go after they passed overhead of drydock #1.

9. Shortly, I saw Captain C.D. SWAIN, U.S. Navy and Lieutenant Commander B.E. MANSEAU, U.S. Navy coming down to the drydock. I went out to meet them and was requested to close up both destroyers preparatory to flooding drydock even though about 30 ports below main deck forward were off on *Cassin* preparatory to blanking and shell plating on both destroyers forward was off preparatory to replacement by heavier plating.

10. All hands except the machine gunners were directed to close up the ship as well as possible. This was done from lower decks up which later facilitated abandoning as closure was practically completed and most men were on main or forecastle deck. Power cables led form one compartment to another and had to be cut. Also leads from large portable blowers forward had to be disconnected.

11. After I returned to the bridge I saw another group of five high altitude bombers pass overhead the same as in paragraph 8 above.

12. About 0830 the *Pennsylvania* called by semaphore and sent a message "Senior destroyer officer report aboard". This message was interrupted by signalmen having to lie down due to terrific gun fire from enemy and own ship and came in two attempts.

13. About this time Lieutenant (jg) J.D. PARKER, acting commanding officer of *Downes*, requested permission to open fire with 5"/38 caliber on blocks which I immediately granted. His #3 gun was assembled in time to fire two shots before he was hit.

14. Closure being well underway and .50 caliber shooting rapidly I started from bridge for the *Pennsylvania*. I had secured phones and called to signalman to notify Ensign F.M. CULPEPPER I would be right back. When I was almost to bow of *Pennsylvania* the *Downes* was hit by a small bomb on after deck house. Smoke and dust were rising as I ran along the dock.

15. The 3"/50 caliber on the *Pennsylvania* quarterdeck were firing fast, quietly and efficiently.

16. I climbed amid terrific blasts of fast shooting guns to *Pennsylvania* conning tower then to next level above to Captain C.M. COOKE. He asked me if we were preparing for flooding of dock stating that even without propellors he wanted to get it flooded. I told him "Yes" and left. Apparently Captain SWAIN and Lieutenant Commander MANSEAU had not seen the Commanding Officer of the *Pennsylvania* regarding flooding at the same time they saw me.

17. At sometime between by arrival at brow of *Pennsylvania* and my departure the *Downes* had apparently been hit again at about 0850 and hug flames were rising all over her and on starboard side of *Cassin*. A hug hole in dock abreast of *Cassin's* stern was emitting clouds of smoke.

18. I skirted this hole on the double realizing from the nature of the flames that the fire could not be fought successfully. I later found out that there was no water at all with which to fight the fire. #3 .40 caliber gun was on fire due to lack of cooling water. There was none in men's washroom due to interrupted service from Yard. As soon as I was past this hole I started waving for men to get off. The word had been passed to abandon ship, which word was repeated all through the ship. The men were all converging toward brown from forward and aft. I kept shouting for the men to "step out" as the flames and heat as I passed the stern of *Cassin* were terrific and I feared a magazine explosion. I arrived at the brow as the last group of men came off. I estimate that there was another five minutes in which men could have gotten off. Ensign CULPEPPER was the last man off. I thought there was a hole in the brow, which I later found was caused by a small bomb which dropped through just a few feet ahead of Ensign M.E. CALLICOTT, USNR. This bomb went through the ship without exploding. I believe another small bomb hit in galley passage, but am not sure.

19. Within a few minutes the first hose arrived from the yard then others. The first six or eight hoses I kept on the port side of the *Cassin*, because wind was carrying flames over the *Downes Cassin's* depth charges and torpedo tubes to keep them from exploding. Nine of the twelve torpedo warheads melted off.

20. It was necessary to move back from the dock several times due to heat and to fragments from several small explosions which followed each other at close intervals.

21. About 0915 there was a terrific explosion on the *Downes* and flames shot about 60 feet in the air, which was filled with fragments. Hoses were practically torn away from fire fighting parties consisting of men from *Cassin*, *Downes* and yard employees. All hands retreated from the dock and sprawled on the road. Lieutenant (jg) PARKER, a few feet to my right, was hit and TALBERT, C.L., F1c of the *Cassin*, to my left, was hit. I at first thought PARKER's neck had been badly cut due to large amount of bleeding and seeing a small truck stop close by, I directed him and TALBERT to get in and go to the hospital. Within a short time he was back, minus his coat and with his head bandaged, rejoining the fire fighting forces. I believe his hospital corpsman fixed him on the spot.

22. The fire on the *Cassin* was brought under control about 1045. The Gunnery Officer arrived shortly after we abandoned ship and joined Lieutenant SPEER, of the navy yard, at one end of the *Cassin*. Both of these officers did excellent work.

23. Commander L.P. LOVETTE, Commander Destroyer Division FIVE< and the Executive Officer of *Cassin* arrived while the fire was raging. With one quick look, the Division Commander told me to take charge of *Cassin* and *Downes* as he would got at once to Reid or Conyngham to sortie. Emergency signal for sortie had been hoisted before *Downes* and *Cassin* were hit (neither had a mast). Commander LOVETTE returned in about ten minutes from Cummings to tell me he would go out on her and would take 25 men from *Cassin* to include the best gunnery and torpedo personnel. About 60 went to the Cummings, but 40 were returned.

24. It has not been possible as yet to salvage .50 caliber ammunition remaining or to check on amount expended.

25. The conduct of the men was superb, particularly the quiet over all supervision by the Chief Boatswain Mate, J.T. STRATTON, who seemed to be everywhere at the same time directing closure and abandoning. At no time was there any fear or panic, but merely rage not only at enemy attack but at inability, after months of training, to be able to return the fire. The entire crew behaved in accordance with the best traditions of the Service.

[signed]
D.F.J. SHEA.

U.S.S. *DOWNES* (DD375)

DD375/A16-3

(412)

December 17, 1941

From: The Commanding Officer.
To: The Commander-in-Chief, U.S. Pacific Fleet.

Subject: Report of Action with Japanese Aircraft During Attack on Pearl Harbor, T.H., December 7,1941.

Reference: (a) U.S. Navy Regulations, Articles 712, 873(6).

Enclosure: (A) Statement of Lieutenant W.O. Snead, U.S. Navy, Executive Officer, U.S.S. *Downes*.
             (B) Statement of Lieutenant (jg) J.D. Parker, U.S. Navy, Senior Officer on Board during Attack.

1. At the time of the surprise attack of Japanese aircraft on fleet units in Pearl Harbor, T.H. during the fore-noon of December 7, 1941 the *U.S.S. Downes* was docked in drydock No. 1, Navy Yard, Pearl Harbor. The *Downes* and *Cassin* occupied the southern end of the dock with the *Downes* to starboard. The *Pennsylvania* occupied the remainder of the dock astern of the two destroyers. The wind was from about 225 relative, force 2. The ship was receiving steam, electricity, fresh and salt water from Navy Yard sources. Navy Yard work was in progress on the stern tubing, strut bearings, shell plating forward, replacement of tripod mast with stick mast, and various minor jobs. Large sections of the shell plating had been removed on both sides forward preparatory to replacement with heavier plate.

2. The following officers were ashore on authorized liberty: Lieutenant Commander W.R. Thayer, U.S. Navy, Commanding; Lieutenant W.O. Snead, U.S. Navy, Executive Officer; Lieutenant W.A. Hunt, Jr., U.S. Navy, Engineer Officer; Ensign J.B. Balch, U.S. Navy, Gunnery Officer. Four members of the crew were absent on authorized liberty leaving a total of 142 enlisted men and five officers on board. Lieutenant (jg) J.D. Parker, U.S. Navy was the Duty Officer and senior officer on board.

3. The offensive weapons of the ship were in the following condition:

   a. 5"/38 caliber guns. Breech plugs and tripping latches removed for an approved BuOrd alteration.

   b. 5"/38 caliber ammunition. 310 rounds removed to Naval Ammunition Depot to permit yard work in connection with depth charge stowage. The remainder of the 5"/38 ammunition was distributed through-out all magazines.

   c. .50 caliber machine guns. Dismounted and stowed in locker.

   d. All belted .50 caliber ammunition removed to Naval Ammunition Depot to permit yard work. Remain-der of .50 caliber ammunition in forward magazines, unclipped.

   e. Twelve torpedoes with war heads fitted in tube mounts with air flasks bled down.

   f. Eight depth charges in racks.

   g. Six F.S. tanks charged and mounted.

h. Several battle telephones under repair.

4. The following account of the action is based upon reports submitted to me by all officers and men on board during the attack. While the action in the later stages was very rapid and the ship subjected to several bombings in rapid succession, it is believed that the essential facts can be set forth with reasonable accuracy.

5. The attacking planes were sighted coming in out of the clouds at about 0755 by several men on deck including the Chief Petty Officer with the day's duty. The C.P.O. with day's duty immediately had general quarters sounded and notified the duty officer, Lieutenant (jg) J.D. Parker, U.S. Navy. The crew proceeded to their stations quickly, set condition Afirm, except where prevented from so doing by the temporary ventilation ducts forward, checked closure of sea valves, and began intensive efforts to prepare the ship for fighting. The machine guns were quickly prepared for firing and work was begun on assembling the breech plugs of the 5" battery. Ammunition details broke out ammunition for both the machine guns and the 5"/38 caliber. As there was no belted .50 caliber on board, two magazines of this ammunition were obtained from the *Cassin* in order that fire might be opened as soon as possible. yard power was lost at 0810 which necessitated passing much of the 5" ammunition up by hand. Ammunition passers worked in total darkness until flashlights could be obtained, and as a result no tracer ammunition was located for the machine guns. Men not occupied, which included men of the engineers force and most of the 5" gun crews, were turned to belting machine gun ammunition. The speed with which this operation was carried out was most gratifying. The machine guns were firing within 15 minutes of the start of the attack. The 5" guns crews were retained in the ammunition supply and belting details until their guns could be made ready to fire.

6. After loss of yard power at 0810, several men of the engineers force under Chief Machinist's mate JOHNSTON and Chief Electrician's Mate RAIDY succeeded in starting the emergency diesel generator. As the ship was in drydock, it was necessary to connect a hose to the fire main to supply circulating water to the diesel. This was done by the light of the battle lanterns. At 0823, the power and light load was taken by the emergency diesel generator. Switches were thrown to supply power to the ammunition hoists. The hoist for gun No. 2 was used thereafter in bringing up ammunition.

7. During the first hour the *Downes* was untouched. The first attacks were made by torpedo planes against the battleships. These were followed a few minutes later by horizontal bombing attacks on the battleships. During these attacks the *Downes* opened fire with machine guns, but the range was too great for effectiveness and fire was stopped. The horizontal bombers attacked in groups of about five planes each, at an altitude of about 9,000 to 12,0000 feet.

8. With the loss of yard power, no power was available for the operation of the 5" battery or director. however, as soon as gun No. 3 could be made ready (about 0845), it was loaded by hand and fired. This was a test shot to see how the ship would stand the shock of firing while drydocked. The test successful, Ensign Robinson, who had been in charge of the forward machine guns, took charge of gun No. 3 and stood by to open fire in local control. Ensign Stewart had been sent to control the after machine guns. Ensign Sebbo took control of the forward machine guns. Ensign Comly was in charge of the ammunition details. lieutenant (jg) Parker directed operations from the bridge.

9. At about 0850, there was a lull of some six minutes. Lieutenant (jg) Parker was asked at this time if the *Downes* was ready for the dock to be flooded. After a quick check, he replied in the affirmative. Shortly thereafter, dive bombers attacked the ship. Three dive bombers came from the Southeast in a steep dive. They were immediately taken under fire by the forward and after machine gunners. Attempt was being made to get 5" gun No. 3 on the horizontal bombers attacking the battleships. Almost simultaneously with

the first bomb hit, this gun got off one shot at the horizontal bombers. At 0827 the dive bombers dropped an incendiary bomb, which hit in the drydock between the *Cassin* and *Downes* about abreast of gun No. 4. Two men were killed outright. Fire enveloped the after part of the ship instantaneously. The diesel fuel oil tank was ruptured and set afire, and the emergency diesel generator stopped. The ship was now without power or lights. Flames spread very rapidly covering the after deck house and gun shelters. The heat was intense. The incendiary material used was described as a yellowish-green liquid. Fire hoses were quickly manned by the repair party and gun crews aft and water turned on the flames. The initial flow of water was inadequate; after this had been corrected, it was found that water was ineffective, spreading rather than reducing the fire.

It was soon evident that the fire was out of control. The engineroom was abandoned at 0912. Lieutenant (jg) Parker ordered the abandonment of the after part of the ship, however the flames were already driving the men off the ship. Orders were given to flood the after magazines, but it is not known whether this was accomplished or not. A few seconds later, at about 0920, the situation then being hopeless, Lieutenant (jg) Parker gave orders for all hands to abandon ship. Shortly after orders had been given to abandon ship another incendiary bomb hit between the *Cassin* and *Downes* abreast the bridge structure setting the quarter-deck and the forward part of the *Downes* afire. Lieutenant (jg) Parker attempted to make a personal check to see that all men were off the ship but was prevented from doing so by the flames, and was forced to leave himself. The flames, fed by diesel and fuel oil as well as the painted surfaces of the ship, and fanned by the wind, swept diagonally across the ship, setting it on fire from bow to stern.

10. Most of the men escaped over the brow which was located on the 02 deck just forward of the chart house but some men, finding themselves trapped aft, were forced to escape over the sides into the dry-dock. As the last survivors were leaving the ship a bomb, velieved to be a small high explosive one, struck the bridge completely destroying the director platform, bridge, and chart house.

11. Having released their bombs, the Japanese then made a strafing attack on personnel on the dock, but none were injured. Upon completion of these strafing attacks, some of the *Downes* men proceeded to the windward side of the dock to man yard fire hoses, others assisted in removing the wounded to the hospital or first aid stations, while several others, including two gunner's mates proceeded to the Marine Barracks to assist in giving out arms and ammunition. Two of the latter obtained guns and ammunition and returned to take up stations where they might fire on attacking planes.

12. Soon after the ship was abandoned, a terrific explosion occurred amidships, at torpedo tube number 3. After the fire had been extinguished it was discovered that the warheads in tube 3 had blown up leaving a large hole in the side and main deck in the vicinity of the tube mount and demolishing the number 2 stack. Fragments of the tube mount were found on the bow of the *U.S.S. Pennsylvania*.

13. The powder in the forward magazines blew out through the sides of the ship, however most of the projectiles and the .50 caliber ammunition in the forward magazines were apparently unharmed.

14. The men who manned the hoses on the dock displayed unusual courage. Some of these men had already been badly burned on the ship and were later hospitalized. The 5" ammunition in the gun shelters exploded, sending out frequent showers of metal fragments in all directions. lieutenant (jg) Parker and several men tending hoses were injured by these fragments. The explosions became so dangerous that, for a few minutes, it was necessary to abandon the hoses, which, however, were futile against the fire at that time. Later the hoses were concentrated on the sterns of the two ships to save the depth charges.

15. One depth charge of the *Downes* dropped into the dock, but all others were later removed, apparently in a serviceable condition. The torpedo warheads on the torpedoes in mounts number 1 and 2 melted off.

16. Flooding of the dock was considerably delayed, commencing sometime after both *Downes* and *Cassin* had been abandoned. The flames were brought under control after the dock had been flooded, and the fire was extinguished in the late afternoon.

17. The conduct of the officers and crew in these trying circumstances was magnificent. Each officer and man did his job. All are deserving of the highest praise. It is difficult to single out individual men or acts of bravery among such a fine crew, but the conduct of the following was outstanding:

1. Lieutenant (jg) J.D. Parker, U.S. Navy.
   As Senior Officer on board, Lieutenant Parker commanded the *Downes* during and for some time subsequent to the attack. He displayed leadership, good judgement, resourcefulness, coolness, and courage to the highest degree. his handling of the emergency under the most trying conditions was above reproach. With utter disregard for his own safety, he remained on the ship until further efforts to insure that all personnel had left the ship were blocked by the fire. After leaving the ship, he engaged in fighting the fire. During this phase, he suffered head injuries from flying fragments, but after first aid treatment he returned to continue fighting the fire.

2. Ensign R.L. Stewart, U.S. Navy.
   Ensign Stewart was placed in control of the after machine guns. Together with the two after machine gunners, he remained at his station and continued firing until the entire machine gun platform was enveloped in flames. He suffered a broken foot when forced to jump to safety. In spite of his injury, Ensign Stewart commandeered an automobile and made several trips to take injured personnel to the hospital.

3. Riley, John B., C.B.M.(PA), U.S. Navy.
   Exemplified the highest type of leadership. Always cool, self reliant, and resourceful, he refused to leave his station after being badly injured, he continued to fight the fire from the dock.

4. Cradoct, Henry E., C.G.M.(PA), U.S. Navy.
   Cradoct was largely responsible for the speed with which the machine guns were mounted, ammunition belted and supplied to the machine guns, ammunition gotten up for the 5" battery, and 5" guns number 2 and number 3 made ready to fire. His leadership, coolness, knowledge of his specialty and of the ship, energy, and loyalty are deserving of the highest commendation. Both officers and men considered his work to have been outstanding.

5. Odietus, Michael G., G.M.1c, U.S. Navy;
   Schulze, Curtis P., G.M.2c, U.S. Navy.
   These two men did a splendid job of getting 5" guns number 2 and number 3 ready to fire as quickly as possible. When the ship caught fire Odietus tried to connect the hose on dock single-handed, but was unsuccessful. After abandoning ship, they both proceeded, on their own initiative, to the yard marine armory to assist in giving out arms and ammunition. They were issued two Browning Automatic rifles by the Marines and returned to take up stations to fire upon enemy planes.

6. Johnston, Charles B., C.M.M.(PA), U.S. Navy.

Knew his job thoroughly and did it. He was cool, collected, and courageous. Successfully fought minor fires in the engineroom, ordered men to abandon engineroom when flames were out of control, then fought flames on deck until forced to leave the ship. He undoubtedly saved the life of Raidy by rolling him on deck to smother the flames which had caught on his clothing.

7. Raidy, James M., C.E.M.(AA), U.S. Navy.

The spirit shown by this man was remarkable. he fought the fire on the topside until nearly everyone else was off the ship and his person set on fire by an incendiary bomb. After abandoning ship he manned a hose on the dock. He was taken to the hospital with severe burns.

8. Richardson, Shirley W., C.Ph.M.(AA), U.S. Navy;

Blaszak, Adam A., Ph.M.3c, U.S. Navy.

Both men performed their duties in an excellent manner during the engagement and afterwards. Blaszak continued dressing a man at after battle dressing station with flames all around outside. he barely escaped in time. Richardson tried to lead several men off the ship, but they were lost.

9. Hite, Lewis, G., B.M.1c, U.S. Navy.

Displayed real leadership. Instrumental in saving life of Kemp, whom he led part way off ship. Returned to connect fire hoses. Chased other men off ship in time to save them.

10. Ernst, William, M.M.2c, U.S. Navy.

Tore Kemp's burning shirt from him. Passed word in crew's washroom to abandon ship when after part of ship was on fire. After leaving ship proceeded to lumber pile in yard to stand by fire plug there.

11. Skjerven, Mylo H., Y.2c, U.S. Navy.

His presence of mind and training saved the Muster Rolls and Transfer and Receipt Book the only records saved from the ship.

12. Hooke, Charles M., Sea.1c, U.S. Navy;

Stadelman, Elmer S., Sea.1c, U.S. Navy;

Foundation, James J. Jr., Sea.1c, U.S. Navy;

Thompson, Eric L., Sea.1c, U.S. Navy

Hooke and Stadelman on the forward machine guns and Foundation and Thompson on the after machine guns displayed remarkable courage and coolness in the face of grave danger. They all fired whenever a target was available notwithstanding the fire, strafing and bombing to which the ship was subjected. They way they remained at their posts was superb.

13. Rau, Armand F., Jr., Sea.1c, U.S. Navy.

Displayed complete disregard for personal danger and a high degree of loyalty when he was the first to volunteer to handle the hose on the dock even though large splinters were being thrown out of the dock by the explosions on the ship.

14. Kwolik, Edward T., F.2c, U.S. Navy.

This man remained on the ship in the face of grave danger even after being ordered off in order to keep a fire hose on the after engineroom hatch. his conduct permitted the men in the engineroom to escape.

15. Postlethwaite, Paul O., Sea.2c, U.S. Navy.

This man was injured while checking the setting of condition Afirm prior to reporting the ship ready for the dock to be flooded. He continued in his duties, fighting a fire in the ship then fighting the fires from the dock until hit by fragments and wounded severely. He was forced to leave the ship over the fantail.

18. The ship was lost, but the Commanding Officer has naught but praise for the officers and men of the crew who fought her under such unfortunate circumstances. They did their utmost to inflict damage on the enemy, working against almost unsurmountable odds. They did all in their power to save the ship from fire. They showed that they were real shipmates with a concern for each other's safety. They were loyal and determined. Their primary concern during the engagement was to get the guns in action, and their biggest regret was that they couldn't meet the enemy in a fair fight at sea. I am proud to have commanded the U.S.S. *Downes*.

[signed]
W.R. THAYER

The Downes *(top) was ready in March 1944 and sailed from San Francisco escorting a convoy to Pearl Harbor. Followed in April when the* Cassin *(bottom) also reported to active duty at Pearl. Both ships operated practically un-interrupted during the rest of the war. The sister ships performed air-sea rescue operations, radar picket duties, ocean escort tasks and fire support missions during the island hopping campaigns. By war's end* Cassin *earned six battle stars and* Downes *earned four battle stars.* PHPC

U.S.S. NEVADA (BB-36), BATTLESHIP

The refloating and drydocking of *Nevada* showed unmistakably that such work should be under the direction of a person familiar with floatability, trim, list, and stability. The availability of a technical group knowing these facts about a particular ship as well as about the strength of various bulkheads is important to a satisfactory outcome. As was clearly shown later, the same applies to all ships which are flooded with water or filled with oil, ammunition, and stores. The close cooperation which existed between the Salvage Officer and the Pearl Harbor Navy Yard was of invaluable assistance in finding a satisfactory solution in the case of all vessels which were sunk at Pearl Harbor.

At this time, the Assistant Salvage Officer was a reserve officer named George M. Ankers. He had had some practical experience in Alaska but was quite unfamiliar with large naval vessels. Through hard work he progressed in the Navy from Junior Lieutenant on the *Nevada* job to Captain in the Bureau of Ships in charge of all salvage work.

In addition to Lieutenant Ankers and Carpenter Mahan, other officers and men became available. Most of these were reserves who, as on regular shipboard duty, were assigned specialty jobs and continued on that specialty. Thus some had charge of cleaning, or of diving work, or of pumps, or of internal watertightness. These specialty officers progressed from ship to ship under salvage, while the Salvage Officer, himself, covered all projects, but spent most of his time on the ship destined for early drydocking.

Nevada was beached to prevent sinking on 7 December. She was located near the entrance channel with stern up against the shore and bow in deep water. Her draft when flooding of compartments had been completed on the following day was about 48 feet forward and 39 1/2 feet aft at high tide, which was about two feet above zero. This position was maintained by several anchors laid out astern, and she remained in such position until refloated in February. Her list at the time was about two degrees to starboard. This was to prevent any possibility of the ship's sinking in the channel which connected Pearl Harbor to the sea.

The Salvage Officer, Captain Homer N. Wallin, was optimistic with respect to *Nevada* as she had reciprocating engines as compared to the electric-drive battleships California and West Virginia which were in much worse shape. But, he was taken aback somewhat by the words of the new Commander-in-Chief of the Pacific Fleet, who, when viewing *Nevada* for the first time, remarked that satisfactory salvage seemed impossible and that we should not be over-optimistic. It should be stated here that when Admiral Nimitz arrived on 31 December 1941 he wanted very much to be shown the various "wrecks" in the harbor. Captain Wallin, who was then the Senior Material Officer of the Battle Force, was assigned to him for this purpose. What Admiral Nimitz saw was a ship entirely filled with water, with her bridge and forward controls entirely burned out, and with the forecastle wrecked by the bombs which exploded beneath. No wonder he was pessimistic!

Nevada was struck by a torpedo at frame 41 about 0810 about fourteen feet above the keel. The innermost torpedo bulkhead held but the joints permitted considerable flooding below the first platform. The original list was four to five degrees but this was soon corrected by counterflooding. The ship had started warming up the machinery and was able to get underway at 0840. While underway near the Air Station the signal was received that the ship should not leave the harbor but should continue to the west side of Ford Island.

About 0950 five bombs hit the ship almost simultaneously. Two struck the forecastle near frame 15. One passed out through the side of the second deck and caused near-miss damage. The other exploded within the ship after penetrating the structure near the gasoline tank. This caused gasoline leakage and vapors in that part of the vessel. This added to the many fires and the difficulty of extinguishing them. Another hit was near number I turret inboard from the port waterway. It blew large holes in the upper and main decks. A fourth bomb struck the port director platform in the foremast and exploded at the base of the stack on the upper deck The fifth bomb exploded directly over the crew's galley, at about frame 80.

New fires broke out immediately. They were intense around the foremast, the officers' quarters forward, and the crew's galley. The forward magazines were flooded, and by mistake the after group was flooded too. When the fires burned themselves out, the foremast structure containing the bridge was entirely destroyed. Air from the intakes was smoky and caused the boiler rooms to be abandoned.

Flooding was progressive and emanated primarily from the "bull ring" where the main ventilation air intakes were located. By Monday nearly the whole ship was flooded including the machinery spaces. This flooding continued for a month; only a few compartments were found partly dry when the ship was eventually drydocked.

The new Commander-in-Chief of the Pacific Fleet was concerned about the flooding of the after part of the vessel where practically no damage had occurred. He therefore requested a report for the benefit of future operations. *Nevada*'s officers pointed out that the progressive flooding was due to the following causes:

a. Ventilation trunks permitted water to spread from the "bull ring" to various parts of the ship. There were inadequate closures in the ventilation system.

b. The second deck was not watertight. As water spread on the second deck it reached spaces below through hatches and other openings. The second deck should have a large number of transverse bulkheads to prevent water from traveling forward or aft.

c. There was leakage around piping and electric leads passing through armored decks and bulkheads.

d. Although it was found that practically all "X", "Y", or "Z" closures were properly closed during the action, the flooding of the ship converted *Nevada* into a salvage job instead of a repair job.

Salvage work commenced promptly. The bomb holes forward were covered by wooden patches externally as shown in the illustration on page 217. These are known as "window frames" and are held close to the hull plating by hook bolts manipulated by divers. Of course the water pressure assists.

As the water level is lowered the inflow of water was partially stopped by stuffing rubber mats and kapok material in the bomb holes and using shores to tighten them. In one instance a steel patch was welded by divers in way of a serious leak.

Where the torpedo hit, there was one void and two liquid layers of fuel oil. This was minimal protection against torpedoes and exists in major ships only forward and aft of vital spaces. The damage from the torpedo was roughly 48 feet long by 25 feet in depth. Over this it was proposed to fit a large patch, but it was found that internal bulkheads in this area were reliable and would prevent the spread of flooding. Although the seams and butts of the inner bulkhead were opened somewhat as a result of the explosion, the flooding from this torpedo hit was not enough to scuttle the ship or cause serious flooding.

The large patch was made up at the Navy Yard and made to fit the upturned bottom of Oklahoma, the sister ship of *Nevada*. It was delivered in early January but it was unwieldy for handling. Immediately dredging was resorted to and part of the docking keel was removed by dynamite charges. Divers were busy for a month to fit the patch but it was finally given up and the intact bulkheads properly shored and backed up with water pressure. The patch would have projected at least two feet below the keel, and therefore presented a docking problem. It was ascertained after docking that the blister had blown outboard about two feet, and, unknown to the divers, prevented the patch from seating properly. The large hole was therefore left open to the sea and the internal bulkheads were depended upon for restricting the flooding.

Gradual reduction of the water level in the flooded ship was accomplished by suction pumps ranging in size from 10 inches to 3 inches. As spaces were unwatered prompt steps were taken to plug holes used for drains or sanitary discharges. The ship's crew also cleaned compartments of oil and refuse as the level receded. Personal property was guarded, classified information was turned over to a central point, and steps were taken to assure proper care and preservation of electrical and other equipment.

Ammunition and stores were removed from the vessel, as was oil and fresh meat which was very smelly by this time. The ammunition was sent to the ammunition depot for reconditioning.

Credit should be given to the Acting Commanding Officer for the efficient work performed by the twenty men of the ship's force who remained to handle the salvage work. His name was Commander H. L. Thompson. The working force, which was recruited from the Receiving Ship and from the Salvage Division, performed valiantly in removing stores and ammunition. Oil was pumped into oil barges by the fuel oil pumps in the machinery spaces. These were operated by compressed air furnished by the compressors on barges alongside. The suction pumps on the oil barges were of considerable help. The valves for fuel oil lines were traced out by sense of feel by the divers.

The Engineering Officer should not be overlooked, as he was a true optimist. He predicted that *Nevada* would sail to the West Coast under her own power. It sounded fantastic at the time, but his prediction was correct, not only for his own ship but for all the sunken ships except *Cassin* and *Downes*. His name was Lieutenant Commander George E. Fee.

Naturally the living spaces and other compartments were a real mess. These areas had been under water for two months, and the contents of the compartments were strewn about. The first requirement was general washing down with sea water; thereafter a hot caustic solution was used to cut the oil which had permeated all materials and all spaces which were open.

USS Nevada in drydock, showing window frame patch in place.

It was determined early that the proper uniform for men of the salvage crew and ship's crew were rubber boots and a one-piece overall. These permitted the men to wade in oily water and to contact oily objects. Again, care was taken to guard all personal belongings and official papers.

Unwatering was a step by step process, in order to give the salvage crew time to plug leaks and to give the working crew time to clean up the spaces which were unwatered. Care was taken later when the ship was afloat to reduce to a minimum the free water surface. The use of small suction pumps in lower spaces facilitated this purpose.

The electrical gear held up remarkably well. At least ninety-five percent of it was salvaged, at least for temporary or limited duty. As the machinery spaces became free of water the motors were removed and sent to the Navy Yard for drying out and reconditioning. On account of the number involved, a Honolulu firm was requisitioned to assist with the work. Even the delicate electrical instruments like ammeters and wattmeters were found to be satisfactory and capable of salvage if prompt steps were taken for their proper preservation following unwatering. About this time "tectyl" was "discovered" by the salvage crew although the Bureau of Ships had become familiar with it before. Generous quantities of "tectyl" were used by all ships beginning with *Nevada*.

"Tectyl" is the trade name of a liquid substance which does wonders for machinery submerged in salt water. It not only absorbs what water remains, but furnishes a thin protective film over all parts. The treatment should be given before the air is allowed to cause corrosion after the removal of salt water.

The electrical wires or leads were found in relatively good shape. They could be dried out and used satisfactorily. The vital leads were finally replaced by the Navy Yard when the ship was sent to the Yard.

At about this time two fatalities occurred on *Nevada* due to poisonous gas. On 7 February Lieutenant James S. Clarkson removed a cap from the air test fitting of the steering engine room. He was in a trunk which had limited space and air volume. Several men went to his rescue, but too late as escaping gas killed him. Machinist Mate DeVries who reached him first, later died at the hospital. In all, six men were overcome by the gas. At once a Board of Investigation was called, and the Navy Yard chemist ascertained that the gas was hydrogen sulfide. It is odorless in high concentrations and acts without warning; it originates in stagnant water which has a quantity of paper products in the pressured space. Thereafter frequent samples of air were taken for analysis, and temporary ventilation was greatly increased on all ships under salvage. Confined spaces were not entered without wearing rescue breathing apparatus.

Besides the temporary ventilation which was provided as spaces were unwatered, temporary lighting lines were run. Both were essential for the efficient performance of the work.

As weights were removed and water was pumped out, *Nevada* gradually came afloat. She floated on 12 February and was drydocked in Drydock Number Two on 18 February. It had been the original intention to drydock the vessel in Drydock Number One which is a smaller dock and has less clearance over the sill. This was given up gradually as trouble was encountered with fitting the large patch over the torpedo hole forward. As recounted, the patch was finally discarded and the magazine bulkheads were depended on for relative watertightness. The holding bulkheads were backed up by water introduced in the magazines. This water was pumped out as the vessel took up on the blocks of the drydock.

The operating forces, especially Admiral Nimitz were concerned lest *Nevada* sink in the channel when jostled by the tugs which conveyed her to drydock. To forestall this, gasoline pumps were kept running and there was no re-sinking. Accordingly, on 18 February Admiral Nimitz and Admiral Furlong stood at the head of the drydock to show their support of salvage work. A commendation was received from Admiral Nimitz for all hands whose hard work and persistence made possible the satisfactory outcome of the operations.

The work of the divers is worthy of mention. Much of the diving forward could be done with shallow water diving outfits, which were widely used until it was discovered that the water was polluted. *Nevada* divers were helpful in finding the valves in machinery spaces and operating the right ones to permit the transfer of fuel oil from the ship's tanks to the oil barges. All of this work was done underwater and without lights. The ship had only two divers but they made 80 dives. Widgeon and Ortolan had over a dozen divers each and together they made over 150 dives. Even the Destroyer Repair Unit had a few divers who participated in the salvage work. Of major importance were the four civilian divers of the Pacific Bridge Company who made 160 dives for over 950 diving hours. In all over 400 dives were made on *Nevada* totaling over 1500 diving hours. The divers performed all manner of work from underwater cutting with oxy-hydrogen and electric torches to hydraulic and syphon excavating, to using dynamite to remove sections of the docking keel, to the use of hand and pneumatic tools for drilling and setting patches. They also did much interior work for pumping operations, adjusting watertight closures, etc. The successful accomplishment of all assigned diving tasks without casualty or injury was the result of excellent supervision on the part of Lieutenant Commander H. E. Haynes, who was in general charge of all diving, plus Gunner Duckworth of Widgeon, Gunner Arnold Larson of Ortolan, and Carpenter Mahan of the Salvage Division.

The Pearl Harbor Navy Yard took *Nevada* in hand once she was in drydock. The torpedo hole was temporarily made watertight. The bomb damage was also repaired, although it was necessary to build a new structure and new decks in various locations. The galley was made suitable for limited service. The damaged starboard shaft and propellers, and the rudder, were put in temporary good condition. These were damaged as the ship backed into the shore at Waipio Point. The six boilers were all rebricked, reinsulated, and properly tested.

The Navy Yard worked assiduously on *Nevada* and the vessel was undocked on 15 March 1942. The main and auxiliary machinery was thoroughly overhauled and tested. All Navy Yard work was completed on 22 April 1942. On that date *Nevada* joined a convoy for the West Coast and set sail for Bremerton, Washington. She traveled on her own power with both screws in use, arriving at the Puget Sound Navy Yard on 1 May 1942.

There the ship was thoroughly overhauled and modernized. She left Bremerton before the end of the year with a bristling array of modern antiaircraft guns. She participated in the Aleutian Campaign in December 1942, and later took an important part in the landings in France. Thereafter she joined forces in the Pacific and took part in the campaigns which brought victory at Iwo Jima, Okinawa, and Japan itself. Here was a ship which at one time looked like a total wreck but now was a formidable foe of the Axis Powers.

Nevada won seven stars in World War II as follows: one star for Pearl Harbor-Midway, one star for the Aleutian operations, one for the Invasion of Normandy (including bombardment of Cherbourg), one star for the Invasion of Southern France, one star for the Iwo Jima Operation, one star for the Okinawa Gunto Operation, and one star for the Third Fleet Operations against Japan. She also received the Navy Occupation Service Medal (Asia clasp).

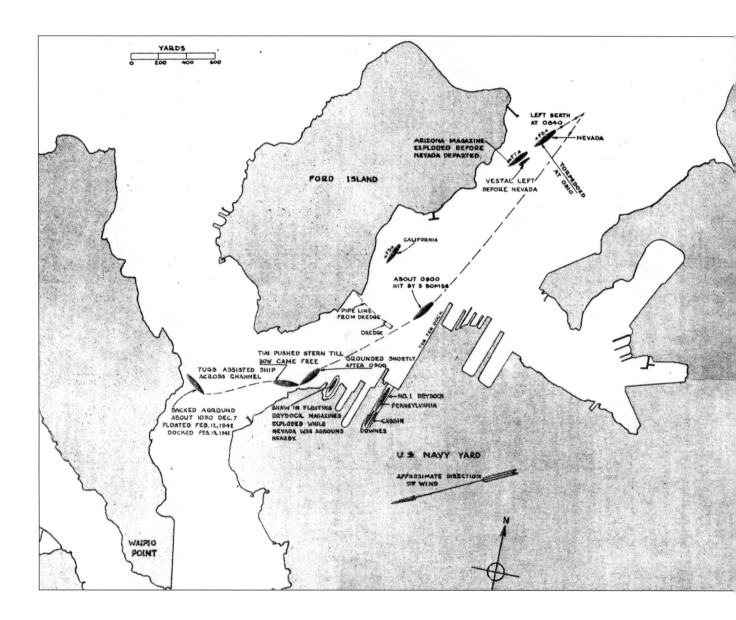

The morning of December 7th Nevada *was moored at Fox-8, astern of the USS* Arizona *at Battleship Row. At 0755, as the ship's band started to play the National Anthem for the raising of morning colors, they spotted some strange airplanes in the distance heading in their direction. Suddenly a torpedo smashed into the ship's port side between turrets #1 and #2. As the ship's crew ran for battle stations, the band never skipped a beat and managed to finish the Anthem, though at a much quicker pace.* NA 80G-455922

In the event of an attack standing orders for ships in harbor were to make for the open sea. Damaged and flooding forward but still seaworthy, lines holding the Nevada *to its mooring were hastily cut. The engine room had enough steam pressure up so that the ship (right) was able to back out without the assistance of yard tugs.* Nevada *was the only battleship to get underway during the attack. The battleship* California *(left) is listing from torpedo damage.* NA 80G-32635

The Nevada *carefully maneuvered into the channel past the blazing* Arizona *and set course to stand out of the harbor. The ship was immediately spotted by a large formation of Japanese "Val" dive-bombers from the carrier* Kaga. *They attacked hoping to sink the battleship in the channel and block up the harbor. Within minutes the ship suffered extensive damage forward and amidships from 5 or 6 direct bomb hits and many near misses.* NA 80G-3255

At 0910 with fires forward and amidships and taking on water, the heavily battered Nevada *received orders not to proceed out of the harbor. The ship moved out of the main ship channel and was intentionally run aground in the shallow waters between the floating dry dock and Hospital Point ending her gallant journey. In the foreground is the small seaplane tender* Avocet *with her gun crews at battle stations.* NA 80G-32583

The Nevada *tried to drop anchor but due to damages was unsuccessful. Then two harbor tugs, the* Hoga *and YT-153, came alongside to assist in fighting the heavy fires forward and remove some of the wounded for transfer to the Naval Hospital or the hospital ship* Solace. *The tugs then pushed* Nevada *across the channel stern first into the shallow waters of the opposite shore off Waipio Point (now called Nevada Point) above the channel entrance where she settled in the mud.* NA 80G-19940

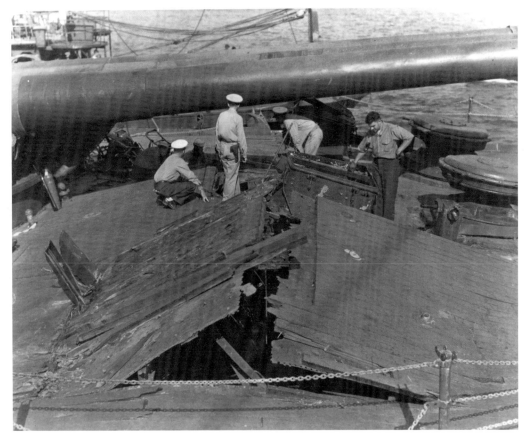

On December 12, 1941 officers and crew of Nevada examine the ship's ruptured deck on the bow just forward of turret No. 1. The 250-kg bomb that crashed through the main deck blew open a hole about 25 feet long and 18-feet deep caused extensive flooding in the forward section. The forecastle section from the bow to turret No. 1 was completely wrecked including the anchor handling gear and all compartments below decks were flooded. USN NH 64484

The bomb hits that crashed into the forecastle blew out several watertight bulkheads on the second and third decks leading to uncontrolled flooding in the forward area. One bomb continued on out through the starboard side of the ship about 13 feet below the main deck and exploded in the water leaving a hole six feet in diameter. Amazingly the path of this bomb went through a gasoline storage tank without igniting the contents! USN NH 50104

122

Another bomb smashed through the forward superstructure setting fires that completely gutted the Navigation Bridge, the Signal Bridge and the Charthouse. That bomb continued on through the boat deck completely wrecking the captain's cabin, the crew's galley and other compartments. The explosion caused the galley's upper bulkheads to breakaway from the supporting stanchions and the concrete and tile deck was blown downwards about a foot.
HA PPFUR 2-17

Heavy duty pumps were used to control the constant flooding while work was in progress to patch up the ship enough to be refloated. Gasoline driven suction pumps up to 10 inches in diameter were used with some pumps able to move water out at 4,000 gallons a minute. Once the pumps were able to move water out faster than it came in Nevada would become buoyant enough to be moved into a dry dock.
HA PPFUR 2-17

A large temporary wooden patch reinforced with steel, 55-feet long and 32-feet deep, was fabricated by navy yard shipwrights to place over the damaged section on the port side of the hull from the torpedo hit. For the proper shape of the patch measurements were taken from the overturned hull of Nevada's sister ship, the Oklahoma. USN NH 64476

The patch was transported to the Nevada by the floating derrick/dredge Gaylord on February 10th for installation. After several attempts divers found they could not fit the patch properly to the port side for a watertight seal. The torpedo and bomb explosions had distorted the hull enough that the unusable patch was finally removed on February 17 and scrapped. USN NH 50104

After nearly eight months at Puget Sound the Nevada *underwent a major change to her appearance. Her bridge superstructure was completely reconstructed. The ship's aft tri-pod mast was removed and the latest radars were installed. She now mounted 16 rapid fire 5-inch dual purpose guns in twin mounts and numerous 40-mm and 20-mm antiaircraft guns. The* Nevada *was the first of the battleships sunk on December 7th to return to active service.* NA 19N-38057

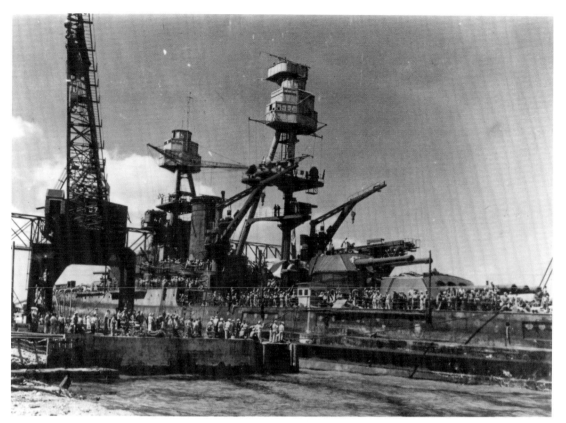

While in dry dock permanent repairs were made to all underwater damage in the hull, and where possible, interior bulkheads were repaired or shored up. The ship was undocked on 15 March 1941and moved into the yard's repair basin. There clean up continued, electrical systems were restored and the ship's main and auxiliary machinery put into working condition. All Navy Yard work was completed by mid-April 1942. NEVADA STATE ARCHIVES

The ship was finally ready for sea and on April 22, 1942, Nevada joined up with a convoy for the West Coast and sailed from Pearl Harbor under her own power to Bremerton, Washington, to complete major repairs and modernization at the Puget Sound Navy Yard. Nevada's salvage had involved more than 400 individual dives by navy and civilian divers who spent over 1500 hours on their work. The refloating of the battleship Nevada was the first success of the Pearl Harbor Salvage Team.
NA 80G-64768

CIGARS FOR THE CREW

On Oct. 8, 2010, a ceremony was held at the *USS Nevada* Memorial at the Veterans Memorial Plaza in front of the *Nevada* State Capital in Carson City honoring surviving sailors from the ship and completing a promise of then-Governor Edward Carville in 1944. He promised all 2,500 of the men on the ship a silver dollar, a handshake, and a cigar.

The crew received their dollar in 1944, but it was not until earlier in October 2010 that the handshake and cigar were provided. *Nevada* Lt. Governor Brian Krolicki shook hands and presented the cigars, as well as a specially struck commemorative coin to the surviving members of the ship's crew. Fifty Churchill-sized cigars were offered by local cigar retailer Carson Cigar Company.

By the Spring of 1943 Nevada was ready to rejoin the fleet after nearly eight months at Puget Sound where the battleship underwent a major change to her appearance. Her bridge superstructure was completely reconstructed. The ship's aft tri-pod mast was removed and the latest radars were installed. She now mounted 16 rapid fire 5-inch dual purpose guns in twin mounts and numerous 40-mm and 20-mm antiaircraft guns. Nevada was the first of the battleships sunk on December 7th to return to active service and also the only Pearl Harbor battleship to serve in both the Pacific and Atlantic Theaters of War. Nevada would earn seven battle stars for World War Two service. NA 19N-38057

CONFIDENTIAL   December 15, 1941.

From: Commanding Officer.
To: Commander-in-Chief, United States Pacific Fleet.

Subject: Report of December 7, 1941 Raid.

Reference: CINCPAC Despatch 102102 of December 1941.

1. The following report is submitted in compliance with reference (a).

2. <u>OFFENSIVE MEASURES TAKEN.</u>

a. Enemy air attack first observed at 0801. General quarters sounded immediately. Two machine guns forward and two aft were already on continuous watch. The 5" antiaircraft battery was partially manned for routine daily 0800 battery and fire control check.

b. At 0-802 machine guns opened fire on enemy torpedo planes approaching in port beam. one plane was brought down by machine gun fire and crashed about 100 yards off *Nevada's* port quarter. One plane dropped a torpedo which struck the *Nevada* on the port bow.

c. At 0803 (about) 5" AA. battery opened fire, local control, as guns were manned, and without waiting for control to be manned. These guns fired at torpedo planes, low altitude and high altitude bombers. Fire from these guns as well a .50 caliber machine guns, was almost continuous until 0820 when the attack slackened somewhat.

d. During the periods mention above, at a time undetermined, but probably about 0803, the port 5" broadside battery opened fire on low flying torpedo planes; members of the *Nevada* crew state that this battery scored a direct hit on one of these planes, the shell probably striking the torpedo, resulting in the disintegration of the plane in midair.

e. Firing was intermittent until 0830 when a heavy bombing attack was made. Both AA. batteries opened continuous fire on enemy planes until 0908. At this time the attack slackened.

f. About 0915 the 5" AA. battery opened fire intermittently on enemy planes to the eastward. These planes, as far as is known, made no direct attack on *Nevada*.

3. <u>DAMAGE TO ENEMY</u>.

a. Officers and members of the crew vary in their accounts of the number of enemy planes seen brought down by gun fire. It is probable that at least five planes were destroyed in the vicinity of the *Nevada*.

b. One torpedo plane was destroyed by .50 caliber machine gun fire about 0-802 and fell about 100 yards on the *Nevada's* port quarter. The plane had not dropped its torpedo. A considerable number of person saw this plane destroyed.

c. Before getting underway at 0840, the forward machine guns are believed to have brought down three enemy torpedo planes that were strafing. These planes were said to have been hit within 200 yards of the ship.

d. It is reported among the crew that one enemy torpedo plane was brought down by a direct hit from the 5" secondary battery, exploding the torpedo and blowing the plane to bits.

e. Just before grounding off Hospital Point, three enemy planes, probably dive bombers, were fired upon until a range of 200 yards was reached. members of the crew observed these planes to crash, one in a cane field toward Ewa, one near the Naval Hospital and one in the channel.

4. <u>OWN LOSSES AND DAMAGE</u>.
    a. The list of killed, wounded, and missing has been previously forwarded.

    b. Damage to *Nevada*.
        1. Hole in Forecastle Deck at frame 15, six feet outboard of the ship's center line to starboard, from bomb hit. Staterooms wrecked below, impossible to tell how far down the bomb traveled due to water level six feet below Forecastle Deck. Sides of trunk to paint storerooms deflected inward considerably, water fills trunk within six feet of Upper Deck. Size of hole in deck about 12 inches in diameter, just aft and to starboard of paint storeroom trunk, and aft and inboard of after starboard hawse pipe, through wearing plate.

        2. Hole in Forecastle Deck at frame 15, 8 feet from center line of ship to port, 12 inches in diameter caused by bomb hit, depth of penetration unknown due to flooding on deck below. This hit and the hit above apparently went through to the second deck and caused fires in the Officer's Quarters. The force of the explosion also caused considerable deflection upward of the Forecastle Deck in this vicinity. On the port side, about 15 feet from the center line, the deck is split and deflected upward from frame 13 to frame 21. All of the Officer's Quarters forward of the Wardroom are either badly damaged or completely destroyed by fire. The hole is aft and to port of paint storerooms trunk, and aft and inboard of after port hawse pipe, through wearing plate.

        3. Hole of approximately the same size as the previous two hits, about three feet in from the port waterway, frame 25. This is outboard of the anchor windlass capstans. The bomb probably went through the Wardroom to the second deck before exploding. The deck inboard of this hole is deflected upward about 4 feet and split across the center line at a point about 6 feet aft of this hole. The deck is also split aft on a direct line from this hole to frame 32, as a result of this and apparently other hits. Across the Forecastle Deck in this vicinity the entire deck from port to starboard is deflected upward considerably. The two anchor engine vertical shafts are bent forward at about an angle of 20° and the top of the capstans apparently flew upward with the deck, and hit the two outboard gun barrels of No. 1 Turret. The vertical shaft on the portside has broken away from the one coming up from below. The Main Deck in the Wardroom has been blown upward from below, and the Wardroom is a tangled mass of deck, supporting beams, and stanchions. The port skylight hatch at frame 25 has been blown partly clear of the deck wreckage.

        4. There is some reason for believing that a much larger bomb than the ones noted previously struck the Forecastle Deck at a point ten feet to port of the ship's center line at about frame 27, just forward of No. 1 Turret, and went through to the second deck before exploding. The Forecastle Deck at about frame 29 is bent sharply downward from about three feet to port of the ship's center line to a point about 8 feet inboard of the port waterway. Due to the size of the opening in

the upper deck at this point it is difficult to determine the exact outline of such a hit, but the great wreckage indicates an extremely large explosion. The forecastle is also split forward from frame 265 to frame 22 at a point 3 feet to port of the port skylight hatch. The entire forecastle deck from frame 26 is bent upward and forward to about frame 22. From the starboard side at frame 26 at a point four feet inboard of the waterway the deck is broken open and deflected upward and inboard a distance of approximately 21 feet, at which point the deck is split fore and aft from frame 23 to frame 31. At the outboard point the deck is split fore and aft from frame 25 to frame 30. The deck winch at this point was blown upward at an angle of 25°, but remained intact. The seems to be no other indications of bomb hits on the Forecastle other than the very large bomb hit or several smaller hits which apparently went through as described above. One of the reasons for being very sure that there was such a large bomb hit is the size and number of fragment holes which have penetrated the Main Deck from below at frame 25 to port of center line. Both the Wardroom and the Junior Officer's Country below appear to be completely wrecked.

5. Considerable damage was done by one bomb, of apparently about the same size as the two forward ones in the Forecastle, which struck the deck just forward of the port AA. director, coming down at an angle of about 30° to the perpendicular, from about 3 points forward of the port beam. This bomb continued downward through the port wing of the Navigation Bridge, and the Signal Bridge, penetrating into Casemate 6. There was no damage sustained to any part of the mast structure above the Sky Control Shack. Sky Control Shack was completely burned out, very little being salvaged from it. Sky Control deck was punctured in several places from metal fragments from below and the starboard side is badly warped from the fire below. Apparently no damage of any kind was sustained by any of the three mast supports. The only damage suffered by port AA. director, except for broken glass, appears to come from external heat, and this is very minor. The stack structure above the Boat Deck has suffered very little; mostly holes caused by an exploding 5" AA. Ammunition Ready Box at about frame 567 on the starboard side just outboard of the stack.

This bomb was apparently 12 inches in diameter, and it hit the Sky Control Deck at frame 62 port, about 6 feet outboard of a point where the port after tripod pierces the Sky Control Deck just above and outboard of the chart house. Range V (Forward Rangefinder) is apparently undamaged, but the deck aft of it is warped slightly by heat. The Navigation Bridge structure was completely burned out from below. The deck of the Navigation Bridge is deflected downward considerably at the vicinity of the wheel. There is also a burned out part of the deck inside the Navigation Bridge aft and to starboard of the forward mast support. Nothing of any value remains in the Navigation Bridge. The heat of the fire from below apparently caused the deck of the Navigation Bridge inside of the Chart House to burn completely through and fall clear leaving a hole the size of the interior of the Chart House plus about three feet further to starboard and all the way aft. The rest of the deck to starboard is badly warped, and although the starboard after tripod leg is very badly burnt externally, it does not appear to have suffered any structural damage or deflection. The starboard bridge gyro repeater and pelorous has been practically destroyed by fire. Absolutely nothing remains of the Chart House, except a partial shell. The Conning Tower structure has suffered no damage.

The bomb hit just forward of the port AA. director penetrated through the Navigation Bridge, the Signal Bridge, the Boat Deck inside of the Captain's Office and exploded on the Upper Deck inside of Casemate 6 against the forward edge of the stack, blowing a hole downward through to the Main Deck to the Officer's Galley and back to No. 2 boiler uptake. The explosion blew up through the Captain's office; and forward into No. 4 Casemate, starting a fire which spread through the Captain's quarters and up to the Signal Bridge, navigation Bridge, and Sky Control. The fire spread to the Boat Deck and set off the AA. Ready Box previously mentioned. The flag bags on the Signal Bridge were burnt out, as were the life jacket lockers. A hole of approximately 30 feet square amidships was burned in the deck of the Signal Bridge beneath and aft of the Chart house. The four compartments on the Signal Bridge were completely wrecked by fire. Nothing of value remains inside of them. Practically all of the Chart House deck hangs down through the hole in the Signal Bridge. This hole extends also through the top of the Captain's quarters and is about the same size there as on the Signal Bridge. The entire enclosure on the Boat Deck, which held all the Captain's quarters and office, was completely destroyed, mostly by the fire, and partly by the explosion from below in No. 6 Casemate. Everything of value therein has been destroyed, including all the records in the Captain's Office. A safe in the Captain's Cabin appears intact, although badly scorched on the outside.

The explosion also blew out a seam amidships of the stack on the portside for a distance about 4 feet just above the Boat Deck level; splinters were also blown through the stack from below and a number of rivets were blown out. Casualties sustained to the starboard 5" AA. Battery during action were loss of air ramming at Nos. 1, 5, and 7 AA. Guns. No. 5 was due to a rupture in the air line due to vibration. The uptake from the Officer's Galley was badly damaged by the explosion.

When the bomb struck the Upper Deck at Casemate 6, frame 65, and exploded, it ruptured the stack back as far as frame 688 port, and pushed the smoke pipe in all the way to the top. The explosion blew out the bulkhead between No. 6 & 4 Casemates, and bulged out the bulkhead to No. 3 Casemate. The Canteen was completely destroyed by fire and the explosion blew a hold overhead into the Captain's Office and Cabin. A fire was started in No. 4 and No. 6 Casemates which was extinguished before it did an excessive amount of damage. The Upper Deck in the after starboard corner of Casemate 4 was badly warped downward; hammock nettings, lockers, Canteen, and drinking fountain were destroyed. Stanchions and overhead beams in the vicinity were pulled away from the deck. Ship's Service Office was badly damaged by fire. The explosion blew back into the Incinerator Room damaging some pipe in its forward end, blowing two holes in the after bulkhead of the Incinerator Room, one particle passed through the Bakery, penetrated the Dynamo Trunk on the portside and continued through the after bulkhead of the Dynamo Trunk into the Galley.

This explosion of the bomb on the Upper Deck, Casemate 6, blew a hole about three feet square through the Main Deck in the after portside of the Officer's Galley. The Officer's Galley was wrecked; as was the Dry Cleaning Room. The after bulkhead of the Dry Cleaning Room blew back into the laundry and the port bulkhead blew out into the 6th Division living space (B-171-L). Very little damage was done in the Laundry, or living space B-171-L. Ventilation system 1-68-2 in the port forward part of the laundry was wrecked. The after bulkhead of the Officer's Galley on the starboard side was pushed back slightly into the Laundry Distribution Room. A fire main riser at frame 66 port was broken just above the upper Deck; this helped keep the fire main pressure down until it was discovered and the valve closed on the third deck. This, however, was after most of the fire had been extinguished.

6. A bomb hit the Boat Deck, about frame 80, just aft of the ventilator trunk to the Evaporator Room, about 12 feet to starboard of the center line (about one-half way from stack to break of the boat deck.) it apparently struck some obstruction on the Boat Deck where it appeared to have exploded, blowing a hole through the Boat Deck into the Galley and deflecting the Galley Deck downward somewhat. It is understood that there was some exposed five inch AA. ammunition laid out on the Boat Deck at this point which exploded at this time. this might account for the failure

of the bomb to go deeper into the Ship. The Boat Deck was sprayed very heavily with exploding fragments which went through the after part of the stack, and ammunition hoist inboard of AA. Gun No. 7, the Evaporator Trunk Ventilator, and the Ventilators directly aft and inboard of it. Fragments also pierced the starboard forward tripod of the Main Mast, Starboard Galley, Skylight Hatch, the Deck Locker on the Steel Deck, and the fuse setter aft of No. 7 AA. Gun. Some fragments even pierced the after Search light Platform. The hole in the Boat Deck is about 12' across and 6' fore and aft. The explosion wrecked the ranges along the forward bulkhead of the Galley, and many flying fragments ruined the center table. Some pierced a few of the steel kettles, they also pierced the starboard bulkhead, and the force of the explosion deflected it outward toward No. 10 Casemate. The oil tanks on the portside were not damaged. All of the other equipment in the Galley was very badly damaged, possibly beyond repair. The explosion blew open the starboard door of the Galley in Casemate 9, starting a fire which apparently swept the entire casemate, and all of the instruments on gun No. 9 were burned up. Very little of any value is left in No. 9 Casemate. on the Main Deck inside of the Crew's Reception Room, the overhead was deflected downward from the explosion in the Galley. All the beams fore and aft were bent downward, cracked, or broken, except the one on the far port side.

7. There was a torpedo hit at about frame 42 port, even with the forward edge of No. 2 barbette, which tore a hole in the lower blisters A-32-V, and A-34-V. Upper blisters A-66-V and A-68-V were also ruptured. The hole was from frame 38 to frame 45 in length, and about 300 feet in depth. Another small split opening was found at about frame 36 extending about ten feet down from the second deck and about three feet in width. The explosion is believed to have penetrated the lower blisters to fuel tank A-14-F, and then to void A-426-V, to magazine A-424-M. It is believed that many compartments in the vicinity were damaged by this explosion and that practically all of the compartments forward of frame 60 and below the Main Deck are now flooded. The flooding spared aft along the second deck down into practically every compartment below the second deck so that it is believed that all the compartments except those aft of frame 122 are now flooded with the exception of certain storerooms and compartments which may have been completely water-tight.

8. The Engineering Department suffered few, if any, casualties from bomb or torpedo hits. Boilers are believed to be in good condition except for salting up, du to trying to keep steam up using salty feed water when the feed bottoms became contaminated by flooding from above.

The damage expected to other equipment in the machinery spaces will result from boiler priming or salt water immersion. electric wiring above the main deck is destroyed in the way of any fires. Piping is in fair condition except where actually destroyed by explosion or fragments.

SUMMARY. From the above it is apparent that the *Nevada* suffered at least six (6) bomb hits and one torpedo hit. It is possible that as many as ten bomb hits may have been received by the *Nevada*, as certain damaged areas are of sufficient size to indicate that they were struck by more than one bomb. However, direct evidence is not available to determine the exact number. The holes created. by bomb hits indicate that all, with one possible exception, were 12" in diameter (very Nearly). It is possible that all were of that size. Some may have not exploded or may have contained less explosive than others.

The damage, while considerable, should be capable of speedy repairs once the ship is afloat and alongside a dock in the Navy Yard.

[signed]
F.W. SCANLAND.

U.S.S. CALIFORNIA (BB-44), BATTLESHIP

The Salvage Organization studied all jobs which lay ahead and came to some conclusions regarding the salvage of each particular ship. As a result there was little difference of opinion as the work progressed. The officers and men of the Salvage Division, the Navy Yard, and the Pacific Bridge Company were all included.

While work was proceeding on *Nevada*, the wooden cofferdams for *California* were well underway, and the patches for *West Virginia* were being put in place. Moreover, personnel were transferred from a ship which had been completed to the next ship scheduled for drydocking. Thus Lieutenant Ankers and Chief Carpenter Mahan were transferred, among others, from *Nevada* to *California*. The Salvage Officer, Captain H. N. Wallin, divided his time among all ships and concentrated on the one that seemed most in need of his services.

The crew of *California* affectionately referred to her as "The Prune Barge," because that state produced a large quanity of prunes for export. It did not seem possible that the old "Prune Barge" was helpless on the bottom of Pearl Harbor. The salvage of *California* was studied by many interested persons.

The salvage of *California* was somewhat similar to the work on *Nevada*, but the first ship was damaged much more severely and recovery of human bodies was involved. It was the recommendation of experts from Washington that a sheet steel bulkhead be driven entirely around the ship. But because of the nature of the bottom of the harbor, it was decided that the first work should be to close the torpedo holes with concrete patches. Before that could be done, it was necessary to wall off the water by driving steel sheet piling around the torpedo holes. But as work progressed it was

The USS California, *Flagship of the Battle Force, was moored starboard side to berth Fox-3 off the southern end of Ford Island. The weather was clear with scattered clouds early that Sunday as the ship prepared for morning colors. The stillness of the morning was shattered by an explosion at nearby Hanger Six. The crew immediately rushed to man battle stations as General Quarters was sounding over the ship's PA system.* EA

133

At 0805 California was struck by two torpedoes on the port side, one after the other, both exploding below the ship's armor belt. Japanese "Val" dive-bombers attacked the ship 30 minutes later. One bomb crashed through the second deck killing 53 men. A close miss off the bow stove in the hull while other near misses sprayed the ship with shrapnel. The damage to the battered hull started extensive flooding into the ship's interior that soon disabled the engineering plant causing the ship to lose all power and lights. NA 80G-20047

Despite the valiant efforts of the ship's crew working in hazardous conditions to keep their ship afloat, the "Prune Barge" as the crew lovingly called her, the flooding continued to gain headway. It was a losing battle for three days ending with the California finally settling in the soft mud of the harbor bottom with her decks awash and only her superstructure remaining above the surface. PHPC decided to reduce leaks through these holes from inside and to eliminate entirely the patches on the outside.

While *Nevada* lost some men, none of the bodies were in the ship. All men had been blown overboard or killed near the impacts of the bomb hits. In the case of *California*, however, it was assumed that about 50 bodies remained in the ship.

Another important difference was that the whole quarterdeck and a part of the forecastle of *California* were underwater. While *Nevada* was driven by reciprocating engines, *California* was electric-driven. The experts at hand figured that the salvage of electric-drive battleships would require at least four years. All in all, the salvage of *California* was much more difficult job than the salvage of *Nevada*.

California was struck by two torpedoes and one bomb. Serious damage was done by a bomb near-miss and minor damage resulted from bombs which exploded at a distance. A bad fire resulted from the bomb which struck the ship before it stopped by the armored second deck. The vessel sank over a period of three days. This fact indicated that the torpedo bulkheads were reasonably intact.

Flooding of the ship was progressive due to open manholes, ventilation systems, and ruptured pipelines. Water and oil permeated the ship and caused abandonment of fire rooms and engine rooms. Unfortunately a serious oil fire from Arizona swept down upon *California* at 1000 on the day of the attack. This caused temporary abandonment of the ship and interfered with the steps being taken to keep the ship afloat. Except for this, *California* would no doubt have been saved from sinking.

The list of the vessel was to port, and at one time was nearly 16 degrees. There was considerable concern lest the ship turn turtle as *Oklahoma* had done, or that she slide into deeper water on the port side. In order to reduce the list, counter flooding was restored to, and two boiler rooms on the starboard side were purposely flooded. The Commanding Officer, Captain Joel W. Bunkley, asked the Material Officer of the Battle Force, Captain Wallin, if flooding by hose of the outboard starboard blisters would not be helpful, and this step was taken. The result was that the list to

port was greatly reduced. It was about five and a half degrees eventually.

Unlike *Nevada*, *California* was not in battle condition at the time of maximum damage. Although attempts were made to assume condition Zed after the surprise attack was begun it must be realized that passing from X-ray to Zed at breakfast time on a Sunday morning was no easy task. The fact that unwatering showed many Zed closures open substantiates the fact that the ship never attained the proper closure.

A number of the manholes of the port blisters were off or were loose, which contributed to the loss of the ship. This permitted fuel oil to flow to the fuel tanks near the torpedo hits and eventually to find its way to the lower parts of the vessel. This together with non-closure of eight-inch fuel lines and ventilation ducts, permitted gradual seeping of fuel oil and water to vital parts of the ship.

California was well designed. The holding bulkhead near the torpedo holes was adequate to its task. Expect for a few discrepancies in the location of fuel oil lines and water lines the ship was entirely able to withstand the punishment received on 7 December. Staying afloat for three days and drydocking without a single patch attests to the toughness and ability of the ship. Adequate pumping if it could have been supplied at the time, would have kept the vessel afloat.

The two torpedo hits at frames 46-60 and frames 95-100 respectively were the most serious damage sustained. The torpedo protection at these areas is approximately 17½ feet deep consisting of five bulkheads. In each case the inboard bulkhead was practically intact. The torpedo hits were below the armor belts

The near-miss forward was a serious threat because of the 3000 gallons of gasoline carried in this area for the seaplanes and motorboats. The gasoline lines were not ruptured although some leaks occurred. Most of this gasoline was drained out during salvage operations. Flooding was general in this part of the ship, and this put the bow down several feet. A "window frame" patch was installed over the hole blown by the near-miss on the level of the platform deck. This was effective but was blown off a few days before docking by the explosion of gasoline vapor in the area. The explosion was severe and did additional damage

The Salvage Division decided that the first order of refloating the California was to lighten the ship as much as possible. The ship's anchors and chains, two aircraft catapults, ammunition, ship's boats and tons of miscellaneous equipment and supplies that could be re-used later were removed This also included nine of the battleship's main battery of twelve 14-inch guns that were lifted from their turrets as well as all secondary battery guns. PHP

The mainmast was cut off at its base on the 01 level and lifted off by the yard's 150-ton floating derrick. The mast was not scrapped but refurbished and erected on a new concrete base at the supply depot on Kuahua near the entrance to Southeast Loch. It was used as a control tower for small craft operating in the harbor for the remainder of the war. A month later the ship's flag and conning tower was removed and shipped to the Mainland as scrap metal for use in the war effort. PHP

to the structure. Fortunately all hatches and doors were tightly closed and dogged at the time of the explosion. It is likely that a naked light, possibly with defective wiring insulation, caused the explosion. Later additional ventilation was provided to prevent such explosions. Some additional areas were opened to the sea, but it was possible to isolate the damage and to proceed without attempting further patching. By this time it was ascertained that the pumps in use were more than enough to keep up with the water which found its way into the ship.

A 250 kilogram bomb did considerable damage at about 0845 on the day of attack. Although it killed a large number of sailors, it did not directly affect the ship's stability of floatability. It entered at the starboard upper deck level at frame 60, passed through the main deck, and exploded on the armored second deck. It caused a great deal of structural damage and a fire which was difficult to extinguish on account of the failure of water pressure at the time. The smoke from this fire which was fought with carbon dioxide extinguishers by men using old type rescue breathing apparatus infiltrated the second and third decks. The smoke found its way into the forward engine room through the ventilation system. By causing the abandonment of the engine room it had a bad effect on the fortunes of the ship. The fire was finally put out by three minesweepers which same alongside.

A few high-level bombs were dropped on the starboard side, but these had little effect on the ship aside from slight damage from near-misses and some fragmentation damage to smoke stacks and starboard anti-aircraft guns.

After three days the ship came to rest with a list to port of about 5½ degrees with a draft of about 43 feet forward and 57 feet aft. This put sea water over the port side forward and over turret IV on the quarterdeck. The ship was settled deeper in the mud than anticipated.

The first requirement was to unload the ship. This was partly accomplished by the removal of all guns from the turrets except turret IV which was below the water level. Eventually the ship and flag conning towers were taken off, the broadside guns removed, and mainmast, which had previously been recommended for removal, was cut

off at the base and taken off the ship. Plans were made to remove all safes aboard, the catapults, the boats, the cranes, and the anchors and many shots of anchor chain.

While this was being done a wooden fence-like cofferdam was erected around the quarterdeck, and in the forecastle area, which was flooded. The thickness of the timbers depended upon the pressures which were encountered; they varied from four inches to eight inches. The cofferdam was usually installed from barges in 30 foot sections. Each section was made watertight at the deck coaming was bracing, was braced by divers against fixed objects, and was fitted with bins for sand bags to overcome the positive buoyancy of the lumber. The weight of the sections was taken by a fore and aft timber which rested in the waterway. The heights were sufficient to prevent seawater from entering in case a greater list was experienced, or if the vessel should take a starboard list when afloat.

About this time, material from the mainland began to arrive. The most important were the electric deep-well centrifugal pumps up to 12 inches in diameter. Although the ship received power from Ford Island it was self-sufficient with generators, air compressors, and drying out machines. These were set on the upper deck or some other dry spot on the ship. The Navy Yard received some mechanics from the mainland who were extremely useful in the heavy workload ahead. Among these were carpenters to fabricate the cofferdams and make them tight against water pressure.

Most of the work was done by divers at this and later stages. A large part of it was done by the Pacific Bridge Company, which fabricated and installed the wooden cofferdams. Their six divers were kept busy bracing and making watertight the cofferdam around the quarterdeck. When the water level inside was below that outside, the flow of water was checked by stopping small leaks. At the deck coaming and between sections a soft material, or pudding, was used to attain watertightness. This was usually oakrum enclosed in canvas.

Other divers were busy below decks plugging sanitary drains, rupturh piping, sea scuppers, and ventilation lines. The closing of all ports was one of the most important tasks. They also closed off the leakage resulting from open or loose manhole covers. This was done by driving shores or wooden wedges in ruptures admitting seawater or oil.

One big job efficiently performed by divers was the closure of gun ports on the port side. The Navy Yard made strongbacks which permitted the closures to be drawn up tight. After removal of guns it was hard to make the closures watertight except by strongbacks and wedges.

When the electric and the gasoline-driven centrifugal pumps were placed in the various trunks and compartments the water was circulated to overcome stagnation. This was kept up every day. It was then discovered that the outflow of the pumps was greater than the inflow of water, and it was decided that with additional plugging it would be possible to float the vessel without patches over the torpedo damage.

The lowering of the water level was kept in step with the removal of stores and oil, the care and preservation of the equipment which was uncovered, the removal of human bodies, and the cleaning of the compartments which were unwatered. A definite schedule controlled this work. As soon as turret IV was above water, inspection was made of turret rollers. It was found that aside from slight corrosion and discoloration the rollers and their paths were perfectly all right.

The Salvage Division never did get enough men to do a satisfactory cleaning job although men from the Receiving Station were added from time to time to augment the ship's force available. The amount of cleaning which is necessary in a sunken battleship is well-nigh incalculable. The maximum number required was about 500 men; at first only six officers and 48 men were available.

As the ship was pumped down in accordance with the schedule, divers plugged leaks in the structure and steps were taken to preserve machinery. A hot caustic solution was applied to machinery equipment as well as to all surfaces immediately after original washdown with seawater. This was followed by fresh water, and machinery items were treated to a bath of "tectyl" to prevent corrosion. Many items were put on a barge and sent to the Navy Yard. They were tagged for identification under the able direction of Lieutenant Commander J.A. McNalley who was in charge of preservation and identification. Eventually these items were sent to the Navy Yards at Puget Sound

and Mare Island, but those needed for the homeward voyage were retained at Pearl Harbor. Because of the large number of electric motors on *California* all those not needed for the voyage to the mainland were preserved in place aboard ship.

On the second and third decks of *California* a number of human bodies were encountered. It was the practice to stop pumping in time to leave two feet of water above the deck. The bodies were then floated into large canvas bags. These were securely tied and transported to the Naval Hospital at Aiea for correct identification and burial.

The removal of oil, ammunition, and stores went on continually. About 200,000 gallons of free oil were collected from various compartments. The free oil had a good effect in protecting machinery items from the seawater although, of course, it was also responsible for causing loss of life and the abandonment of certain battle stations. Stores were easy to remove when the water level permitted. The refrigerator spaces containing fresh meat were a notable exception. Ammunition was a valuable factor in reducing weight, especially the 14-inch shells and powder.

Mention should be made of the oil-skimming operation, which was followed in all ships. This was a part of the free oil recovered, and was used at all times particularly before final pumping at any deck level. All classified information and personal effects were turned over to the Commanding Officer for proper handling and disposal.

The experience aboard *Nevada* warned of the danger of toxic gases. Great care was taken to avoid subjecting the men to this danger. Before any compartment was entered the air was analyzed by the Yard expert, Lieutenant Commander C.M. Parker (Medical Corps) of the Industrial Department. He was available at all times and was a frequent visitor to the ships under salvage. Lieutenant Ankers and Carpenter Mahan were charged with watching for gas hazards. One of these officers was aboard at all times. Temporary ventilation was furnished for all spaces and temporary electric lights were installed in all compartments. All men were outfitted with boots and coveralls.

As the machinery spaces were emptied, great care was taken to preserve the electric-drive alternators and motors. It was hoped they would be usable for the voyage to the mainland. The mechanical parts were washed out with fresh water and "tectyl." The electrical parts were cleaned and dried. The instruments in the control room were sent to the Navy Yard as quickly as possible following removal from the instrument board.

Shortly after docking Commander Hyman G. Rickover arrived from the Bureau of Ships. He had a plan for reconditioning the electric-drive machinery and had consulted with General Electric and Westinghouse companies as well as with the Puget Sound Navy Yard. He held a conference on 11 April. He had with him a representative of the Puget Sound Navy Yard and the General Electric Company. It was decided that the electric motors which were subjected to high voltages could not safely be dried out and re-impregnated. This method was only suitable for low voltages especially in a ship which was 20 years of age at that time.

It was not long before General Electric had 53 men working on the alternator and two motors. It was their estimate that the electric machinery necessary for a trip to Puget Sound could be completed in about four months. It was decided that one set, consisting of one alternator and two motors, would be cleaned in place and dried out for the voyage, and finished while other work was being performed at Puget Sound. All vital wiring and instruments were replaced at Pearl Harbor. The machinists, electricians and riggers from the Puget Sound Navy Yard were partly responsible for the fine record made.

The turbine end of the electric-drive machinery gave no important trouble although it required the usual attention due to corrosion in some degree and presence of fuel oil. As for the boilers which had been submerged for four months, they were found to be in good condition. As done on *Nevada*, it seemed best to rebrick and test them.

California came afloat on practically an even keel or a slight list to port on 24 March 1942 and was placed in Drydock Number Two on 9 April. At that time her mean draft was about 40 feet. Before docking, the wooden cofferdam around the quarterdeck and on the forecastle was removed from the vessel. As customary, the Commander-in-Chief of the Pacific Fleet and the Commandant

Engineers and divers from the Pacific Bridge Contractors built two wooden fence-like structures called cofferdams. One was installed forward off the port bow and the other aft completely around the quarterdeck. Divers worked continuously with plugging up the many leaks as they occurred during installation of the cofferdams. The purpose of the heavily braced cofferdams was to keep out the harbor waters once pumping operations were underway to de-water the ship. PHPC

of the Navy Yard were at the head of the dock to welcome *California*. In the spring of 1942 the office of Fleet Maintenance was established under Rear Admiral C.A. Dunn; after arriving at Pearl Harbor he was never absent from significant events in the salvage operations.

California remained in dock, subject to 72 hours notice, until 7 June 1942. During this time the Yard made permanent structural repairs to al-most all the ship's damage. After a few trial trips she left Pearl Harbor under her own power on 10 October and arrived at the Puget Sound Navy Yard on 20 October. There she was modernized and fitted out with 40 40-millimeter Bofors in quadruple mounts and 48 20-millimeter Oerlikons in single mounts. The ship was entirely new with greater beam, stability, protection and 154 miles of new electric cable.

With most of the leaks in the cofferdam now under control and heavy duty pumps keeping ahead of the inflow of water into the ship, the California *finally came afloat on an even keel on 24 March. Divers began working in the interior of the ship closing hatches, manholes and other openings. It was determined that her basic watertight integrity was reasonably good eliminating the need to put patches over the torpedo damage. Note the large number of sandbags piled atop the cofferdam, they were used to counteract the natural buoyancy of the wood.* USN NH 55036

The cofferdams were removed and sixteen days later on 9 April 1942, with pumps working full time, yard tugs carefully moved California *across the harbor and into Dry Dock Two. Over the next two months in dry dock, yard craftsmen worked around the clock to repair the damage. Structural repairs were made in the interior of the ship while work continued on removing unusable stores, fittings and equipment for scrap. Cleaning up the ship was an enormous job with constant risks from toxic gases and fire.* PHP

Leaking fuel oil had permeated the ship's interior leaving everything coated with a black gooey substance. The resulting mess and filth was indescribable, but there was some benefit in that various metals covered with oil were preserved for reclamation. Otherwise they would have corroded beyond usefulness. Over 200,000 gallons of loose oil leaking from the ship's bunkers was recovered in the months prior to the ship moving into dry dock. PHP

The torpedo that struck forward smashed into the ship about 18-feet above the keel just below the ship's 14-inch thick steel armored belt (top). The damage to the hull extended over an area 64-feet long by 16-feet high. The aft torpedo damage was similar in size and also struck below the armor belt. Note remnant of air flask from the Japanese torpedo. PHP

The California's *main propulsion was provided by four turbo-electric drive engines deep within the hull. They were manufactured by the General Electric Company who hurriedly sent out a crew of 58 experienced men to Pearl Harbor. Working alongside yard electricians they began the difficult repairs to the motors once the engine spaces were un-watered. Not only were the motors covered with thick oil and grime and some corrosion from salt water, the men worked in and foul cramped conditions.* PHP

Once the water was pumped out of the dock the repair work on the wounded battleship could begin. Adding to the difficulty of the salvage work on the California *but also the work on other sunken ships in the harbor as well, was the recovery of human remains wherever they were found. When workers came upon any casualties, work was immediately halted in that section until Navy Corpsmen were called in to remove the bodies from the ship. This procedure was always done with the utmost respect and dignity.* PHP

Hundreds of cheering men, naval personnel and civilian workers alike, gathered around Dry Dock One on the seventh of June 1942 to watch as yard tugs moved the California *out of the dock. There was still a lot of work to be done but this was a day of pride at the Pearl Harbor Navy Yard for all hands.* PHPC

The yard tugs then towed California *to Berth 22 in the Navy Yard where over the next four months salvage work and structural repairs were carried out. Only the necessary repairs to the make the ship seaworthy was done and the messy job of cleaning up interior spaces continued. The main battery of 14-inch guns were reinstalled and two of the turbo-electric engines were completely reconditioned, enough for the ship to steam under her own power when ready.*
NA 80G-10031

U.S.S. CALIFORNIA

Pearl Harbor, T.H.,
December 13, 19411

From: Commanding Officer.
To: Commander-in-Chief, U.S. Pacific Fleet.

Subject: Report of Raid, December 7, 1941.

Reference: (a)CincPac despatch 102131 of December 1941.

In accordance with reference (a) the following information is furnished herewith.

OFFENSIVE MEASURES TAKEN

0750   Sounded General Quarters and manned all battle stations, started setting Condition ZED.
0803   Commenced firing with M.G.s 1 & 2 (Ready Guns) on Torpedo Planes.
0810   Opened fire with 5" A.A. Guns #2 (Ready Gun) and #4 on Dive Bombers.
0825   Opened fire on dive bombers with 5" A.A. and fwd. machine guns, and continued intermittent fire until end of attacks about 0915.

DAMAGE TO ENEMY

At 0830, shot down one enemy dive bomber with fwd. machine guns which crashed in flames.

At 0832, one enemy plane shot down over Ford Island by either own fire or that of another ship.

OWN LOSSES AND DAMAGE

Five (5) officers killed.

Three (3) officers wounded.

Enlisted men - estimated 125 killed and 100 wounded. 37 dead and wounded have been positively identified. There are still 116 men missing.

0805   Two torpedoes struck port side, frame 10, making a hole about 40' long, extending from the first seam below the armor belt to the bilge keel.
0820   A torpedo struck port side, frame 47, making an irregular hole covering an area about 27' X 32', the top of which is some 6' below the bottom of the armor belt.
0840   Ship shaken by four (4) near bomb hits and splintered considerably by fragments.
0900   One (1) bomb (possibly a 15" A.P. projectile with tail vanes) struck abreast of Casemate #1, frame 59, penetrated to the second deck where it exploded in A-611, rupturing the forward and after bulkheads of the compartment, and the overhead into compartment A-705. The armored hatch leading into the Machine Shop was also badly sprung and could not be closed. A serious fire started about 0905 below main deck as a result.
0925   Plane 2-0-5 capsized and was sunk while removing from ship to remove gasoline fire hazard.
0930   Fire broke out on main deck, starboard side, "F" Division compartment and Casemates #'s 3, 5, & 7.
1002   Oil fire on surface of water enveloped ship, starting many fires and became intense on forecastle.

DISTINGUISHED CONDUCT PERSONNEL

KEENER, J.C., S.K.1c, PEARSON, G., CSK(PA), and NEWMAN, J. CSK(PA) were outstanding in their work during battle in the ammunition supply and endangering themselves in pulling wounded to safety.

CELESTEIME, B., M.Att.1c., BACOT, J.D., M.Att.1c., and WALLACE, H., Jr., M.Att.2c. were outstanding in their work assisting the Medical Officer with wounded.

REEVES, T.J., CREM(PA), deceased, was outstanding in his conduct in that upon being forced to abandon Main Radio, at request of Gunner PHARRIS, he assisted in a burning ammunition passageway, attempted to continue the flow of ammunition until overcome by smoke and fire.

Gunner J.C. PHARRIS, although injured, was outstanding in his work to continue ammunition supply in spite of fire and other hazards, during which he organized and reorganized able personnel and personally provided ammunition while men were dying in fuel oil and in rescuing many men from oil and vapors.

Pay Clerk H.A. APPELGATE and PAVLIN, B.F., E.M.3c. went beyond their required duties in taking a boat and obtaining ammunition from other ships while under fire.

Boatswain S. OSMON, who, although injured, did outstanding work in directing repairs and the rescue of injured. Commander J.D. JEWELL (MC), although burned about the face and arms from fires nearby his station, continued to administer effectively first aid without interruption.

BALDWIN, R.M., CY(PA) for his outstanding work in performing duties of Damage Control Officer in a very efficient manner while the First Lieutenant commanded the ship.

Ensign H.C. JONES and Ensign I.W. JEFFERY (both deceased) who organized a party and were attempting to get ammunition up by hand when killed.

FLEMING, W.S., B.M.1c., Gun Captain of 5"/25 gun #4, who, although wounded, continued to direct his gun crew and by his coolness and example under fire instilled confidence in the men about him.

WARD, D.E., B.M.2c. for bravery and coolness in action and in fighting fires and rescuing trapped personnel.

GARY, T.J., Sea.2c., (deceased) was killed while carrying out rescue work of men, after having rescued three or four.

The following officers and men conducted themselves in a distinguished manner in effecting the rescue of personnel trapped below decks in the Center Thrust Block Room, Forward Battery locker and Forward Distribution Room:

Ensign C.H. CHAMPION		Ensign W.A.J. LEWIS	
Ensign C.A. LABARRE		Ensign L.S. TAYLOR	
Ch.Elect. R.W. MILLER		*BLY, C.L.	MM1c
HELDEN, E.W.,	MM1c	CAROUTTE, J.H.	F1c
BEZVODA, S.F.	EM1c	MAXWELL, G.R.	EM1c
EBBERSON, L.F.	F3c	PLUARD, F.D.	F3c
ISENHOUR, R.A.	MM2c	MINCKLEY, R.F.	EM2c
NUNNELLEY, L.E.	F3c	FLEMING, C.E.	EM2c
BOTTOLFSON, R.L.	F3c	TOTH, R.J.	F2c
COON, R.V.	EM3c	WAITE, J.E.	EM3c
ROUNTREE, W.H.	F1c	KOIPPLINGER, C.F.	Bmkr2c
LITZ, C.L.	EM3c	GREENBAUM, H.	EM3c
GALYEAN, C.W..	F3c	STREETER, C.L.	EM2c

| ILLIAN, E. | EM1c | ALFORD, L.B. | EM1c |
| SAMUEL, H. | F3c | FRANCK, D.E. | EM3c |

An additional report of Distinguished Conduct may be made later when more facts are obtained.

OTHER ITEMS OF INTEREST

At the time of the raid, Lieutenant Commander M.N. LITTLE, First Lieutenant, was senior officer present on board. he immediately took command and ordered battery manned and preparations made for getting underway. Lieutenant Commander F.J. ECKHOFF, Navigator, relieved the Officer-of-the-Deck and assisted Commanding Officer. Lieutenant Commander H.E. BERNSTEIN, Communication Officer, had the head of department duty aboard ship, rushed immediately to insure the keys for the magazines were broken out and ammunition supply started promptly and then took his station in the Conning Tower. The senior Gunnery Officer was Lieutenant G. FRITSCHMANN who manned Control and took charge of all batteries. All other officers aboard went to their battle stations and performed their assigned duties. At 0915 Captain J.W. BUNELEY, Commanding *U.S.S. California* returned to ship and assumed command. At 1015 the order to abandon ship was cancelled, flames from the water having cleared the ship and battle stations topside were manned and a large number of men returned from the beach to resume work. The fire aboard ship was fought with all available fire equipment on board and much that was obtained from Ford Island - and extensive salvage operations were started. The ship was listing about 8° to port and the engineering plant was disabled. There was no light or power on board, and no water service, fresh or salt.

The conduct of all *California* officers and men during the attack and subsequent fire was excellent and cool and they performed their duties in the manner fitting the best traditions of the Naval Service.

J.W. BUNKLEY.

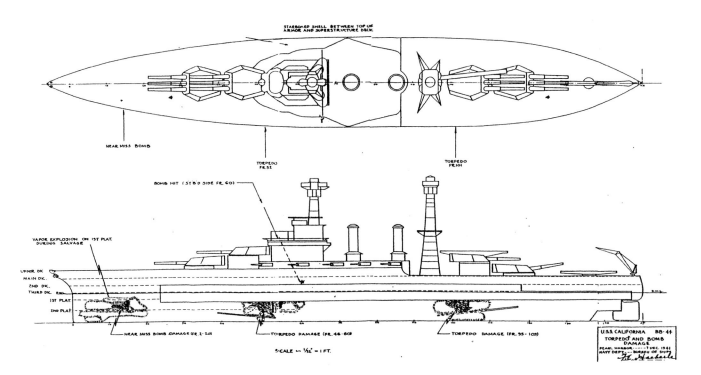

Near-miss and torpedo damage to the *California*. This drawing is from her war damage report.
National Archives

In the summer months of 1939, the clouds of war were gathering over Europe. In September the West Virginia, *along with other ships of the United States Fleet visiting New York City for the 1939 World's Fair, were ordered to the Pacific. In 1940 the Battle Fleet was permanently based at Pearl Harbor operating in Hawaiian waters for intensive training and exercises. On Sunday 7 December 1941,* West Virginia *was in port for upkeep and was moored outboard of the* Tennessee *at berth F-6.* EA

U.S.S. *WEST VIRGINIA* (BB-48), BATTLESHIP

Here was a ship much more severely damaged than *California* or *Nevada*. Salvage was getting harder as the work progressed. Few were there in the early days after the Japanese attack who believed that *West Virginia* would ever float again, much less be a formidable ship against Japanese sea power. Yet, so it turned out to be!

The pet name for this battleship was the "Wee-Vee." Most of the crew and officers were transferred to other ships and only a skeleton crew remained on board. The high command was hard pressed for experienced men to man the ships of

the fleet, and after all, it did not seem reasonable to assume that "WeeVee" would ever fight again.

The vessel was hit by as many as seven torpedoes; the exact number is questionable because of the extent of the damage on her port side. At least three torpedoes struck below the armor belt and one or more hit the armor belt knocking it askew. Seven armor plates and their keys were ordered by the Puget Sound Navy Yard. One or possibly two torpedoes entered the ship through the holes made by the first torpedoes when the vessel was listed about 20 to 30 degrees. These exploded on the armored second deck; and one hit the steering gear and wrecked the area aft, besides knocking off the rudder. Two bombs struck the ship but fortunately they were both duds.

The torpedoes virtually opened up the whole port side. It was the composite opinion that a patch was required over the two major holes extending from the waterline to the turn of the bilge. One such concrete patch was needed at frames 43 to 52, and another of ample proportions from frames 611/2 to 971/2. The steering area could be isolated, and the rudder picked up from the bottom of the harbor in due course.

The torpedo bulkheads were severely damaged. The holding bulkhead was ruptured far more than in the case of *California,* and the intervening transverse members were badly accordianized. The bombs which struck 16-inch turret III and the foretop respectively did little damage. Both were the armor-piercing type 15-inch projectiles. The first passed through turret III's top but failed to explode within the turret. The other passed through the foretop and was found later unexploded in the debris on the second deck.

Serious damage occurred due to an oil fire which was not extinguished for 30 hours. Part of the oil was washed in from *Arizona* and part of it came from the ship itself which was about 70 percent loaded with fuel oil. This fire caused warping of a large area of deck and bulkhead plating amidships. A peculiar aspect of the fire was that it was put out in one area it broke out in another.

West Virginia suffered some damage from being pinched by *Tennessee* when the ship wedged against the forward quay. Some damage in the bilge amidships was caused. But this may have prevented *West Virginia* from capsizing in the early stages of the attack before counter flooding was effective. In any event it reduced the amount of heel. Salvage work began while similar work was underway on *Nevada* and *California.* The experience which the salvage crew gained on those two ships was useful for the *West Virginia* job.

One significant aspect of the work was the use of underwater concrete. By this time, too, the electric driven deep well pumps of up to a 10-inch discharge were available. Also, the gas hazard was recognized and steps were taken to consult Commander Parker of the Medical Corps frequently.

In fact, regular tests were run in various parts of the ship, especially those recently un watered, to assure that the air was safe before men entered without gas masks. By this time, too, the men had regular "tank" suits, as coveralls were now called, which were laundered continuously by a contractor in Honolulu. Men engaged in particularly dirty work were furnished knee-length rubber boots which were readily cleanable.

The underwater concrete was a great success. It extended from above the waterline to below the turn of the bilge. This material was used to seal the ends of the large patches as well as the bottoms of each individual patch. Its efficiency was proven by the fact that in drydock it struck so well to the hull of the ship that small dynamite charges were required to break the concrete loose. We were extremely fortunate that the Pacific Bridge Company was present and available to handle the design and installation of these patches, and to make the large number of dives which was necessary to make the patches watertight.

It 1s not practicable to give a complete description of the concrete-sealed patches, but some information should be included. In the first place, the patches were usually in 131/2 foot sections. Each section was about 50 feet long or deep. The bottom portion followed the contour of the ship, and the patch was pulled up snugly by means of hook bolts spaced horizontally every 12 feet or so. The hook bolts were spaced by divers and hooked into the side plating through holes burned by an underwater gas or electric touch. These bolts passed through the patches and were fitted with butterfly nuts. The mud which covered the bilge was washed away by waterjets. The bilge keel was cut away where it fouled the patch, but in most instances the patch fitted over it. The joints between patches were made watertight by using old rubber hose for gaskets and drawing one patch to another by lug bolts.

The patches were made of four-inch planking. The four-inch steel "I" beams and the 10-inch steel "H" beams were set vertically. This ingenious structure took the inward thrust of the patch. Fore and aft wales of 12 inch x 14 inch timbers were spaced about four and a half feet apart. These members were shored directly to the armor belt. Negative buoyancy of the time of placement was

In the opening minutes of the assault on Battleship Row eight torpedoes quickly slammed into the West Virginia *on or above her armor belt, ripping open over 200 feet of her port side amidships. A ninth torpedo blew off the ship's rudder and two 1,700-pound bombs struck the ship that did not explode but caused extensive damage. The torpedo explosions ignited oil fires that burned on the devastated battleship for nearly 30 hours before finally being extinguished.* NA 80G-19947

obtained by a lead weight placed on an angle iron shelf on the outside of each patch. The clearance between the armor and the inside of each patch was about 18 inches. This gave sufficient room for a person to work between the armor and the patch. The forward patch had one door and the after patch three doors for divers to pass from the outside to the inside of each patch. After concrete was poured these doors were secured.

The final operation was the pouring of the underwater concrete to seal the bottoms of all sections and the sides of end sections. All were poured in succession from a steel barge on which had been placed a mixing machine. The concrete

was a rich mixture consisting of one part cement to three and one-half parts of aggregate. The contractor utilized the Tremie process which he used in drydock construction. Ten-inch Tremie pipes were about 10 feet apart. Care was taken, as is usually the case that the concrete mixture did not disintegrate in the water. The concrete was installed about four feet deep along the bottom of each patch and at each end. In all 325 cubic yards, or about 650 tons of concrete were used.

As soon as the concrete patches were finished the deep-well pumps were started to reveal large leaks in the patches, or elsewhere. It was easy to exceed the inflow when the leaks were rectified

150

Despite the danger of exploding shells, Chief Boatswains Mate J. L. Jansen, Commander of the little YG-17, *a garbage lighter nicknamed "the honey barge," brought his vessel alongside the burning* West Virginia. *Pumping heavy streams of water onto the flaming inferno, the* YG-17 *and her brave crew stayed alongside the battleship fighting fires till early evening when ordered over to the blazing* Arizona. NA 80G-19930

by the divers. Soon the salvage crew was in command, and it remained to reduce draft by removing weights still in the ship.

These weights consisted of free oil which was skimmed from the surface of each level by use of a skimmer operated by an electric motor. Fuel oil, which totaled about 800,000 gallons, was also removed. About 40,000 gallons of free oil was picked up by skimmers. This was only half of the free oil in *California*. However, *West Virginia* had only 70 percent of its fuel oil aboard whereas *California* had 100 percent. The fuel oil was taken out by ship's pumps operated by air, as in *California*. All of the 16-inch shells and powder were sent ashore. This was a sizable weight.

Many of the regular stores and canteen stores were landed also. Experience proved that the removal of fresh meat and dairy products was an unwholesome job, but a new method was devised. The consisted of pumping sea water into the compartments for several days, after which the meat was in shredded form and could be removed in its original bags without a noticeable stench.

The hazard of capsizing was always present because of possible failure of the concrete patch due to an enemy air attack or structural failure. Steps were taken to prevent this, especially when the ship was en route to the drydock. Temporary patches, similar to a collision mat, were made to draw over any damage which might be stained.

Taking on water rapidly, the wounded battleship was in danger of capsizing. The order to counter-flood failed to reach some of the repair parties below decks. Lt. Claude V. Ricketts on his own responsibility, rushed below with a party of enlisted men ordering the closing of watertight doors and flooding of the starboard voids thus preventing the ship from capsizing. The "Wee Vee", as she was affectionately called, came to rest on an even keel in the shallow depths with the main deck barely above water. NA

As with previous work on salvaged ships it was necessary to lighten West Virginia *as much as possible before it could be refloated. The ship had over 800,000 gallons of fuel oil reserves that would have to be pumped out. Deck equipment, secondary armament, catapults, ammunition, decaying ship's provisions, along with tons of trash from interior spaces were removed. The mainmast was lifted off 24 March by the yard's floating crane YD-25.* NA

It was asked to drydock in Number One instead of Number Two Drydock, if possible, because of the long time that *West Virginia* would require to make even temporary repairs/ It should be understood that Number Two was a much larger dock with a greater depth over the sill and blocks. Therefore it had to be available for damaged ships returning from a fray with the Japanese. The use of Number One Drydock established our goal for a draft of approximately 33 feet, which was hard to attain for this severly damaged ship. But it was reached by removing the fresh water from the double bottoms and all unattached weights on board. Air pressure was used extensively in *West Virginia*. It was tried out successfully in the area near the steering mechanism, and elsewhere wherever isolation of damage was possible.

Human bodies were handled as in *California* and were taken out almost unknown to the working parties. Sixty-six bodies were found throughout the ship. Several bodies were found lying on top of steam pipes which were in the air bubble existing in the flooded areas.

Great care was taken with the main propulsion plant. Little oil was allowed to percolate into the main units, and as they were unwatered prompt steps were taken toward preservation. The General Electric Company and Puget Sound working parties on *California* became available and went to work promptly on *West Virginia*. They reconditioned the steam end without much trouble, and were able to start at once on the alterations and motors. As a result *West Virginia* had all her electric-drive machinery restacked and rewound before the voyage to the mainland. This was the biggest job ever undertaken on a ship afloat.

West Virginia came afloat on 17 May and was received in Drydock Number One with blocks cut down to 33 inches on 9 June 1942. At that time she was practically on an even keel although she had been heeled to a maximum of 28 degrees. When the salvage crew started working on her the draft was 50 1/2 feet forward and nearly 41 feet aft, with a list to port of about three degrees.

It might be observed that the smaller pumps were pumps to reduce the water level in storerooms and smaller compartments. Even the Barnes three-inch suction pumps were put to work. As were the four-inch and the six-inch suction pumps. The 440 volt Pomona and the Peerless ten-inch deep-well pumps were extremely effective in reducing the ship's water level.

Adequate ventilation was a must in *West Virginia* in order to reduce the gas hazard. Temporary lines were run by the Pearl Harbor Repair and Salvage Unit and hooked up to the ship's ventilation system. Temporary lights were rigged by the same crew, as lower compartments were unwatered.

Nearly all electric motors and auxiliary machinery were saved. This was due to the care exercised by Commander McNalley's crew. Preservation was the watchword. All vital items were reconditioned at the yard; all others were retained on the ship for delivery at a West Coast Navy Yard. As usual, personal effects and classified material were turned over to the ship superintendent by order of the Commanding Officer. Great care was exercised, especially when personal lockers were emptied of their contents.

The enthusiasm and spirt of the crew deserves high praise. The Commanding Officer, Lieutenant Commander W. White, and his first assistant, Lieutenant Commander Levi Knight, were fine leaders, and performed through the months most admirably. They, with less than 500 men at any time, tackled almost a hopeless job. Yet they were able to clean up the ship, remove the dead, take off every weight that could be moved, set up and man an anti-craft battery of nine machine guns, and reduce the draft to permit docking in Drydock Number One. At the same time they established temporary living quarters on Ford Island, built a walkway to the ship, recommissioned the officers' gallerys aboard ship, and from 27 April served three meals a day to all hands.

The Navy Yard's design and planning specialties were important to the success of salvaging *West Virginia*. Various shops also applied their talents to the work. Without them the operation of air compressors and ventilation blowers would have been greatly handicapped. The Navy was fortune indeed to once again have the personnel and the experience of the Pacific Bridge Company. Their abilities in diving work, and in design and installation of the patches was an achievement which excited the admiration of all.

Some reference has been made to the work of the divers. Without them it would have been im-

The extensive torpedo damage would require the construction of a huge cofferdam to cover the wrecked area amidships to float the ship. The cofferdam was designed and built by the Pacific Bridge Contractors in the Navy Yard and would be constructed of wood, steel and concrete in individual sections. Steel A-frames were installed on the main deck to support the patches as they were lowered in place and then bolted to the hull. A removable 4-ton lead weight was used at the bottom of each patch to counteract the natural buoyancy of the wooden patch. NA

Once divers secured a patch to the hull the 4-ton lead weight was removed and used on the next patch. Divers were kept busy constantly sealing up leaks as they occurred. A four foot layer of Tremie underwater cement was used to seal the patches at the bottom, the same type used in bridge and dry dock construction. The cement was mixed on the contractor's barge alongside the ship. A crane on another barge alongside lifted the buckets of cement to the hopper feeding the 10-inch pipes leading down to the bottom of each patch. NA

As soon as the patches were considered reasonably watertight the unwatering of the ship was commenced. A total of nine heavy duty deep-well pumps were installed on deck and a number of smaller pumps in interior spaces. With all pumps working, the water level within the hull was slowly reduced and on 17 May 1942 the West Virginia came afloat. Three weeks later, battered, bruised and barely afloat yard tugs carefully towed the battleship to Dry Dock One. NA

possible to salvage *West Virginia*. They performed hazardous work, both inside and outside, without a casualty. These men came from the Salvage Division, *West Virginia*, *Widgeon*, the Submarine Base, the contractor, and the Navy Yard. In all from January to June, 527 dives were made totaling nearly 1400 hours. Nearly half of the hours underwater were done by the contractor.

In drydock *West Virginia* received the attention of the Navy Yard. It was agreed that the ship could be undocked to make way for any battle casualty, but none appeared. The electric-drive machinery was the governing job, so final repairs in lieu of temporary repairs were possible in most cases. She sailed under her own power, as was the habit of Pearl Harbor's sunken ships. She was modernized by the Puget Sound Navy Yard with greater torpedo protection, increased stability and floatability, and a vastly improved anti-aircraft battery.

West Virginia left the Puget Sound Navy Yard on 4 July 1944 and took up the fight with the Japanese at the Battle of Surigao Strait where she poured 93 16-inch projectiles into the Japanese fleet. Before this she helped the landings at Leyte by bombardment. Later she took part as the flagship in the Mindoro Operation, and still later she participated at Luzon, Iwo Jima and Okinawa. She was present on 2 September 1945 when the Japanese surrendered formally on board the *Missouri*. *West Virginia* was the first of the "old" battleships to steam into Tokyo Bay and to anchor off the Japanese capital.

Such is the history of the ship which was "lost" on 7 December at Pearl Harbor. She had won five battle stars.

West Virginia in drydock showing damage on her port side. To expedite repairs of the damaged ships, work was started on the vessels well before they were drydocked. Draftsmen, planners, shop superintendents and supervisors of various shops inspected the ships in advance to plan for the work ahead. The drafting room made plans for the new welded sections to repair the damaged hulls. In the shops, the ship lines were laid down on the mold loft floor, templates lifted and

156

To seal the extensive damage to the West Virginia's hull the huge cofferdam consisting of eleven patches was constructed of wood in the navy yard. Each wooden patch, braced with steel reinforcement, was 13½-feet wide with 12x14-inch timbers running longitudinally and vertical 4-inch wood planking on the waterside. Each patch was 48-feet in length and shaped like an "L" so the lower part of the "L" could be attached securely under the turn of the port side bilge. A derrick lowered the weighted patch in position one at a time. Then divers bolted them securely to the hull and to each other to form one huge outer wall.
USN NH 64489

Looking aft most of the upper section of the cofferdam has been cut away in an area where three of the nine torpedoes that struck West Virginia had detonated. The lower section, still filled with the tremie cement, has yet to be removed.
NA 80G-13075

Much of West Virginia's damaged interior spaces and equipment was coated with a film of grimy fuel oil. Compartments and passageways were cleared by spraying with cleaning fluids and high pressure steam hoses. Cleaning up was backbreaking dirty work with much of the task done by hand. On 31 May a 1700-pound Japanese armor piercing bomb was found unexploded in the second deck port side. After a demolition team safely removed the fuse from the bomb it was sent over to the West Loch Ammunition Depot for further disposition. USN NH 64305

View of the port side looking aft towards the stern two days later on June 13th. A large section of the main outer wooden patch has been removed amidships about frame 64 showing the distortion above and below the armor belt and the damaged hull structure. Note the piles of broken cement at the bottom of the dock. The hardened cement was blasted off by using light charges (½ stick charges) of dynamite. The total amount of cement eventually removed from all eleven patches was 650 tons. USN NH 83058

Another view of West Virginia's *extensive damage. Several weeks before the ship was placed in dry dock another tragedy of the Pearl Harbor attack was discovered. The bodies of three men were found in a storeroom deep inside the hull. In the compartment was a calendar with the days marked off through 23 December 1941. Finally succumbing due to the lack of air the trapped men had lived on emergency rations for sixteen days waiting for the rescue that never came.* WEST VIRGINIA STATE ARCHIVES

The work of removing hundreds of tons of torn and twisted metal wreckage was done by civilian shipfitters and burners from the navy yard. Riggers had to improvise means of handling and removing the damaged sections as they were cut away. A crane offloaded the awkward pieces onto dump trucks which hauled them away to salvage scrap piles for eventual shipment to the West Coast and recycled for use in the war effort. WEST VIRGINIA STATE ARCHIVES

The cutting away phase of the damage portions of the ship proceeded until all the weakened and distorted structure was removed. Replacement sections were fabricated in the workshops and brought out to the dry dock. Dockside cranes swung the new sub-assemblies, some that weighed as much as 40-tons, into their final position to be welded to the ship and to each other. Work to restore the ship's watertight integrity took three months to complete. PHPC

The underwater hull structural repairs were completed, the compartments all tested and leaks corrected. A new rudder was built in the machine shop and re-mounted. The propellers and shafts were back in place and properly aligned and on 9 September the West Virginia *was moved out of the dock. Further repairs continued at pier side in the navy yard until April 1943. Now only a shell of her former self, but seaworthy, the "Wee Vee" departed Pearl Harbor on 7 May 1943 under her own power for a major rebuilding at the Puget Sound Navy Yard Bremerton, Washington.* USN NH 84005

On 4 July 1944, she left the Puget Sound shipyard, in many respects a new ship, having undergone a complete modernization, The West Virginia *would be the last of the severely damaged ships in the attack on Pearl Harbor to be salvaged and returned to combat duty. On 31 August 1945 the* West Virginia *proudly steamed through the narrow Urago Channel into Tokyo Bay to anchor off the Japanese capitol city not far from the* USS Missouri. *Two days later the formal surrender ceremonies ending World War Two took place on the decks of the "Big Mo".* NA 80G-307998

SYL PUCCIO'S STORY
Courtesy Roger Hare

By April 1940 I was assigned to the *West Virginia* as a Seaman 3/c, so I studied hard and became A Shipfitter 3/c.

On the morning of December 7th, I had the 3rd section "stand by" duty, when "away fire and rescue party" sounded just before 8 am.

The 1st section party responded to the call, so I went topside, just outside the Shipfitters shop. "Colors" sounded and all on deck were required to stand at attention. If you are wearing a hat, a salute is mandatory as the flag is raised. I wasn't wearing a hat, so I simply stood at attention.

That's when I saw the smoke and heard the noise coming from "10-10" deck across the harbor. If I'd been saluting, I would not have seen the airplane flying over the harbor toward us.

I thought it was ours at first, but then it dropped low and launched a torpedo at our port side. Peeling up, it straffed #2 turret and revealed the big red "meatball" insignia on the bottom of the wing. I knew then it was an attack.

I took a few stops down the Shipfitters shop hatch and yelled "Japs are attacking". My friend, Jimmy Camm yelled back "You're full of shh. . .," but he didn't get the word out when the first torpedo hit.

The ship jumped, then settled with a crash.

I headed aft, passing the Paymasters office to my Battle Station. My duty was to set "condition Zed"—closing water-tight hatches and sealing ventilator shafts; all critical for controlled counterflooding.

Roy Wallace Powers (S/F2c from Seattle, Washington) was with me at this battle station and after a few more torpedo hits I said "what do we do now Roy?" He was strangely silent and I suggested we get in touch with "main repair 3" forward. He gruffly replied "alright."

As we went to the hatch, Navy training kicked-in and I stopped to feel for heat and sniff for smoke. None present.

"Roy and I opened the hatch and ran forward to "main repair 3". We had no orders, but knew counterflooding must be started immediately.

WeeVee was now listing badly and the handles to operate counterflood valves were in a locker. It was pad-locked!

I saw Rucker (Murell B. Rucker S/F 1c) and he yelled "Pooch, I forgot my keys to the locker—they're back in my quarters."

I thought "oh no . . . how can we quickly counterflood when all the stuff we need is locked away?"

While all stood shuffling in confusion, I noticed a large spool that carried towing cable. It had a big handle on the side made from 2 inch solid steel stock.

I was pumped with adrenalin and anger, but knew a sledgehammer couldn't break a Navy padlock. Being in the metal business, I figured the locker hinges were made from soft metal, so I took the handle and attacked those. I took a big swing back first and almost clobbered Carpenters Mate Stevens, standing just behind me.

I don't know how many times I hit those hinges, but as soon as they broke I grabbed the locker door and ripped it open backward. I then took a counterflood crank handle and tossed it to Rucker while I grabbed a battle lantern.

I followed him to the first valve and helped him open it.

Handle in hand, Rucker then ran aft to meet with Lt. Claude Ricketts and Bobbick (James F. Bobbick S/F2c). They quickly opened the other valves just in time. WeeVee was listing at 28 degrees and we all thought she was turning over.

It took about five minutes for counterflooding to halt and reverse the list—the longest five minutes of my life!

[By contrast, neighboring *Oklahoma* reached 28 degrees and never stopped rolling.]

Why did *West Virginia* stay upright while *Oklahoma* rolled? Puccio's succinct answer: "*Oklahoma* was scheduled for a double open bottom hull inspection and had all areas wide open for review. She filled fast and couldn't be counterflooded."

As we sank straight down, I was worried. Rucker, an experienced diver, had told me there was only 12 to 15 feet between our bottom and the harbor mud. We didn't have far to go.

Shortly after, word was passed to abandon ship, just as the second wave of bombing started.

I ran to the quarterdeck and was getting ready to jump down to the starboard armor belt "fender line" when I saw Rucker again. "Pooch, stick with me—I don't want to go alone".

We both ran forward along the armor belt until we were close enough to inboard USS *Tennessee's* armor belt line. Jumping over, we joined other WeeVee sailors patiently waiting their turn to climb the Jacobs ladder to her main deck.

When my turn came, I made the mistake of looking up. That's when I saw all those bombs coming down, and they all looked like they were aimed at me!

I climbed that ladder so fast it was a blur. A big guy was ahead of me and thankfully he was thinking the same thing because if he had slowed I'd have carried him up on my head.

We rode out the second wave bombing on the *Tennessee*, then reported to the Administration building on Ford Island. It was here I saw who I considered my big brother in the Navy, Robert Adams (S/F2c).

Later that evening, we took a ferry over to the Navy Dockside and went to the Receiving Station. There we were given a mattress and a sandwich and were told to bed-down at the arena across the street.

I was tired and depressed when our Division Officer, Fred White, appeared and asked for two volunteers to go back to WeeVee and fight fires. I was about to volunteer when Robert Adams reminded me "never volunteer for anything."

It didn't matter because (in true Navy fashion), White just growled "Puccio, Adams, front and center—you just volunteered".

We were taken to Fleet Landing to catch a motor launch back to the *West Virginia*. After passing the sub base, we entered mid-channel and were nearing the over-turned *Oklahoma*. An armed guard on its keel suddenly opened fire on us with his .306 rifle. I ducked below the gunnel launch and yelled as loud as I could "Ahoy *West Virginia*!"

He stopped shooting.

The shattered *Arizona* was leaking fuel oil that was streaming into WeeVee's stern area and igniting. Robert Adams and I were given 3 inch fire hoses and instructed to play our streams at the oncoming slick.

Well into the night we kept that oil at bay until Adams and I were relieved. Time meant nothing by then, so I don't know when I finally went to sleep, but we were back the next day. This time to retrieve 5 inch shells for shore batteries to fight off an invasion we thought was coming.

Two days later we were assigned to the Submarine Base for temporary duty, but were again called back to the WeeVee for five more days of salvage work.

I was permanently assigned to the Sub Base, but I kept asking for re-assignment back to my ship. I was always denied. "I loved that ship and her crew."

A simple story of counterflooding, luck, and fire fighting. Details still fresh after all these years.

I sat speechless, but eventually mustered a weak "thank you" and stammered my gratitude for his service.

Next to me was a man I believed saved my Father's life and the future lives of WeeVee families. But when I spoke of this sentiment he seemed uneasy.

I attributed this to typical Navy vet humility, but future conversations always featured others actions instead of his—especially Rucker, Adams, and Powers.

Roy Wallace Powers was killed that day, as were over one hundred of his shipmates. Syl doesn't know how it happened.

"Torpedoes, bombing, flooding, fire or gas. Take your pick—there were hundreds of ways to die that day."

TO THE NEW YORK TIMES
VIA THE NEW YORK TIMES WASHINGTON BUREAU
FROM ROBERT TRUMBULL

REPAIR: IV.

PEARL HARBOR, Dec. 18 (Passed by naval censor)---When
the subject of the USS West Virginia is mentioned to the men
who worked on her salvage, they seldom say anything. They
just whistle.

The Japs on Dec. 7, 1941, left this $27,000,000 beauty
a model for destruction. It will be amazing and disheartening
to them now to learn that she will return to the war a better
ship than she was before.

Rear Admiral William R. Furlong, commandant of the Pearl
Harbor Navy Yard, pulled out a bulging manila envelope of
pictures when the writer and Keith Wheeler of the Chicago Times
requested details of the damage and repair of the West Virginia.

"Look here", Admiral Furlong said, pointing to the West
Virginia's hull. He showed a long section welded in to replace the dark, ragged cavern blasted out by Japanese torpedoes.
The new side was spotless, and smooth as the glossy paper the
Admiral held in his hand. The old hull, he reminded us, had
been riveted---a style that is passe' in this age of stream-
lining and economy of weight.

The West Virginia's 31,800-ton mass lay deep in the water
when the Japanese flew away on Dec. 7, 1941. She listed far
to port her starboard bilge hooked into the adjacent battleship

(More)

164

REPAIR: IV, Page 2.

Tennessee---a circumstance that prevented her listing even
more. *delete sups con Furlong. She was resting on bottom*

~~Seven~~ Eight torpedoes had hit the West Virginia on her port

side, blowing out a series of gashes above and below the armor

belt 120 feet long and so wide from lip to lip that two tall

men could stand, one on the other's shoulders, in the vent.

The boat deck was a shattered mass. Bombs laid open

this was after rough side taken off four decks the way an earthquake might tear away the wall

of a four-story building, leaving the rooms indecently exposed.

Up on the bridge Capt. Mervyn S. Bennion had lain grievously

wounded, refusing to be moved and there he died. Posthumously

he was awarded his country's highest honor, the Congressional

Medal.

The ship's plaque naming all her commanders has been

salvaged, and under Capt. Bennion's name Admiral Furlong had

a line engraved, "Killed in action........Pearl Harbor".

Back in the list of captains is the name of William R. Furlong,

skipper in 1936-37, and before that executive officer. The

with runs down flag plaque hangs again aboard the gallant West Virginia.

Japan's dive bombers did their work well on the West

Virginia. The heavy bomb abaft the bridge, that had damaged

all the upperworks, had pushed one deck clear down upon

another, and a five-inch gun in a rended casemate fell a full

deck below, as if sprung from a trapdoor.

(more)

165

The heavy armor belt showed the marks of **six torpedoes.**
Another tore into her vitals under the stern, breaking the
rudder and the giant steel castings that held the ~~stern~~ posts. *rudder or stern*
[word to get anyone to cast them.
Inside, the West Virginia looked as if she had been
crumpled like paper in a giant hand. Such damage as fire can
do was ~~everywhere~~. *on me rode* To top it, her bottom was **wrinkled where**
she struck the ~~floor~~ *bottom* of the harbor.

When the engineers went to work on the West Virginia,
almost the only point in her favor was the fact that the
ship was not capsized. Neither of the methods used to raise
the Nevada and the California would do in this case, because
the great **alash** in her port side was too large for **any patch.**
Delicate matching of the timber frames to the lines of her
hull was out of the question, for the sides of the ship had
writhed in their agony, and she no longer fitted her blueprints.

But the engineers found the cofferdam principle **still**
workable, with a remarkable variation as to the method of
making them watertight. Because of the grotesque irregularities
in the ship's tortured hull, it would be impossible to seal them
at the bottom by ordinary means.

The huge cofferdams were built, huge wooden sections
braced with steel. They were lowered, bolted to the hull as
on other ships
before, and meeting so as to form one tremendous outwall. The
cofferdam was further secured by long steel rods running
vertically upward from their attachments inside the timber
structure to "A" frames fastened to the deck above.

(More)

186

The support from the top was given by frames of steel "I" beams, from which the cofferdams hung as from a coat-hanger.

Now for the troublesome problem of sealing at the bottom, where a snug fitting of the wood was impracticble: Hundreds of tons of tremic concrete was poured from hoppers into funnels high above the water. This quick-setting cement, which hardens under water and gets its name from the French word for hopper, oozed through thick pipes and formed about the West Virginia's uneven crevasses far below. It hardened and made the cofferdam part of the ship, watertight.

As the pumps strained to suck out the fouled sea inside, the West Virginia rose, inch by inch. Each new day disclosed a new surface-ring of oil and black muck from the harbor bottom marking on the cofferdam the laborious progress of the ship's flotation.

There followed a period of heartbreak amid the indescribable filth only to be found in a ship that has been blown to bits between decks and left to the mercy of salt water for months. During this annoying time, the workers lived close ashore in rude huts built for them so they could stay near the job. They came to work on foot, over a bridge laid on floats. These were sailors all. The "yard workmen", civilians, had their customary quarters elsewhere, and were taken to and from the ship by boat.

(More

When the time came to nurse the West Virginia over the
sill and into drydock, the engineers held their breath, for
the battleship now was in great danger of striking some small
obstruction that would rupture her again.

On the keel blocks, the West Virginia had to take rough
treatment to remove the concrete. The only workable way
was to blast it out with small sticks of dynamite.

This done, the job before Admiral Furlong's big and
hard-bitten organization could be stated simply, but the
implications were staggering. They just had to rebuild a
large portion of the ship. Still, they had considerable
foundation for the new construction, for the seams---where the
torpedoes had left any hull at all---were opened only slightly.

Today, the West Virginia's port side has been renewed,
half of it new material. Behind the outer hull, considerable
rebuilding has taken place. In many parts of her, the West
Virginia is a new and better ship.

An incidental point of interest is that the West Virginia
yielded to the clean-up crews a fine reservoir of powder that
conceivably will be used to propel missiles at the Japs.
The powder was not in usable condition when recovered, but
was suitable for re-blending.

Admiral Furlong dwelt, with reason, on the repair of
the West Virginia.

(More)

168

"The spectacular salvage is re-floating", he said. "The hard work is cleaning up, then the repair."

This job was to be immeasurably more difficult on the West Virginia than it has ever been found elsewhere.

The compartments below decks were half-filled with rubble--rotting stuff that exuded an over-powering stench. Discoveries odd and gruesome were frequent as the men set about righting and cleansing the charnel. This work was arduous and discouraging, but the work crews, supervised by the West Virginia's own officers and men who treated the maimed battleship as a mother would tend a sick child, carried on.

There were instances of heroism in the salvage that deserve to go permanently into the annals of Dec. 7. One day an unexploded 1,750-pound bomb was discovered, held in a section of steel that it had penetrated. An officer risked his life to unscrew the live fuses.

Another time the workers came upon the uninjured air flask of a Japanese torpedo. The officers spent an uncomfortable time searching for the war head. They came to the conclusion that it had dropped off before the fish entered the ship. This torpedo, weirdly, was encircled, when found, by one of the ship's barber chairs.

Workmen prowling the ruins below decks made several tragic discoveries of the type that can only be expected when a city of more than a thousand men is hurled to the bottom of the sea in a space of minutes.

(More)

169

The West Virginia's larder was well stocked on Dec. 7. The refrigeration tanks belched hideous gases when air was again let in to the rotten food. Carrying this mess topside and loading it onto barges was a noisome task.

Clothing and other personal belongings were sorted when possible from the wet and stinking gobs of refuse, to be tagged if identifiable.

The electrical equipment, with its hundreds of miles of wiring, was also brought on deck and cleaned preparatory to overhaul. Some fifty specialists from the General Electric Company, which had built the motors and generators, were brought from the Mainland for the complex re-wiring. The tax-payer may rest assured that the Navy isn't throwing away anything that can be fixed.

Summing up the West Virginia job, Admiral Furlong said:

"We built her new from the inside out. We went right to the bottom, like a dentist drilling out a rotten tooth, and we burned away all the damage, then renewed the hull and decks."

The Admiral paid the highest tribute to the yard workers of the Industrial Department, the plumbers, carpenters, coppersmiths, tinsmiths, artisans of every kind, who labored untiringl, with Lt. Henry P. Rumble, the superintendent on the spot.

BB48/A16-3

10/2k

CONFIDENTIAL

Hawaiian Area,
December 11, 1941.

From: The Senior Surviving Officer, *U.S.S. West Virginia.*
To: The Commander in Chief, Pacific Fleet.

Via: The Commander Battleships, Battle Force.

Subject: Action of December 7, 1941 -- Report of.

Reference: (a) Article 712, U.S. Navy Regulations, 1920.

Enclosures:

(A) Statement of Lt.Comdr., J.S. Harper, U.S. Navy.
(B) Statement of Lt.Comdr., T.T. Beattie, U.S. Navy.
(C) Statement of Lt.Comdr., E.E. Berthold, U.S. Navy.
(D) Statement of Lt.Comdr., D.C. Johnson, U.S. Navy.
(E) Statement of Lieut., L.J. Knight, jr., U.S. Navy.
(F) Statement of Lieut., C.V. Ricketts, U.S. Navy.
(G) Statement of Lieut.,(jg) H.B. Stark, U.S. Navy.
(H) Statement of Lieut.,(jg) F.H. White, U.S.N.R.

1. In accordance with the instructions contained in reference (a), the following report of the action of December 7, 1941, is submitted:

The Senior Surviving Officer was at the time of the engagement the Executive Officer. I was in my cabin just commencing to dress, when at 0755 the word was passed "Away Fire and Rescue Party". This was followed about thirty seconds later by "General Quarters"; at the same time, 0755, the marine orderly rushed into the cabin and announced "the Japanese are attacking us". Also, just at this time two heavy shocks on the hull of the *West Virginia* were felt. It seemed as if these shocks were somewhere forward on the port side.

By this time I had reached the Quarterdeck, and the ship was beginning to list rapidly to port. I proceeded along the starboard side until just forward of Number Three Turret, when there was a third heavy shock felt to port. The planes on top of Turret Three caught on fire, and there were flames all around the Turret Top. The quarterdeck sentry informed me that the Captain had already gone to he bridge, so I remained aft to assist in extinguishing the fire around Turret Three and on the quarterdeck. There was another heavy explosion at this time, that threw me flat on the deck. During all this time the ship was continuing to list to port, and at that time of this latest shock, I should estimate that the list was about 20° or 25° (this is purely an estimate). I called to the sound power telephone watch to tell Central to counterflood, but do not know whether or not this word got through.

Immediately following this latest explosion, I saw a flash of flame about fifteen feet high somewhere forward on the Arizona and had just gotten to my feet again when there was a terrific flash of flame from the Arizona, this second flash being higher than the foretop. Burning debris of sizes from a fraction of an inch up to five inches in diameter rained on the quarterdeck of the *West Virginia*.

During all of the above the ship's batteries continued firing, and shortly after the *Arizona* explosion, the list on the *West Virginia* stopped and she gradually started right herself. Meanwhile, efforts to push overboard the burning embers on the quarterdeck and to extinguish the fire on top of Turret Three and in the planes was continued. There was another heavy shock, distinguishable from the shock of the ship's own guns firing, and it was reported that a large fire had broken out amidships. I went in to the deck-house and found the repair parties already working against a fire, but without much success, as the fire increased by leaps and bounds. At this time, a Telephone Talker said "Central Station says Abandon Ship". As it was evident the fire fighting party had no chance to extinguish the fire, they were ordered to leave the ship. The fire had by then, from all appearances, from aft, isolated the after and forward parts of the ship. I went out on the port side of the quartered, and seeing on boats on that side went over to the starboard side. By this time the stern of the *Tennessee* was burning, and a wall of flame was advancing toward the *West Virginia* and the *Tennessee* from oil on the water from the *Arizona*. I looked around and saw no one else aft on deck and then I dove overboard and swam to the *Tennessee*. On getting on deck of the *Tennessee* I found about ten *West Virginia* people gathered under the overhang of the *Tennessee*'s Number Three Turret. As the *Tennessee* people were busily engaged in fire fighting but in no need of any extra help, I took the *West Virginia* people over the starboard side on to the pipe-line to help in extinguishing the fire that had started in the rubbish and trash and oil covered water between the *Tennessee* and Ford Island. Several of our people that were hurt were loaded into a truck and taken to the dispensary. I then brought the truck back to that part of Ford Island opposite the *Tennessee* and kept on with efforts to extinguish the fires among the trash and oil on the water. More and more *West Virginia* personnel kept arriving at this point, some by swimming, some by hanging on to wreckage, and, I think one whaleboat load.

After the fires in the water were out, I went back by the pipe-line climbed up a Jacob's ladder to the forecastle of the *Tennessee* and went up on the bridge and reported to the Commanding Officer of that vessel. The *West Virginia* at this time was blazing furiously amidships, and the Commanding Officer, *Tennessee*-wanted to know if the magazines of the *West Virginia* were flooded. I assured him they were. Finding the greater part of the personnel of the *West Virginia*'s A.A. battery on the *Tennessee*, I gave instructions that they were to remain on board under the orders of the *Tennessee*.

O then returned ashore, visited the survivors of the *West Virginia*, who were lodged in the Bachelor Officers Quarters, Ford Island, and in a bomb shelter. While there, I learned that the Navigator, Lieut-Comdr., T.T. Beattie, and a working party had returned aboard ship to assist in extinguishing the fire, so I gathered up a working party from among the personnel who were able and unhurt and went back aboard the *West Virginia*.

Fire fighting parties, in relays, continued efforts against the flames, which finally were extinguished Monday afternoon.

2. Throughout the entire action, and through all the arduous labors which followed, there was never the slightest sign of faltering or of cowardice. The actions of the officers and men were all wholly commendable; their spirit was marvelous; there was no panic, no shirking nor flinching, and words fail in attempting to describe the truly magnificent display of courage, discipline, and devotion to duty of all officers and men. Some examples of outstanding performance of duty are:

Lieutenant Commander J.S. Harper, U.S. Navy, the First Lieutenant and Damage Control Officer, who by prompt action in counter-flooding prevented the *West Virginia* From capsizing. He continued at his post in Central Station until forced to abandon it by the entrance of water, then abandoned it through the Conning Tower escape hatch and even then made a search through the ship before abandoning it.

Lieutenant Commander T.T. Beattie, U.S. Navy, the Navigator, who remained at his post alongside the Captain throughout all the action and made extreme and strenuous efforts to get the Captain, wounded, to a place of safety and to a first-aid station. Lieutenant Commander Beattie then returned aboard and continued in attempts to extinguish the fire on board.

Lieutenant Commander D.C. Johnson, U.S. Navy, the Communication Officer, who remained on the bridge, under fire, aided the Captain when the latter was wounded, and was untiring in the work afterward.

Lieutenant W. White, U.S. Navy, the Assistant Damage Control Officer, who was ashore at the beginning of the action, but returned aboard and performed prodigies in the attempt to extinguish the fire. His untiring and intelligent efforts were an essential aid to getting the fire finally under control.

Lieutenant C.V. Ricketts, the Senior Gunnery Officer aboard, and regular Secondary Battery Control Officer, who, as his battery was not firing, busied himself with aiding the Damage Control Officer in counter-flooding, in caring for the Captain when wounded, in attempting to get additional ammunition to the Anti-Aircraft battery, and was unsparing of himself in his efforts during the action and during the fire-fighting which followed.

Lieutenant F.H. White, D-V(G), U.S.N.R., who aided by MILLER, Doris, Mess Attendant second class, U.S. Navy, was instrumental in hauling people along through oil and water to the quarterdeck, thereby unquestionably saving the lives of a number of people who might otherwise have been lost.

Ensign H.W. Sears, D-V(G), U.S.N.R., who was ashore when the attack started, made his way back to the Navy Yard, but could only get aboard the U.S.S. PHOENIX. As that vessel started out, Ensign Sears asked the Commanding Officer if he needed a turret officer. The answer being in the negative, Sears, as the PHOENIX passed near the U.S.S. *West Virginia*, dove over the side and swam to the *West Virginia*.

Boatswain E.R. Weaver, U.S. Navy, who made himself unusually valuable in effecting repairs and fighting fires during the action, and then continued untiringly afterwards.

Because the above named people are particularly mentioned, it must not be construed that the actions and work of their shipmates and associates was any less valuable or less courageous. The entire ship's company is deserving of the highest commendation, both for their work on December 7th and on the days following. All the ship's company, officers and men, ask is another chance at the enemy. Their devotion to duty and their performance of duty have given new meanings to those phrases.

3. Statements of various officers are enclosed herewith.

(signed)
R.H. HILLENKOETTER.

Built in 1907 as the SS Massachusetts *for Eastern Steamship Company to operate as overnight passenger service between Boston and New York. Acquired by the U.S. Navy during World War One, the vessel was converted to a minelayer and commissioned as the* USS Shawmut. *In 1927 the Navy renamed the ship the* USS Oglala, CM-4. *On December 7, 1941* Oglala, *flagship of the Mine Force, was tied up outboard of the light cruiser* Helena *at Ten-Ten Dock.* NA 80G-466200

U.S.S. OGLALA (CM-4), MINECRAFT

Immediately after the *Oglala* sank in the forenoon, men from her crew (about 75%) were pooled and details sent to various other units of the Fleet; among them a party to both the *Pennsylvania* and *Helena* to assist those ships in manning their batteries, 45 men to the *Tennessee* to assist in firefighting, 30 men to the *Mugford*, which went to sea soon thereafter, and repair parties were also sent to the *Pennsylvania* and *Helena*. Approximately 75 men were sent to the Naval Ammunition Depot at West Loch. In addition, the *Oglala's* medical personnel assisted in receiving and distributing dead and wounded men from the battleships being landed at the end of 1010 dock. Commencing Monday, 8 December, working parties were sent to various

activities ashore and afloat. The crew, officers and men, were split up and assigned to various ships and activities in the 14th Naval District.

After *California* and *West Virginia*, *Oglala* ("Lalie" for short) was indeed a small ship, but she presented to her salvors new problems. She was on her side almost submerged, she was an old ship designed in 1906, her construction permitted a maximum of free water, and her stability during salvage was of the worst. Because of the uniqueness of *Oglala's* damage she became a historic ship in salvage operations.

On the morning of 7 December *Oglala* was moored outboard of *Helena* at the 1010 dock of the Pearl Harbor Navy Yard., an eight foot camel

A Japanese aerial torpedo passed under the shallow depth of the Oglala *and struck the* Helena *(left) in her starboard engine room spaces. However,* Oglala *got the worst of it, the pressure wave from the explosion ruptured her thin hull plating amidships causing uncontrollable flooding into the portside boiler room and inner lower spaces. Admiral Furlong, fearing his flagship would capsize against the* Helena, *hailed two nearby tugs to assist in moving the* Oglala *and moor her aft of the damaged cruiser.* NA 80G-464887

separating the two ships. An aircraft torpedo, fired from 500 yards, passed under the shallow draft *Oglala* and exploded against the starboard side of *Helena* causing great damage in her machinery spaces. The pressure wave from the explosion ruptured the lower port shell plating abreast of *Oglala's* fireroom. Although watertight closures had been rather well secured, the crew of this old vessel was unable to isolate the flooding. The ship gradually took aboard large quantities of water and finally capsized to port about two hours after the explosion.

The Commander of the Mine Force, Rear Admiral William R. Furlong, was aboard *Oglala* at the time and saw that the sinking of his flagship alongside *Helena* would foul the cruiser and prevent her removal from the dock. He therefore commandeered several tugs to pull *Oglala* clear and alongside the dock. In that position every effort was made to save *Oglala* but she finally capsized with her masts and top hamper resting on the dock. As she rested on the bottom only the middle area of her starboard side was above water at two foot tide which was the maximum at Pearl Harbor. Fortunately the crew suffered no loss of life nor serious injury.

Oglala was initially written off as a total loss. Any planning for her future pertained to getting

175

her clear of 1010 dock by fair means or foul. For the next several months manpower and material were made available only for salvage and repair work of the highest priority. The only work done on *Oglala* during these days was to remove her masts and topside structure, with the thought of preparing her for beaching or for burial at sea. The purpose was to free the urgently needed dock site.

To accomplish this worthy objective, much thought and discussion was involved. A logical and simple method was to unwater the flooded areas by means of compressed air, at least sufficiently to float the vessel on her side, and then tow her to the beach, to drydock for further handling, or out to sea for sinking. But tests soon proved that the ship's hull would not hold enough air pressure to utilize this method.

Finally after three or four months it was determined that all the methods which seemed to promise an easy way out were unworkable or impracticable. So somewhat in desperation the decision was made to undertake the orthodox procedures of first righting the ship, refloating her, and then drydocking her for repairs. All of this was accomplished within a period of about three months but not without many problems and interesting episodes.

The righting of the vessel was primarily a parbuckling operation. Ten submarine salvage pontoons, each of 80 tons lifting capacity, were sunk inboard and attached to destroyer-type anchor chains which girdled the ship. The chains were positioned under the hull by divers, and their free ends were secured to large steel stoppers which had been welded to the starboard side above water. In addition, compressed air up to three pounds pressure was injected into the hull to remove as much water as it would: two barges were heavily anchored outboard to exert a rotational pull by means of winches which were placed aboard; and two 75 ton hydraulic jacks made ready at the dockside to push against the deck edge if required to start the rotational movement. All preparations were meticulously made, and this part of the resurrection of *Oglala* was scheduled for 11 April. In spite of an enthusiastic audience the righting operation was a failure, the first of several mishaps in the *Oglala* job.

The cause of the failure was that several of the pontoons broke loose and rose to the surface when their chain bridles parted at the welds. However, it was observed that plenty of power was available to do the job. So the defective bridles were discarded and the pontoons re-rigged more securely for a second try on 23 April. This was entirely successful, although the initial list was about 20 degrees to port. Various steps were taken to reduce the list, including dredging, and new hitches by the pontoons. In a few days the list was less than seven degrees. This was considered acceptable for the next step, which was refloating.

At this point the ship was sitting on the bottom in about 45 feet of water, so very little of the remaining structure was visible. The wooden deckhouses had been removed, so only a few feet of the bow and a bit of the superstructure amidships were above water.

The method of refloating was the same used successfully on *California* and *West Virginia*-that is by extending the shell of the vessel upward from the deck edge to a point above high water. This was accomplished by the wooden fence-type cofferdam which was secured to her gunwale. Then with sufficient pumping capacity and gradual control of the inflow of water the ship is sure to float in obedience to Archimedes' Principle. The salvage crew had definitely learned that successful salvage work follows the proper application of the immutable laws of nature.

Extending the shell upward is basically a simple operation although usually beset by obstacles and design complications. A fence type caisson of wooded vertical sections was bolted to the waterway coaming. In this case they ranged in height from six feet to 26 feet, and the thickness varied from four inches to 10 inches to withstand the maximum computed water pressures. These high pressures necessitated a great amount of shoring from the inside to insure no failure at critical periods. A point of interest, too, is that for the floating cranes to properly position the 30 foot sections of heavy lumber in deep water required negative buoyancy. This was attained by placing a large number of sand bags in boxes built into each section.

While the caisson sections were being installed the diving detail was busy securing an 18 by 20 foot wooden patch over the ruptured shell area. Also

Flooding of the interior spaces could not be controlled. The ship soon lost all power and the crew was ordered to abandon ship. About two hours after being wounded the Oglala *finally capsized with part of her superstructure hard up against the dock. The* Oglala *lay on her portside about 45-feet underwater leaving the ship's starboard mid-section only a few feet above the water's surface. At first considered a total loss the first option was to remove the ship as soon as possible to clear valuable pier space.* NA 80G-23253

they were active in closing all hull openings and calking cofferdam sections. A tremendous amount of first class diving work was performed under excellent supervision. During the *Oglala* salvage some 15 to 18 divers were available, mostly from *Ortolan*. They made 542 dives totaling nearly 2000 hours under water. The divers experienced not a single injury or casualty in this work. The water level was lowered about three feet per hour, and at 1000 on 23 April 1942 *Oglala* came afloat. This was a proud moment for the salvage workers and for *Oglala*, but she still had several ordeals to withstand.

Calculations had been made which proved that with the vessel afloat her stability, both transverse and longitudinal, would be questionable and would soon become negative as the draft was further decreased. There were several reasons for this. An important one was that we had added over 1300 tons of cofferdams, sand ballast, shoring, and pumps high above the ship's deck edge. Another was the large area of free water surface, especially on the open mine deck.

In order to improve transverse stability it was decided to remove the anchors, some 350 tons of sand bags, a few of the higher shores, and consid-

A number of methods for removing and/or salvaging of the vessel were considered. After inspecting the wreckage it was decided that the ship could be fully recovered and repaired. However the decision would be wrought with delays and one mishap after another. The first attempt was to use four crane barges and lift Oglala *from the bottom enough to move the ship to a nearby shallow beach for later disposition. This operation was abandoned when Crane Barge #4 sank in an accident on 20 January 1942. Also the uneven strain put on the old minelayer would prove impractical.* PHPC

erable loose water which was trapped in various locations. But improvement was meager because it required the removal of 150 tons of main deck weight to gain one inch of righting arm. Under existing conditions *Oglala* was certain to be cantankerous regardless of mathematical manipulation. This fact became clear as the pumping continued. The ship kept on an even keel until the draft was reduced to 40 feet at which time she took a port list of eight degrees.

Additional topside weights could have been removed but it was decided that this should await further developments, and it was fortunate that we did. On the night of 25-26 June the Salvage Officer was awakened by the mess boy on watch at a Makalapa bachelor domicile with the dolorous announcement that "the Og-la-la, she is sinking again." What had happened was primarily a lesson in longitudinal stability. First a forward pump stopped when its gasoline line became clogged. This permitted the inflow of water to exceed the outgo at the bow because the other pump in that location took suction several feet higher. As the bow went down a bit some of the water surged forward. This further increased the draft forward and caused still more water to surge toward the bow. The surging water carried some clothing and debris which clogged the strainers of both pumps, thus compounding the situation. Within a half hour the cumulative effect was that

The next attempt to salvage Oglala *would be in two stages. The first stage was to right the ship using a bubble of compressed air blown into the hull and ten submarine salvage pontoons secured to the ship's hull. But on 11 April 1942 this first procedure ended in failure without righting the ship when a number of connecting chains parted causing several pontoons to break loose.* HA PFURR 3-1

During the righting process most of the Oglala's *superstructure and deck equipment was removed to lighten the ship. The pontoons and chain attachments were re-rigged for a second attempt. Twelve days later the pontoons were submerged again then air was blown into them. This time the operation was successful in turning the ship to an upright position without any difficulty.* USN

Though still underwater, Oglala *now rested upright in the mud of the harbor bottom with a slight list to port. The second stage in salvaging the* Oglala *called for a wooden cofferdam to be built around the deck edge from stem to stern similar to the one used to float the battleship* California. *A number of sections salvaged from* California's *cofferdam were altered and re-used on the* Oglala. PHPC

the bow reached the bottom in 48 feet of water, and the rest of the ship soon followed, ending up with a starboard list of eight degrees.

After strenuous work in tightening up the shoring and stopping leaks for three days the ship came afloat again on an even keel. But still another chapter of *Oglala's* ordeal was near at hand. On 29 June while the writer was walking on the top of the cofferdam's stern section he felt a movement of the timbers, and within moments the whole section tilted sufficiently to let in large volumes of water, and again to sink the ship. Removal of the stern section disclosed another "practical" departure from design specifications, in that steel tie-rods between the ship's structure and the bottom of the cofferdam had been omitted. Somebody in the field assembly gang guessed that the two 10 by 12 timbers, inside and out, would be adequate.

Within two days the vessel was afloat again and scheduled for the trip to the drydock two

days later, namely 3 July. Except for some very efficient fire fighting this would not have occurred, for in the early evening of 2 July a spectacular fire raged on the interior water surface fed by oil and gasoline. The oil-soaked timbers of the cofferdam were soon aflame. The picture was ominous, but several fire brigades were soon on the scene and extinguished the flames within a half hour without serious damage. Another sinking of *Oglala* was avoided, and the next day she was in drydock starting a new career. The fire started from a splash of gasoline on a hot exhaust pipe during refueling.

Again, the machinery was entirely reconditionable especially the reciprocating main propulsion drive of *Oglala*. The electric motors were treated to proper care and preservation by the people in charge of this specialty. It had been learned that electric motors and modern wiring subjected to submergence could be preserved and dried out without too much difficulty. Deep submergence

180

When the cofferdam was completed a wooden patch was installed over the area damaged from the torpedo strike. Eight 10-inch pumps were put in place to begin pumping operations. After three unsuccessful attempts to keep the ship afloat, the Oglala *finally came afloat for good on the morning of 3July1942. Barely afloat and looking like the reincarnation of Noah's Ark minus a roof, yard tugs moved the* Oglala *slowly over to Dry Dock Two.* NA

on the other hand, might show satisfactory characteristics in a non-humid atmosphere, but high potential lines were sure to break down ultimately in sea service. All important wiring was renewed by the Navy Yard before the trip to Mare Island.

Oglala had a mean draft of about 16 feet prior to sinking whereas it was over 39 feet when dry-docked. Except for inherent instability the draft could have been further reduced. Great care was taken to avoid damage to the deck edge caissons which had dried out considerably and required constant tightening of shores. Such damage could come from tugs or their lines on the way to dry-dock. Stability could be affected buy accelerated movement in any direction due to the large amount of free surface in the ship. All hazards were guarded against, and the trip to the drydock was made in fair weather with a minimum of difficulty.

After temporary repairs at Pearl Harbor she soon sailed away unescorted under her own power, for reconditioning at Mare Island. However, it was decided that the Los Angeles Shipbuilding Company would do the job and refit her as a repair vessel for diesel propelled craft which by that time abounded in great numbers in the far reaches of the Pacific. The Board of Inspection and Survey had been called in to check *Oglala's* physical condition, especially because of the over-age and the wear and tear of hardy service and the debilitating ordeals of salvage operations. After a rigid inspection the Board reported favorably on her general strength and capability for further service. In February 1944 a fine and almost new repair ship, named *Oglala*, sailed for the South Pacific for duty, and in due time moved with the fleet to Hollandia and Leyte. She was an important unit of our sea forces, rendering essential services to her sister vessels and their crews on their steady approach to Japan.

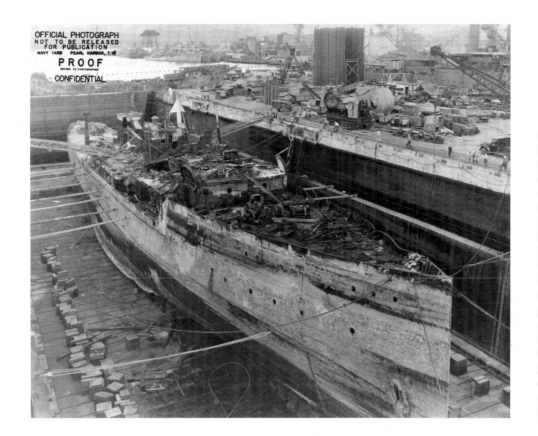

While in dry dock the cofferdam was removed first and work began on repair to the damaged hull. Most of the cofferdam was placed in storage at Waipio Point for later use on the sunken Oklahoma. The pumping out and draining of small interior compartments continued while the ship's work force was engaged in cleaning up and removal of some salvageable materials. Most of the fuel oil was still aboard and pumped into tank cars on the dock. HA PFURR 3-3

After water in the dry dock was pumped out and the wooden patch removed it was found that the damage sustained by the Oglala was comparatively slight. The main damage was around frame 70 on the port side at the turn of the bilge. The section of the hull dished in by the explosive force of the torpedo extended for about forty to fifty feet. Priority was to repair the hole as quickly as possible to clear the dry dock for important work on other damaged ships. PHPC

On other salvage jobs it had been the practice to remove all the fuel oil, ammunition, stores, provisions, trash, etc., from a sunken ship before refloating could begin. With the Oglala underwater most of these materials were impossible to remove without damaging the hull. Once in dry dock the hole in the ship's hull was repaired while very little work was done to clear the decks. After seventeen days, Oglala left the dry dock on 20 July 1942 and moved over to the Navy Yard repair basin where yard forces would remove the remaining huge amount of materials still on board and clean out the ship's interiors. USN NH 64236

The new and completely rebuilt Oglala ARG-1 lies off San Pedro after her first sea trails. The ship is ready for active service following her conversion to a gasoline engine repair ship. For the remainder of World War Two Oglala would operate in the Southwest Pacific and the Philippine Islands serving as a tender for landing craft. NA

UNITED STATES PACIFIC FLEET

FF12-6/A16-3
MINECRAFT, BATTLE FORCE

Pearl Harbor, T.H.,
December 7, 1941.

From: Commander Minecraft, BATTLE FORCE.
To: Commander-in-Chief, U.S. Pacific Fleet.
Via: Commander Battle Force.

Subject: Japanese Plane Attack on Pearl Harbor;
    Morning of Sunday, December 7, 1941.

    Narrative by Commander Minecraft, BATTLE FORCE, Rear Admiral William R. Furlong,
    U.S. Navy, in *U.S.S. Oglala*, sunk by torpedo.

1. At about 0800 this morning, Sunday, December 7, 1941, I was on deck of my Flagship, *U.S.S. Oglala* (CM4) and saw the first enemy bomb fall on the seaward end of Ford Island close to the water. This one did not hit the planes parked there. Another fell immediately afterwards in the same vicinity and caused fires near the water. U.S. planes were on the ground nearby and later flames flared up from structures at that end (south end) of the island.

2. The next bombs fell alongside or on board the seven battleships moored at "F" moorings on the east side of Ford Island.

3. Japanese planes flew within fifty and one hundred feet of the water and dropped three torpedoes or mines in the channel on a line between *Oglala* and the seaward end of Ford Island. A torpedo hit the *Oglala* and the *Helena*, which were moored abreast at berth two at ten-ten dock with the *Oglala* outboard of *Helena*. Fire was opened by *Oglala* and *Helena* antiaircraft battery.

4. I at once signalled Commander-in-Chief that these three objects mentioned above which had just been dropped might be mines because they were dropped in the middle of channel. They could have been torpedoes or mines because no plume went up from them, whereas, plumes over one hundred feet high went up from bombs that hit close alongside of battleships.

5. I then hailed two small contractor tugs which were working with dredges across the channel from *Oglala* to give assistance to haul *Oglala* aft of the *Helena* in order that *Helena* could sortie. I obtained submersible pumps from the *Helena* but then discovered that there was no power in the *Oglala* because of the hit which flooded the fireroom, and she could not use her pumps.

6. One Japanese plane was shot down over the harbor and came down in flames to seaward of Ford Island but probably on land. There was no trouble distinguishing Japanese planes because the red Sun painted on the side showed plainly.

7. Meanwhile planes were strafing as well as bombing. Planes kept coming for quite some time making it difficult to estimate number. I saw four battleships hit with bombs and fires broke out. I saw one battleship turn over. There were six to ten enemy planes visible at any one time over the harbor.

8. The Nevada got underway and passed out of channel near where I had seen the three mines or torpedoes fall. When she arrived in this vicinity her vow apparently hove up as if she had passed over a mine and about a minute later two bombs fell, one of which hit her starboard topside throwing up flame and smoke and the other missed close along the port side throwing up a plume of water.

9. During all this, as these dive bombers flew within five hundred to a thousand feet of the *Oglala*, we were given an excellent opportunity to fire our anti-aircraft battery and did so for over an hour, the *Helena* firing over us.

10. The *Oglala* was got astern of the *Helena* with help of tugs mentioned in paragraph 5 and was hauled and pushed into the pier and secured with many wires and manila lines. As all compartments were closed below she settled slowly.

11. At this time I ordered the two tugs which were assisting the *Oglala* to go to the assistance of the Nevada which was then in the channel between the floating dry-dock and seaward end of Ford Island.

12. On the second attack I saw a bomb drop which hit the forward part of the Pennsylvania or in the dry-dock ahead of the Pennsylvania. Two destroyers of Destroyer Division FIVE were in the dock ahead of the Pennsylvania, and flames went up from them.

13. Another Japanese plane was hit and fell in flames seaward of 1010 dock possibly falling near the entrance of the channel. It went down in a streak of flame as did the first one mentioned. Of the two planes that I saw shot down in this part of the harbor one was in flames after passing over the battleships from north to south about 2,000 feet altitude; the other plane shot down flew over the harbor at about 2,000 feet in the same general direction but closer to 1010 dock and pier, and was engaged by vessels on this side of the harbor. Guns operable by hand proved particularly advantageous, especially where power was knocked out of the steaming fireroom by torpedoes.

14. Following the bombing of the Pennsylvania, I saw a bomb fall near or on the destroyer in the floating dry-dock. This destroyer was later in flames.

15. Meanwhile the *Oglala* had taken a list of about 40°, the wire lines to the dock parted and her port upper deck rail was so far under that she might sink suddenly at any moment. I ordered all hands to abandon the ship shortly after 9:00 a.m. The only ones remaining being the guns' crews and myself. The *Oglala* kept up the anti-aircraft fire until the ship's list was at such an angle that the men on the machine guns were sliding off the deck and the angle was too steep to longer stick on the deck and serve the 3" gun. During this last period the Japanese planes were strafing us, not bombing. As the ship was about to turn over I ordered the guns' crews to leave the ship and left with them. The machine guns were slid off the top of deckhouse to the pier as the ship went over and were set up on the pier.

16. The guns' crews manned their battle stations promptly and stood to their guns during bombing and strafing as if at target practice, keeping up a continuous fire at enemy planes during the bombing and strafing. The signal force manned their bridge stations and sent signals during the action; one to sortie and one to the Nevada warning her of mines during which time the bridge was struck by machine gun bullets. The man on the fires when the fireroom was flooding very promptly turned off the oil fires and no one suffered oil burns. The names of personnel involved will be reported in a separate list.

17. Four men were wounded. One man was wounded seriously, the other three slightly. No other casualties.

18. At about 0900-0930 the four ships of Mine Division TWO of my command sortied from Pearl Harbor.

19. I then reported for further duty to the Commander-in-Chief with my staff.

20. Above dictated at 1100 a.m.

[signed]
WILLIAM R. FURLONG.

U.S.S. OGLALA

CM4/A16-3/(0100)

10/cam
Pearl Harbor, T.H.
December 11, 1941

From: The Commanding Officer.
To: Commander-in-Chief, U.S. Pacific Fleet.

Subject: Action of December 7, 1941; report on.
Reference: (a) CinCPac disp. 102102 of December 1941.

1. In compliance with reference (a), the following is submitted:

A. <u>OFFENSIVE MEASURES</u>.

General quarters was sounded about 0755 at the start of the attack by the enemy. The 3"/50 cal. A.A. gun and three .30 cal. machine guns were manned and firing at enemy plane formations commenced. This firing continued until ship was abandoned.

Machine gun crews report definite hits on the enemy plane.

There is no record of amount of ammunition expended.

B. <u>OWN LOSSES AND DAMAGE</u>.

1. Immediately after sounding general quarters a torpedo plane was observed to drop a torpedo from low altitude close aboard about amidships about 0757. This torpedo exploded under the ship on the port side (perhaps as a result of striking the side of the Helena which was moored alongside). The force of this explosion lifted up the fireroom floor plates and ruptured the hull on the port side. Fireroom started flooding rapidly; personnel secured the boiler fires, closed watertight doors and abandoned the fireroom. At about the same time (0757), several planes strafed the ship with machine gun fire.

One man was shot through the face. He was in the bake shop at the time.

At about 0800 a bomb from an enemy dive bomber fell between the *Oglala* and the Helena and exploded outboard in the vicinity of the fireroom.

At about 0630 extensive flooding of the engine room was reported and the ship took a 5° list. Investigation revealed that the ship was dry forward of the fireroom but was flooding rapidly aft. As all power was off the ship, there was no pumping facilities and it was evident that the ship could not be kept afloat much longer. It was decided to tow the ship clear of the Helena in order to secure her to the dock and also clear the battery of the Helena. Two small tugs which were working with the dredge in the channel were hailed by Commander Minecraft, Battle Force, and they assisted in pulling the ship clear. At about 0900, the ship was secured to Ten Ten dock astern of the Helena.

Flooding continued and the port list continued to increase in spite of all possible lines being secured to the dock. About 0930 with a list of approximately 20° the order was given to abandon ship.

At about 1000 or slightly before, the *Oglala* turned over on her port side. The bridge structure and the main mast were knocked off by striking the dock when the ship turned over. It has not been possible to determine the complete structural damage of the ship.

2. There were no personnel losses. The following were wounded as indicated:

POLER, Howard A., 393 47 34, Sea1c, USN - shot through the face.

PENNELL, Lowell, 342 31 53, CM3c, USN - shell fragment through fleshy part of right knee. Note: This injury was received while man was assisting on 3" battery of Pennsylvania.

HODNETT, "R" "J", 356 23 91, Sea1c, USN - fragments in right hip.

C. <u>DISTINGUISHED CONDUCT OF PERSONNEL</u>.
The entire crew, officers, and men, conducted themselves in a manner that was in accord with the highest tradition of the Navy. The following are especially mentioned:

JOHNSON, J.K., F2c, USN - secured the boiler and fireroom after the first explosion thus preventing possibility of a boiler explosion and reducing the amount of flooding of ship.

ZITO, A., CEM, USN - Promptness in helping getting 3" gun manned and fighting it throughout action. After the *Oglala* was abandoned, ZITO took two men and manned a drifting motor launch and proceeded to the damaged battleships. There he assisted in rescuing personnel and fighting fires. He remained at this until the following morning, December 8.

The regular assigned commanding officer, Commander E.P. Speight, U.S.N., was not aboard during the action. The Ship was under the command of the Executive Officer, Commander R.E. Krause, U.S.N.

The commanding officer arrived at the scene as the ship was turning over.

[signed]
E.P. SPEIGHT.

188

U.S.S. OKLAHOMA (BB-39), BATTLESHIP

The Japanese planes which passed over the officers' boat landing at Merry Point seemed to concentrate their torpedoes on the battleships which were moored outboard near the northern end of the line. *West Virginia* was hit by as many as seven torpedoes, *Arizona* was sunk at her berth, and *Oklahoma* received from five to seven hits. Early in the onslaught she was put out of action and capsized at her berth.

It was realized that the salvage of this ship would require a combination of the steps taken on *West Virginia* and *Oglala*. The size of *Oklahoma* and her general condition made salvage questionable, although it was deemed important to rid the harbor of a derelict and to make the berth available for other ships. Accordingly, plans were made by the Salvage Division to right her and to refloat her for further disposition.

As early as May 1942 the Navy Department indicated a desire that Oklahoma be salvaged. Contractual arrangements were therefore made with the Pacific Bridge Company so that the company could get suitable priorities on required material, and at the same time could hire the right men for the job. A scheme of salvage was therefore drawn up which divided the responsibilities between the Navy and the company. In short, the scheme provided that the ship should first be righted and then floated to a drydock for repairs.

RIGHTING

The righting of a ship weighing about 35,000 tons was no easy task. It was accomplished by various means. The important element was, of course, the installation of shore winches on Ford Island.

The 25-year old battleship USS Oklahoma *entered Pearl Harbor on Friday morning December 5 after several days at sea for drills and battle practice maneuvers. The ship moored outboard of the* USS Maryland *at berth F-5. Shortly after the ship was secured, orders were issued to the various divisions to prepare for an inspection scheduled for Monday. This included cleaning the decks, the securing of battle stations and all work and living quarters to be put in ship shape order.* EA

These twenty-one electric winches were anchored in concrete foundations and operated in unison. Each electric winch was capable of about a twenty ton pull through a flexible one-inch wire cable operated through a block system which gave an advantage of seventeen. The three-inch cable, in order to increase the leverage, passed over a wooden strut arrangement which stood on the bottom of the ship about 40 feet high. Then the cable divided into four "cat tails" which were secured to lugs welded to the shell of the ship at frame stations. Calculations indicated that the hull strength was adequate. To assist the twenty-one winches it was at first proposed that submarine salvage pontoons be used on the port side. This was given up because of the difficulty of proper attachment, and the presence of mud. The air pressure proposed inside the hull seemed ample.

The air bubble method accounted for almost 20,000 tons of weight initially and was highly effective. It was used on the starboard side after the oil had been removed through the bottom. This totaled about 350,000 gallons of the 1,000,000 gallons originally in the ship. It was placed in oil barges as it was pumped out by three-inch steam reciprocating pumps and air-driven pumps. A steam blanket was used to prevent explosions from oil vapors. This was provided for by having ex-Navajo moor alongside and furnish steam and electric power.

The air bubble was divided into five parts to prevent loss of air pressure for the whole ship at a crucial time. The air pressure was about 11-12 pounds, so that the water level was blown down to about twenty-five feet below the surface. This lightened the ship's weight considerably.

There was a large amount of weight in the ship which could have been removed prior to righting or refloating, but difficulty of access made this impracticable. About one-third of the ammunition was taken off but none of the 14-inch projectiles. Some of the machinery was removed from the dry evaporator pump room. The blades of the two propellers were taken off, more to avoid damage to them than to reduce weight.

The above methods assumed that *Oklahoma* would roll instead of slide. Tests, including soil tests, were made to check whether restraining forces should be used to prevent sliding toward Ford Island. It was indicated that the soil of the after two-thirds of the ship facilitated rolling; but the bow section rested in soupy mud which surely permitted sliding. To prevent this about 2200 tons of coral soil were deposited near the bow section, and anchorages along the port side were given up as not necessary.

Consideration was given to some dredging and removal of mud on the starboard side prior to righting, but this was deferred to assure that the vessel would rotate rather than slide. When Oklahoma was righted with a list of about fifteen degrees to port the excess soil under the starboard side was washed away by high pressure water jets operated by divers.

During and prior to the righting operation, care was taken that all purchases were equalized. This was accomplished by the use of strain gauges on the hauling wires at each bent or strut. The one-inch flexible cable was speeded up or slowed down to equalize these strain gauges. Observation posts were established on barges to note the effect of righting movements, and especially to note whether the ship was rotating or sliding.

The wooden bents became less effective as their leverage decreased when the ship gradually assumed a position approaching ninety degrees. When the list was about sixty-eight degrees to port the bents or head frames were cast off and floated clear. From then until the ship reached thirty degrees to port the pull was directly on the lugs welded to the port shell. Then the hauling cables were secured to the ship's topsides, especially to strong portions such as barbettes and the starboard crane foundation.

The ship rolled as desired. The stern section traveled a greater distance than the bow section toward the quays. This was because of the greater area of the stern. In any event, the vessel came to rest with a mean draft of 49 1/2 feet at high tide (high tide is something less than 2 1/2 feet above mean low water). The list to port was only 2 degrees and 10 minutes. The behavior of the ship was in strict accord with the models which were constructed and tested before salvage operations were begun. *Oklahoma* was right side up by 16 June 1943, the work having started 8 March 1943.

Upon hearing an explosion on Ford Island some men on deck turned and spotted some planes flying low over the water towards their ship. The call to "Man Battle Stations" was hurriedly sounded only minutes before three torpedoes smashed into Oklahoma's port side. The ship was taking on water and listing heavily to port as six more torpedoes rapidly slammed into the hull further ripping her open. There was no time to counterflood from the fast inrushing water. The stricken ship finally rolled over with her masts and superstructure settling into the mud of the harbor bottom nearly 151-degrees from upright with only her starboard bilge above water. NA 80G-30550

As the mortally wounded Oklahoma began rolling over men lost their balance and were falling or sliding off the deck into the water. Others abandoned ship by scrambling down the barnacle encrusted starboard hull. Not all made it out. In the bowels of the stricken ship some men were trapped in air pockets or watertight compartments. With seemingly no possible way out they started tapping out "SOS" signals against the bulkheads. NA 80G-33138

Priority was to try and free the trapped men. With the help of twenty civilian yard workers from Shop 11, led by supervisor Julio De Castro, openings were cut in the overturned hull with pneumatic cutting equipment which was much safer than using acetylene torches. After nearly 42 hours of non-stop work, thirty-two men eventually crawled out dazed and weary, but safe, from their ordeal. Rescue crews continued on but no more signs of life came from within the ship. All rescue work was finally halted on December 11. NA 80G-32489

The salvage of the capsized Oklahoma *would be the most difficult and certainly the largest operation confronting the Salvage Division. They would be assisted by the experienced civilian workers and divers of the Pacific Bridge Company who had been working on several construction projects in Pearl Harbor for the Navy since 1939. Despite the difficult and tedious work ahead, it was not to return the* Oklahoma *to service but mainly to clear the much needed berth for active warships.* NA 80-G19941

In April 1942 Oklahoma, remained in her capsized position for many months waiting for a final decision on how to proceed with her salvage. During that time Navy Engineers discussed several proposed plans to right and refloat the ship. A series of tests with a model of the ship were performed in a San Francisco laboratory. Further tests and calculations using a concrete model of a portion of the ship were performed at Pearl Harbor. In the meantime exploratory dives disclosed the extent of the structural damage along the outer port side. NA 80G-64598

FREEING THE TRAPPED MEN

As ships capsized, in particular *Oklahoma* and *Utah*, some men were trapped in the ship's lower compartments. The made their way presence known by tapping on the structures with wrenches or other tools. These were heard by the men on the hulls of the capsized ships and were answered; the Morse Code was used, and the rescue of the trapped men began. *Oklahoma* showed the maximum promise. The bottom of the ship was all that was visible above water. The ship had capsized through 170 degrees so that its bottom was nearest the surface. By cutting holes through the bottom of the ship and rescue party was able to reach the men who had sought refuge in that part of the ship which was near the open air.

A survivor who had escaped through a hatch at frame 117 stated that men were alive in that locality. At about that time, 0915, Commander Kranzfelder and Lieutenant Mandelkorn from the staff of Commander Battleships, were present, and at 0930 Lieutenant Commander Herbert Pfingstag from the Navy Yard arrived. At first they tried to gain access to the inside of the ship by acetylene torch, using it in locations free of oil and water, but found that the fumes from oil and the cork used for insulation were deadly to the men who were trapped in the locality. Accordingly, they thereafter used compressed air and corresponding tools which were furnished by the Navy Yard and various ships, including *Maryland*, *Argonne*, and *Rigel*. The Navy Yard provided submersible pumps, sound powered telephones, and air ducts fro ventilating purposes.

Soon the trapped men were located in the vicinity of frames 131, 116, 78, and 22. The men were all near the bottom of the ship, which at that time was partly visible above the water level of the harbor. It was not until 0800 on 8 December that six men were rescued, and at 1100 eleven more were brought out. Five more were released at 1400 and eight at 1600 on that same date. The last man was not rescued from the *Oklahoma* until 0230 on 9 December. All were in good condition except for lack of sleep, food, and sufficient oxygen. Of course the air bubble gradually disappeared and water rose as soon as an opening was made in a compartment. A watch was maintained on the hull of the *Oklahoma* until 11 December but no further signs of life were detected.

Utah lost fifty-eight men in the action. Of those saved one man was rescued through the bottom after the ship capsized. This was John B. Vaessen, Fireman Second Class, who was later lost. Nearly all of the men who had not been killed or wounded were clear of thee lower compartments except Vaessen who remained at his post in the forward distribution room in order to keep lights on the ship as long as possible. He was rescued by helpers from *Raleigh* as well as by a volunteer crew from *Utah* consisting of Machinist S. A. Szymanski, Chief Engineman MacSelwiney, and two seamen. They heard tapping on the bottom and after answering, they cut a hole by acetylene torch obtained from *Raleigh*, near enough to free Vaessen.

Before any salvage attempts divers had to familiarize themselves with a ship that is now upside down and waters so murky vision was almost non-existent. When a dive team prepared to work in a particular area of the ship, they would study the corresponding section on the model before descending into the opaque mess of oil, ooze and mud. If, while working something did not seem right, they returned to the surface to study the model again while conferring with Navy engineers to note any changes they encountered. HA

"Any sailor can find his way around in a ship that is right side up" explained Admiral Furlong to reporters; "When she is upside down, the whole interior is now unfamiliar to him. He is now walking on the ceiling." A 1:96 scale model of the Oklahoma, *fashioned of composition board, was built by Chief Water Tender R. H. Snow. The model was constructed in transverse horizontal layers that could be lifted individually to expose each deck showing the detailed compartments and sections that would be explored by divers.* PHP

Special safety precautions were adapted and advance planning of the route and task for each dive were worked out using sections of the three-dimensional model of the ship in its capsized position. The dive team who performed the difficult and hazardous underwater work involved in the numerous phases of the salvage operations on the USS Oklahoma consisted of naval personnel from the newly formed Salvage Section and of civilians from the navy yard work force and the private contractor, The Pacific Bridge Company. PHP

In July 1942 work was begun on the pair of concrete anchorages on Ford Island directly opposite and parallel to the keel line of the overturned Oklahoma. *These were designated as Anchor A with 13 anchor rod foundations imbedded in it and Anchor B had eight foundations. At the same time to aid in lightening the ship, workers were drilling a series of fifteen access holes in the ship's starboard hull to gain entry into the fuel bunkers. By 26 August over 350,000 gallons of oil had been pumped out and the access holes sealed up.* HA

On the top of each foundation, an electric winch was installed with a twin 24-inch diameter drum driven at a very slow rate (0.14 revolutions per minute) that was connected to a 5-hp DC motor. The motors were salvaged from the recently retired trolley cars of the Hawaiian Transit System. The 21-winches were intended to operate in unison and each was capable of a pull of twenty tons, which was increased an additional seventeen tons by a carefully worked out pulley arrangement.
NA 80G-431747

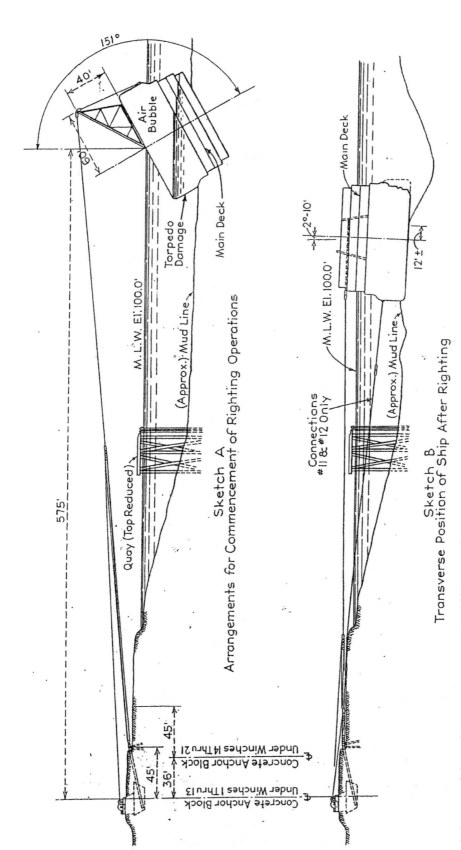

Sketch A
Arrangements for Commencement of Righting Operations

151°

40'

Air Bubble

60°

575'

M.L.W. El. 100.0'

Torpedo Damage

(Approx.) Mud Line

Main Deck

Quay (Top Reduced)

45'

45'

36'

Under Winches 14 Thru 21

Concrete Anchor Block

Under Winches 1 Thru 13

Concrete Anchor Block

Sketch B
Transverse Position of Ship After Righting

Main Deck

2°-10'

12' ±

M.L.W. El. 100.0'

(Approx.) Mud Line

Connections #11 & #12 Only

A diagram of the righting operations on the *Oklahoma*.
Transactions of the Society of Naval Architects and Marine Engineers

U.S.S. OKLAHOMA-SALVAGE 12/11/42 5351-42
PERSONNEL AFTER WORK IN #2 SECTION OF MAIN
AIR BUBBLE SHOWING EQUIPMENT, INCLUDING FACE
MASKS WITH AIR SUPPLY, BATTERY POWERED MINERS
LIGHTS AND SMALL AIR CYLINDERS FOR EMERGENCY
SUPPLY.   ENCLOSURE G

Before the turning operation could proceed it was necessary to create an air bubble within the ship to increase buoyancy. The interior of the hull was divided into seven sections. Heavy duty air compressors mounted on two barges alongside would pump in the air pressure to keep the water out. Six temporary air locks built in the navy yard were installed on the section of the hull bottom still above water. Divers could now enter or exit the ship's interior without losing air pressure. This team of divers covered in slime and oil have just emerged from air lock #2 after their shift was over. NA 80G-431764

U.S.S. OKLAHOMA-SALVAGE 12/11/42 5331-4
PERSONNEL WITH FACEMASKS REMOVED AFTER WORK
IN #2 SECTION OF MAIN AIR BUBBLE.

Due to the near absence of light in the murky waters outside the hull and zero visibility within the ship, divers had to work mostly by sense of touch alone. Divers worked in teams of two. One would proceed to chart a compartment while the other stayed back to assure that life-lines did not become fouled in the damaged and twisted obstructions within the ship. Working in the oily muck also added to the hazardous conditions. When a diver returned to the surface he had to be scraped clean and washed down before he could be removed from his diving suit.
NA 80G-279406

Cmdr. Francis H. Whitaker on 16 January 1943 after exiting airlock No.4 following an inspection of the Oklahoma's *boiler rooms and the ongoing work by divers in the interior. Capt. Whitaker was salvage superintendent from July 28, 1942 to February 18, 1944 during the final preparations and planning in the righting and refloating of the* Oklahoma. *In April 1944, Capt. Whitaker was presented the Legion of Merit medal by President Roosevelt for his performance of outstanding services during the Pearl Harbor salvage operations.* USN

Photographer's Mate 3rd class T. E. Collins of the Fleet Camera Party was assigned to photograph interior compartments that had been dewatered on the capsized Oklahoma. *He entered the ship on 18 January 1943 through airlock No. 4, where air pressure was raised to 10-lbs per square inch. Once inside the ship Collins found an upside down world where everything was covered with a black coating of fuel oil and slime. An oxygen mask had to be worn at all times.*
NA 80G-276601

199

Twenty-one wooden triangular A-shaped forty foot high headframes or bents (as they were called) were built in the carpentry shop. Riggers from the yard force aided by the Haveside Crane No.5 installed them on the starboard side of the hull spaced 16-feet apart. While work on the shore foundations and bents was ongoing, divers were cutting away the ship's stack, masts, damaged plates and most of the bridge superstructure to lighten ship. Red lights were mounted on top of each frame so they could be seen at night by planes approaching Ford Island. USN

The twenty-one headframes were mounted on thrust brackets welded to the outside of the starboard blister so that the bottom of the frame pushed against one side of the hull. Two wire cables secured on top ran down to pads welded to the bottom of the hull just past the turn of the bilge. Each headframe was rigged with a 3-inch cable that ran through a complex block and tackle arrangement to the pulling winches on shore. As a precaution strain gauges were attached to each set of cables to monitor the pull. NA 80G-431763

The winches began the pulling slowly at 0841 hours on the morning of 8 March 1943. As a precaution strain gauges were attached to each set of cables to monitor the pull. If the pull was not uniform the ship might slide on the muddy bottom of the harbor instead of rotating. By varying the motor voltage and thus the speeds of the winches, the loads on all twenty-one winches were kept nearly constant as practicable. Two eyebolts broke away from the connection to headframe No. 11 and were removed. The first pulling period lasted 13 ½-hours with the ship resting at 132 degrees 30 minutes. Earlier divers using high pressure water jets removed about 8-feet of mud from under the port side of the ship from frame 60 aft. NA 80G-410524

Pulling was halted the next day when two more eyebolts gave way after only 2 hours. Replacement eyebolts were forged in the yard and welded yokes were installed to reinforce all the other eyebolts. Pulling resumed again in the afternoon of 17 March 1942 with only a few minor mishaps that were quickly resolved and continued on through the night to 0500 hours the next morning with the ship resting 109 degrees from upright. The next pulling began in the evening at 2027 hours and continued for almost 19 hours. The photo shows the Oklahoma a few hours earlier at 90 degrees from vertical. The ships final position on the afternoon of 19 March was 70 degrees. USN

The pull on 19 March at 1646 hours lasted only 25 minutes with the ship's final position now at 68-degrees. The headframes, which were now almost horizontal to the water level, had lost their leverage and were of no further use. The righting cables had lifted clear of the headframes but retained their tension on the hull to the pulling winches on shore. The headframes were removed and placed on barges for later use on righting the Utah. PHP

On the next day March 20, after the headframes had been cleared from the starboard side work area, there was one more pull scheduled to start in the late afternoon. None of the twenty-one pulling cables had been removed and were still attached to the starboard blister and docking keel. After 7-hours 16-minutes the pulling was stopped with the ship righted at approximately 40-degrees from vertical. PHC

Close up view looking aft from Oklahoma's main deck with the ship's list stopped at 40-degrees on 26 March. With pulling on hold for the next eight days riggers removed nine of the 1-inch pulling wire rope cables from the hull and rewound them multiple times around the base of each of the four turret barbettes, the conning tower and the starboard kingpost and back to the winches on shore for better leverage for the next pull. USN

Pulling resumed on 29 March for a period of only two and a half hours. When the ship had reached 34-degrees work was stopped due to the heavy strain on the aft section of the hull. Another wire cable strap was added to those already around turret barbette No. 3 and then reconnected to pulling winches No. 17 and No. 19 on Ford Island to ease the tension. Note the oily slime and sea growth on Oklahoma's wooden teak decks and equipment from months of immersion under water. PHP

204

On the last day of March, work was stopped again after only three hours of pulling when Oklahoma *had reached 28 degrees. It would be another week before the pull would resume. High stress loads on all winches and partial failure of several multiple wire rope straps connected to several strong points on the hull had to be reworked for added strength. Six tackles were also shifted from the starboard blister connections to higher points on the ship for better leverage. The pulling was started up on 7 April. After only two short pulls the ship reached a position of 17-degrees when work was halted.* NA 80G-410537

Divers using high pressure hoses worked most of this period removing large amounts of mud from under the starboard side while operations were on hold to adjust and repair cables. The next pull was scheduled for the morning of April 20, 1943 and was done in two short phases. Work was stopped again due to heavy strain on all the winches. Now the winches on shore could not handle the excessive loads ending with the ship holding at 12-degrees position. This was caused by multiple failures of the wire rope straps on No.1 barbette and the straps connecting tackles Nos. 2, 8 and 9. The straps had to be renewed and reinforced which would take another two weeks before the pull could resume. HA

Salvage work on the Oklahoma *had been delayed countless times not only due to failure or readjusting of equipment but when workers were needed to assist in other more important ongoing salvage projects. Work was also held up when battle damaged ships limped into Pearl Harbor, all hands, if needed, were made available to repair and return them to service as quickly as possible. Note the blackened oily bands at the different levels acquired when the ship was idle.* PHP

Another attempt at pulling on May 6, 1943 lasted barely 30 minutes when multiple wire straps wrapped around turret barbettes #3 and #4 broke away. With the ship now settled at 10-degrees pulling operations were put on hold. In the next two weeks divers continued to survey internal damage and make preparations for installation of deep water pumps. Work was also begun to preserve Oklahoma's *14-inch guns for future use on other battleships.* USN

207

Wire rope tackles Nos. 15, 18, 20 and 21 on the starboard side aft were removed, strengthened and then reconnected with shorter straps to gain sufficient travel in the blocks needed for the scheduled final pulling. Divers continued removing mud from under the starboard side. This would help later in the final phases of righting the ship to keep the upper deck from submerging. PHP

Riggers and burners continued cutting away and removing sections from the crumpled wreckage of the bridge superstructure. Over the next two weeks several deep well pumps were installed to unwater the intact section of the ship forward of the torpedo damaged areas at frame 30 and the compartments aft of frame 122 on the second deck. The dewatering was a success, further lightening the ship by 3,500 tons. USN

On the upper deck looking aft on May 6, 1943, the buckled deck (center) of the signal bridge was directly over the Captain's cabin. Upon entering into the oil and filth of the cabin, workers found the light bulb over the Captain's desk was unbroken. At one end were the remains of a bed, but on them lay a pair of pajamas, their purple color still evident despite months underwater. Records from the file cabinets were strewn around the cabin, but their notations, in many cases, were still legible. USN

Divers working on the hull had to cut access holes in the third deck to connect air hoses to the four large wing void tanks abreast the engine and boiler rooms. The diving barge moored to the portside was built at the navy yard with a ladder at one end for divers to enter or exit the water. They also dressed and stored their suits, air hoses, phones and life lines on the barge. Also on the barge were two barrels of diesel oil to wash down the soiled diving equipment covered in black grimy bunker fuel. USN

Deep well pumps were installed in the bow and in operation by May 16, 1943. The 14-inch guns of turrets #1 and # 2 were temporarily preserved with a coat of zinc chromate paint. At this time the port and starboard anchors were lifted off including removing the port anchor chain and most of the starboard anchor chain. Divers worked with planners to determine the design and preparation for the installation of patches and cofferdams.
NA 80G-75928

Enough topside wreckage had been cut away and removed to clear enough working space on the superstructure deck. To keep track of the ships position during the righting process two pendulum trim and list clinometers with raised numerals 6-inches high were installed. This one was placed amidships on what was left of the superstructure.
NA 80G-75918

There was one final pull on 16 June 1943 lasting one hour and twenty-two minutes. It was stopped due to generally high strain on all tackles. The Oklahoma was now resting solidly on the harbor floor with a list of two degrees to port. Since this final position was considered satisfactory for the installation of patches and cofferdam sections no further righting was attempted. Three days later, the preservation of her 14-inch main guns began. The righting operation had taken more than three months. NA 80G-279402

FLOATING

When *Oklahoma* was nearly upright, divers investigated the damage on her port side. They found that the port side was pretty well opened up from torpedo explosions which occurred before and during capsizing. They cut away structural wreckage and took necessary measurements for temporary patches. The topside damage was apparent; contact with the bottom had broken off the masts and most other superstructure.

The divers found that a large patch was required from frames 43 to 75. This patch was 130 feet long and 57 1/2 feet high as it extended well under the turn of the bilge. In addition, several patches were installed, usually of wood and sealed with Tremie underwater concrete. For instance, one went between frames 31 and 43, another between frames 74 and 96.

The large patch was in five parts and was primarily steel and wood as shown on page 257. It was sealed by underwater concrete at the ends as well as at the bottom. The sections were made watertight by puddings between the sections. Again, underwater concrete was essential. In all over 1000 tons of concrete were poured. Hook bolts were used by the divers in drawing up the patches to the hull of the ship.

The main deck aft was underwater, but not enough to prevent refloating. However, in order to increase the waterplane area and in order to improve the stability during refloating a wooden cofferdam like *Oglala* and *California* cofferdams was installed from frames 85 to 115.

In the meantime the divers were busy jetting out mud, closing drains and sanitary outlets, cutting sluicing holes, closing watertight doors and hatches, etc. In due time they followed the reduction of the water level and closed off the main leaks in the hull and the patches.

During the last period of righting the weight of the ship was reduced by about 3500 tons through using the buoyancy forward of frame 30 and aft of frame 115. This was done primarily by deep-well pumps which quickly removed the water in those areas.

Then 10 ten-inch deep-well pumps augmented by lesser pumps were more than enough to lower the water level in the ship, but by this time the Navy Yard was in possession of twelve-inch pumps, both electric and diesel. In the main patch eighteen and twenty-inch electric pumps were used at a later date. As in other ships, the water level was reduced according to schedule which permitted adequate testing for toxic gases, plenty of ventilation and lighting, and removal of the 400 or more human bodies which were in *Oklahoma*.

In order to insure positive stability, some ballasting by sea water was scheduled in the machinery spaces. Great care was exercised by the Salvage Superintendent to insure that the ship would come afloat with a minimum of list. Actually she came afloat on 3 November 1943 with a mean draft of about forty-six feet and a starboard list of twenty-six minutes. The list was increased to about one degree to starboard and so maintained by pumping water from the port engine room to the starboard engine room. The hauling tackles were removed after the ship came afloat and the various leaks were well in hand.

Thought was given to the damage caused by teredo worms on patches after long submergence. This was found to be negligible, as was the teredo damage to the teak decking of the ship.

For the purpose of refloating very little weight was removed. However, prior to drydocking, attention was given to this important consideration. It was not practicable to remove stores, but anchors, chain, remaining oil, and so on were taken ashore. Mud in the ship was jetted to electric pumps by water jets in the hands of divers.

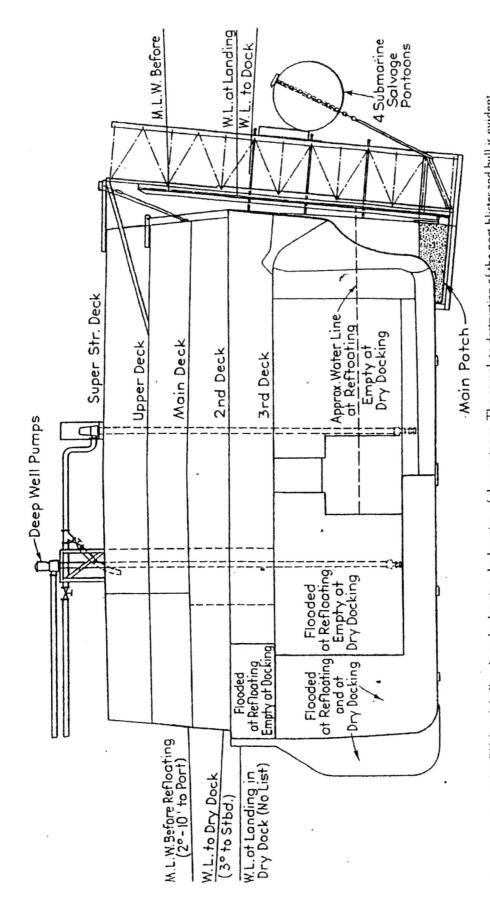

Deep Well Pumps

Super Str. Deck

Upper Deck

Main Deck

2nd Deck

3rd Deck

M.L.W. Before

W.L. at Landing

W. L. to Dock

4 Submarine
Salvage
Pontoons

Approx. Water Line
at Refloating

Empty at
Dry Docking

Main Patch

Flooded
at Refloating.
Empty at Docking

Flooded
at Refloating
and at
Dry Docking

Flooded
at Refloating
Empty at
Dry Docking

M.L.W. Before Refloating
(2° – 10' to Port)

W.L. to Dry Dock
(3° to Stbd.)

W.L. at Landing in
Dry Dock (No List)

A cross-section of the Oklahoma's hull and patch, showing the location of the pontoons. The complete destruction of the port blister and hull is evident. *Transactions of the Society of Naval Architects and Marine Engineers*

213

The five sections for the main cofferdam patches were built at the navy yard shops, mostly with civilian personnel, then barged out to the Oklahoma one at a time. Yard workers and divers constructed shoring and bracing (above) on the hull from frame 45 to frame 74 to support the huge steel girder and timber cofferdams. The finished cofferdam was 132-feet long by fifty-seven feet high extending from above the second deck to well under the turn of the bilge. Pacific Bridge Company used the Navy's 150-ton floating crane, YD-25, to vertically lower (below) the first section in place on August 3, 1943. The final patch was bolted in place on September 12. PHP

214

It took three weeks to secure the five sections in place to the port side of the Oklahoma. *It would take another three weeks to pour more than 500 cubic yards of tremie cement to seal the bottom and sides of the main cofferdam. This work also included fabricating five smaller patches on the hull. To help increase the vessels stability during refloating operations a 10-foot high wooden cofferdam was built on the main deck aft, which was still underwater, from frame 85 to frame 115 port and starboard sides and around turret four.* PHP

Working below decks in dank and dirty conditions in November 1943, a headlamp worn by a salvage worker in the ship's 14-inch magazine space, is useful as he adjusts the discharge hose of a submersible pump. Note the bulkheads and the 14-inch powder cans covered with a heavy coating of oil and slime. Divers worked at removing mud, plugging up leaks, sealing off compartments and cutting away wreckage while pumping operations continued on a daily basis to further lower the water level inside the ship. USN NH 64304

An aerial view of the port side of Oklahoma *three days after the ship had been refloated. With twenty heavy duty pumps operating steadily during an 11-hour period,* Oklahoma *came afloat in the evening of November 3, 1943 with a mean draft of 47 feet. The ship was anchored fore and aft and barges were placed between the ship and the quay to keep the ship from drifting toward shore and prevent damage to the main patches. Pumping operations would continue daily on a 24-hour basis until the ship could maintain and hold a mean draft of 36-feet, enough to clear the entrance sill of the dry dock.* NA 80G-279402

It had been impossible to reach any of the casualties from inside the ship due to the extreme damage and dangerous conditions aboard while the ship was upside down. The first bodies were recovered on October 14, 1943 after Oklahoma was upright. A total of 341 bodies were found by December 27. Having been underwater nearly two years the bodies had decomposed leaving only bones and teeth. None could be identified and were buried in common graves in Halawa Cemetery. Note the stern anchor chains on the stern holding the Oklahoma, barely afloat, in place. PHPC

By December 10, four salvage pontoons were secured outside of the main patch giving the ship a slight list to starboard and for added buoyancy. Pumping operations continued 24-hours daily until the ship reached a mean draft of 36-feet, more than enough to clear the harbor bottom while under tow and over the entrance sill of the dry dock. Divers successfully used kapok, salvaged from life-jackets, to plug up thousands of small leaks. As water was pumped from the hull, the suction created pulled the kapok inwards effectively sealing small gaps and holes. PHP

Seen on December 22, 1943 the Oklahoma is almost fully afloat and one can now see the enormous size of the finished five section cofferdam patch. Electrical power for the pumps during refloating operations had been supplied from sources on Ford Island. To keep the pumps operating once under tow to the newly commissioned Dry Dock Four, a 600-kilowatt Diesel generator was installed on board to supply the necessary 440-volt alternating current power once the cables from the shore were disconnected. PHP

DRYDOCKING

The ship was placed in Drydock Number Two on 28 December 1943 with a mean draft of thirty-six and a half feet and a list to starboard of nearly three degrees. The list was purposely put on the vessel in order to favor the port side and its patches. In order not to lose buoyancy the introduction of water to attain the desired list was not permitted; instead four submarine salvage pontoons, each having a lift capacity of eighty tons, were used on the outside of the main patch.

The total draft of *Oklahoma* was nearly thirty-nine feet because the main patch extended several feet below the keel. During the trip to the drydock the electric-driven pumps were replaced by diesel-driven. The list was taken off in drydock and the ship settled on the blocks provided without undue incident. The pontoons were removed, and the patches were likewise taken off to expose the damage which the ship had sustained. This is seen in the illustrations on page 262. A strict fire watch was maintained on board.

The Navy Yard employees were quick to start with temporary repairs. They worked from inboard to obtain watertightness of the hull inasmuch as the drydock was available for emergency dockings of damaged major ships of the fleet. Thus the drydock had to be vacated on seventy-two hours notice. However, no emergency developed, and *Oklahoma* remained there for several months. During her time at the Navy Yard she was stripped of guns and some of the auxiliary machinery. The ship was unloaded of ammunition and stores. She was decommissioned on 1 September 1944 and sold for scrap for $46,000 on 5 December 1946 to the Moore Drydock Company. On 10 May 1947 she left Pearl Harbor under tow of two tugs but was lost in a storm at sea about 500 miles northeast of Hawaii on 17 May 1947.

Much of the early salvage work was performed by divers under Lieutenant Haynes. This work was difficult and hazardous, but no serious casualty occurred to the naval divers or to the civilian Navy Yard divers. Only one casualty marred a perfect record of the contractor's divers.

Exterior steel work by divers was done with oxy-hydrogen torches; interior work with the oxygen-carbon arc. Precautions were taken to avoid explosions from fuel oil and gases. No serious explosions occurred although several small ones were experienced without serious injury. In all about 1850 dives were made with a total of 10,300 man-hours underwater.

Credit for a great job must go to the Salvage Superintendent, Captain F. H. Whitaker and his corps of assistants. The Navy Yard should be included as should the Pacific Bridge Company which had shown their proficiency in previous salvage jobs. The work of this company in setting up the winches, in making the soil tests, and in designing and installing the various patches is beyond calculation. The feats performed could not have been done without the cooperation of such men as Messrs. Graham, Ginella, Crocker, Davenport, Freeman, and Bisordi. Also, we should include the old Salvage Organization. It was they who made detailed plans of *Oklahoma's* righting and refloating.

After the anchor chains fore and aft were cast off and barges alongside were removed, three tugs slowly moved the Oklahoma *across the harbor. The climax of the long salvage operation ended when she entered Dry Dock Four at 0745 hours on the morning of December 28, 1943. In the salvaging of* Oklahoma *divers made 1,842 dives involving 10,279 man hours under pressure. The overall safety record of navy and civilian divers was almost perfect, only one civilian diver from the Pacific Bridge Co. was lost when his air hose was accidently severed just weeks before the ship came afloat.* NA 80G-279410

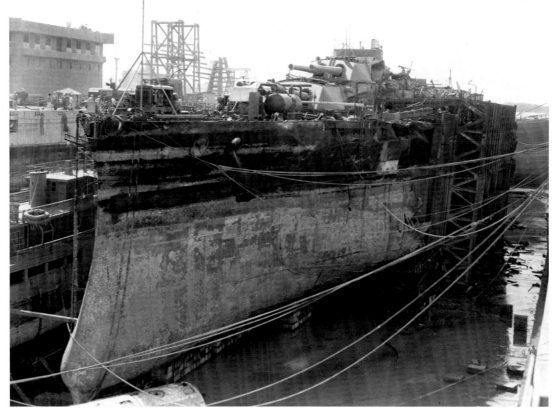

After moving into the recently completed Dry Dock Four, the four salvage pontoons were removed, the water was then pumped out of the dock with the Oklahoma *settling on the blocks. The ship's bow area and two forward turrets appear undamaged. Seen on the port side is the intricate framing of the large cofferdam built around the extensive torpedo damage. It was supported by 10-inch steel beams secured to the upper deck.* NA 19N-109944

The full extent of the enormous damage of the battered and caved in hull was revealed when the cofferdam was removed on December 31, 1943. The Oklahoma's amidships area is completely wrecked and sections of the ships' armor belt was missing. The torpedoes had ripped open holes as wide as forty feet. The shell plating below the armor belt was pushed inwards from frame 33 to frame 115. USN

The armor belt was down and in from its original position and five armor plates were missing between frames 52-115. The armor plates were torn loose by the torpedo explosions against the hull and probably lost in the mud when the ship rolled over or later during salvage efforts. The debris on the dry dock floor is the concrete that was used to seal the temporary cofferdam patches after it was removed by blasting away using small dynamite charges. NA 19N-109949

Draftsmen, engineers and shop superintendents of the various departments had prepared plans months in advance before the ship was raised and moved into the dry dock. First for the righting and refloating operation followed by the repair and rebuilding. Sub-assembly sections were pre-fabricated in the yard shops and were ready for installation as the work progressed. The Oklahoma was on 72-hour notice to un-dock for emergency dockings of damaged major ships of the fleet. Fortunately, no such urgency arose. NA 80G-219089

The shipfitters and burners had the difficult job of removing hundreds of tons of torn and twisted metal bulkheads and decking that was lifted off the ship onto waiting trucks and hauled away to designated scrap piles in the navy yard. Working conditions aboard the battered Oklahoma was dangerous. Everything was fouled with black, smelly fuel oil that had to be cleaned up before any burning could be done safely. There were pockets of noxious gases and mud and debris in almost every compartment. NA 80G-219093

A prefabricated sub-section of the bilge is being lowered down on the hull next to one already in place. Piece by piece, section by section new structures built in the yard shops were moved out to the dry dock where cranes swung the units, some weighing as much as 40 tons, into their final position. There wasn't enough time or labor to remove the main battery guns. The heavy guns would be lifted off later. Her 5-inch guns, most of the 5-inch ammunition, some machinery and rotted stores were taken off. NA 80G-219095

The shell built around the damaged hull was to obtain water tightness that would be sufficient enough to float the ship out of the much needed dry dock. The lower deck will be plated over but the bulkheads would not be rebuilt. After much of the damage had been cut away they were left open and would be sealed off later in the repair basin only to protect the interior from the weather. The main armor belt and most of the superstructure was removed. NA 80G-2768805

The dry dock was flooded on February 10, 1944 after 42 days of work by the yard labor force. Yard tugs moved Oklahoma *out to Berth #12 in the repair basin to finish the structural repairs The navy yard's 200-ton hammerhead crane lifted off the eight heavy guns from the turrets and the 14-inch shells. After four months of work she was moored in West Loch for the remainder of the war. Two of* Oklahoma's *14-inchguns were assigned to the* Nevada, *five ended the war aboard the* Pennsylvania *and two guns were mounted on the* New York. *On September 1, 1944,* Oklahoma *was officially decommissioned.* PHPC

Destined for the scrapyard, the Oklahoma *was sold for scrap value on December 5, 1946 to the Oakland-based Moore Dry Dock Company for $46,127 dollars (that is 1946 dollars!). Two civilian tugs were sent to pick her up in early May 1947. A week later in choppy seas, on May 16, she began taking on water and listing heavily to port. The* Oklahoma *sank shortly before 2 a.m., 540-miles out from Pearl Harbor. The once proud battleship, found a more appropriate grave for an old warrior in 3,000 fathoms under the Pacific.* EA

A9/L11-1

    (01)

December 18, 1941.

From: Commanding Officer, *U.S.S. Oklahoma*

To: Commander-in-Chief, U.S. Pacific Fleet.

Subject: Action Reports.

References: (a) Combatships, Batfor ltr. A9/L11-1/0936 dated December 11, 1941, quoting Cincpac despatch 102102 of December 1941 and extract from Cincpac plain mailgram 111310 of December 1941.
(b) "Report of Rescue and Salvage Work" submitted by Lt. Comdr. W.H. Hobby, USN (Senior officer of the *U.S.S. Oklahoma* engaged in salvage work on that vessel) to Combatships dated 12 December 1941.

Enclosures: (A) Report of Commander J.L. Kenworthy, USN, Executive Officer of the *U.S.S. Oklahoma*, senior officer on board and Commanding Officer during the action at Pearl harbor 0755-0900, December 7, 1941.
(B) "Personnel engaged in salvage work on *U.S.S. Oklahoma*" commendations of, dated December 14, 1941, report of Lieutenant Commander W.H. Hobby, USN.

1. The following is a collation of reports or statements of personnel of the *U.S.S. Oklahoma* who were in positions best to observe and interpret the sequence of events of the attack of Japanese planes on the *U.S.S. Oklahoma* and other naval units in Pearl Harbor beginning about 0750, December 7, 1941: The first indication of the attack was the explosion of bombs dropped at a low altitude (100-150 ft.) on the southwest hangar of Ford Island. Almost simultaneously therewith the ship was struck within a few minutes by three torpedoes on the port side at frames 25, 35-40 and 115. Those torpedoes were definitely seen approaching. The ship began to list to port immediately after the first hit. It heeled to angle of 45 degrees after the third hit. Two or three additional torpedo hits were felt. Great quantities of oil and water which covered the major portions of the weather decks were forced up by the explosions. The ship continued to heel rapidly and turned over through an angle of about 135 degrees in about eight to ten minutes.

2. With the first warning of the attack the call was sounded to man the anti-aircraft battery and immediately thereafter the ship went to general quarters. Although the anti-aircraft battery was manned within a few minutes after the call and the ready ammunition boxes were being opened, because of the rapid heeling of the ship and the oil and water on the decks, it was impossible effectively to service the guns. The port ready machine gun opened fire, but was soon silenced by the force of the explosion and the oil and water thrown up by the first torpedo hit forward.

3. Because of the condition of the *Oklahoma*, capsized and practically flooded, it has been impossible to ascertain the extent or details of damage sustained.

4. Immediately after the overturning of the vessel salvage operations were undertaken and continued as along as the rescue of entrapped personnel was possible and salvage of material was immediately practicable. Thirty-two men were rescued by the salvage party, the operation of which is reported in detail in reference (b).

5. The following is a summary of the latest recapitulation of the personnel of the *Oklahoma* dated December 15, 1951

ATTACHED

Officers	82
Ship's Company (USN)	1,179
Aviation Unit	15
Marine Detachment	77

	OFFICERS	CREW	TOTAL
Survivors	59	850	899
Wounded	2	24	26
Known dead	0	22	22
Missing	21	385	406
Totals	82	1,271	1,353

6. The conduct of the personnel of the *Oklahoma* was consistently and uniformly excellent during the action and in the salvage, rescue and other incidental operations thereafter. All personnel proceeded to their stations and performed their various duties calmly, cooly and quietly with effective efficiency. Approximately 60 officers and men made their way to the Maryland and the *Oklahoma* had capsized where they assisted in the manning and service of the anti-aircraft battery. The report of the performance of duty of the personnel engaged in salvage work on the *Oklahoma*, submitted by Lieutenant Commander William H. Hobby, USN., (the senior officer of the *Oklahoma* engaged in the salvage work), as well as the commendable work of that officer himself, is submitted for consideration as deserving of special notice or commendation. (Enclosure B).

7. The circumstance that the personnel of the *Oklahoma* have been distributed among various commands with limited means of intercommunication and facilities for the preparation of reports has necessitated delaying forwarding additional reports of officers pending their being typed and copied for file.

[signed]
H.D. BODE

U.S. NAVAL AMMUNITION DEPOT
OAHU, HAWAII, U.S.A.

West Loch,
December 16, 1941.

From: Commander Jesse L. KENWORTHY, JR., U.S. Navy.
To: Captain H.D. BODE, U.S. Navy.

Subject: Surprise Enemy Attack and Sinking of the *U.S.S. OKLAHOMA*

1. On Sunday December 7, 1941 the *U.S.S. Oklahoma* was moored outboard of the *U.S.S.* Maryland, starboard side to, at Berth F-5, Pearl Harbor, T.H. At approximately 0757 the word was passed to man the anti-aircraft battery and the sound of gun fire was heard. The word was again passed that this was a real attack and for all unengaged personnel to seek cover. I had started down the starboard ladder to the Wardroom country to go to my office when the first alarm came and immediately ran up the ladder to the starboard side of the upper deck to go to the Conning tower after calling for the crew to go to battle stations. As I reached the upper deck, I felt a heavy shock and heard a loud explosion and the ship immediately began to list to port.

2. Oil and water descended on deck and by the time I had reached the boat deck, the shock of two more explosions on the port side was felt. In the meanwhile, general quarters had sounded and the crew had gone to battle stations and started "Zed" closure.

3. As I attempted to get to the Conning tower over the decks slippery with oil and water, I felt the shock of another very heavy explosion on the port side. By this time the ship was listing from 25 to 35 degrees and was continuing to list further. It was now obvious that the ship was going to continue to roll over and I climbed over the boat deck toward the starboard side. Men were beginning to come up from below through hatches and gun ports and from them it was learned that the ship was filling with water in many spaces below.

4. As I reached the starboard side, I met Lieutenant Commander HOBBY, the First Lieutenant, and with him concluded that the ship was fast becoming untenable and that an effort should be made to save as many men as possible. The word was passed for all hands to abandon ship and the men were directed to leave over the starboard side and to walk and climb over the ship's side and onto the bottom as it rolled over. At about this time another heavy explosion was felt on the port side and the ship began to roll over rapidly. The men went over the starboard side, climbing over the side and bottom and many went into the water to swim to the *Maryland*.

5. After it became impossible to remain on the starboard side longer, I walked up the ship's side over the blister ledge and up over the bottom. The ship settled with the starboard side of the bottom above water and a portion of the keel and the starboard propeller shaft clear. Two motor launches were caught on the keel and propeller shaft aft. One of these was gotten off and sent after men in the water. Life jackets were re-moved from these launches and thrown to men who were still in the water waiting to be picked up by boats that had now come to the rescue. After all men were clear of the hull, I went into a boat and assisted in taking men from the water. When all men in sight had been taken from the water, we proceeded to the boat shed on Ford Island between the California and Maryland and sent wounded and those suffering from im-mersion via trucks to the dispensary. Boats at the boat landing were despatched to pick up personnel from the California and to search the along line of ships. Men arriving uninjured at the boat shed were sent to

assist in putting out the oil and gasoline fires that had started around the fuel dock and near the boat sheds.

6. I then proceeded along Ford Island toward the Maryland, where I met Captain BODE and other *Oklahoma* officers and with them proceeded to the naval air station administration building from where we later went to the naval ammunition depot at West Loch.

7. Throughout the short period of the attack preceding the capsizing of the *Oklahoma*, the ship was subjected to torpedo fire from a large number of enemy planes approaching from the direction of Merry Point. The ship was further subjected to strafing attacks, and two flight of six each high altitude bombers approaching from the direction of the harbor entrance dropped their bombs from around 10 to 12,000 feet, which fell astern and clear of the overturned *Oklahoma*. The exact number of torpedoes that struck the ship is uncertain, but has been variously estimated from five to seven at points from about frame 50 to frame 115 port. No bombs are known to have struck on board for a certainty.

8. While all of the gun crews were at stations immediately after the first alarm, and the ready ammunition boxes were being opened, fire was not taken up by the guns of the 3"/50 and 5"/25 anti-aircraft batteries as the ship listed so rapidly that the guns could not be effectively serviced. Oil and water on the decks made it additionally difficult for men to stay on their feet. Fire was taken up by the security watch on the 30 caliber machine gun on the port side of the superstructure deck but this gun was almost immediately placed out of service by the first torpedo hit forward.

9. The conduct of the crew was excellent throughout. There was no evidence of panic and the men leaving the ship to go into the water were eager to get aboard the Maryland and to assist in the action there on the 5"/25 A.A. guns and pom-poms. A large number of *Oklahoma* men assisted both with the service of these guns and with the ammunition supply until ordered to Ford Island.

[signed]
J.L. KENWORTHY, JR.

U.S.S. UTAH (AG-16), FORMER BATTLESHIP

This ship presented about the same problems of salvage as *Oklahoma*. However, she was a much older ship and was used only for aircraft target practice. She did not occupy a berth essential to the fleet. Some thought was given to using an air bubble to float the hull to the drydock for scrapping, but this idea was abandoned when it was revealed that *Utah* would not hold enough compressed air to make a safe trip to the drydock across the channel.

It was originally intended that the ship should be salvaged immediately after *Oklahoma*, but there was considerable doubt whether the time, energy, material, and cost warranted the operation. The ordnance gang under Lieutenant Commander Stelter and Gunner Manthei had already removed from this ship, and other disabled ships, considerable ordnance material. This consisted of anti-aircraft guns, ammunition, small arms, etc. Most of the fuel oil had already been pumped out through the bottom.

The decision was made by the Navy Department to forego salvage work on Utah as the space was not needed and economy did not warrant further work. The matter was taken up anew in 1956 when the Commandant of the Fourteenth Naval District pointed out that carriers of the Essex class had insufficient space in which to transfer ammunition, special weapons, and guided missile components. The removal of Utah would facilitate such essential transfers. The cost of salvage would be about $4,000,000 whereas the 7,000 tons of recovered steel would bring only about $30-$40 per ton. The Commandant showed, however, that the salvage of Utah would remove an obstruction from the channel and would obviate the necessity of building a new berth for the aircraft carriers.

This view was concurred in by the Service Force, the Fleet Maintenance Officer, and by the Pacific Fleet. The plan was to use the refloating of *Utah* as a training project for harbor clearance. The ship had already been partially righted. The list to port had been reduced to about thirty-eight degrees, but she sat in water which nearly covered her hull.

The Bureau of Ships stated that since the decision of 1944, by the Chief of Naval Operations, the material required for righting the ship had been disposed of by sale, that the divers were no longer available, and that the project would consume one and a half to two years. Further, funds were not available and if the work was to proceed it should be under funds appropriated for the purpose.

The Chief of Naval Operations did not favor further work on Utah but had no objection to using the ship for training of divers and harbor clearance. He saw no emergency requirement which would warrant the project. He was probably influenced by the argument advanced a few years earlier that the final resting place of some fifty-eight men should not be disturbed. It was proposed that a survey be made to determine whether a new pier tangent to *Utah* could not be built for mooring and servicing aircraft carriers.

In any event *Utah* still remains at Pearl Harbor. She rests on the bottom although in a slightly different position than the bottom-up position she originally assumed. The Chief of Naval Operations has been consistent in his decision of April 1942 that because of the minor military value of *Utah* any salvage work should be directed toward her ultimate use as scrap.

The Utah, *a former battleship built in 1909, was converted in 1932 to serve the fleet as an auxiliary mobile target ship and in following years as an advanced gunnery training school. When operating in her alternate mission as a target the guns were covered with heavy steel sheds called "dog houses". The open decks were covered with large 6x12-inch timbers in double layers to absorb the impact of the 100-lb. practice bombs. After several weeks at sea for target duty* Utah *steamed into Pearl Harbor on Friday 5 December 1941. The ship moored at berth Fox-11 on the northwest side of Ford Island her decks still covered with timber and steel sheds over the guns.* USN

On the fantail at 0755 the morning of 7 December the crew was preparing for the raising of morning colors, they paid little attention to the planes in the distance. Coming in low over the water was a flight of Japanese torpedo planes. Two torpedoes in succession slammed into the Utah's *portside blowing massive holes in the hull sending torrents of seawater flooding into the ship. In minutes the list to port approached dangerously to 40-degrees when the order to abandon ship was sounded. Men began scrambling down her barnacle encrusted hull into the water as mooring lines holding the ship snapped.* Utah *finally rolled over at 0812.* NA 80G-266626

The Utah had reached a final position of 165-degrees from upright with her upper decks sitting firmly on the harbor bottom. The ships cage mast, stack and conning tower had broken away. The old Utah was given the least priority for any salvage work by the Salvage Force. The only work done was the recovery of nearly 2,700 rounds of 5-inch ammunition and the ship's safe. Work was halted in mid-January and put on hold for the present and by 14 February 1942 all salvage equipment was removed. NA 80G-32470

After laying idle for 11 months the Salvage Division resumed work on Utah *commencing on 3 January 1943. It was to proceed slowly in tandem with the recovery work already well underway on the* Oklahoma, *but using the same methods. Construction of the foundations for the pulling winches was begun on the western shore of Ford Island in April 1943. A model of Utah's interior decks and compartments was constructed to aid divers in finding their way when working inside the darkened and overturned hull.* NA 80G-410767

Early on a lighter (left) was secured alongside as a service barge with air compressors on board for use by divers and pneumatic tools. At Utah's bow is the ex-Intrepid *(a de-commissioned training ship of 1904) converted for use as a sludge removal barge received the recovered fuel oil. Thrust brackets have been welded onto the hull ready for installation of the headframes being sent over from the* Oklahoma *salvage. After the ship's propellers were removed, a water-tight cofferdam was erected around the stern section and completed by 21 July 1943.* NA 80G-228353

To assist in righting and reducing the weight of the Utah, *sections of the ship's interior would have to be sealed off and dewatered to create a partial air bubble. This is one of six air locks that were installed on the hull to allow divers safe access into and out of the ship to open or close hatches, recover useful materials, cut away wreckage, seal off port holes, air ducts and vents. In the salvage of the* Utah *divers would make 437 dives involving over 2,227 man-hours under pressure. Note the diver (right) with the camera to record progress.* PHP

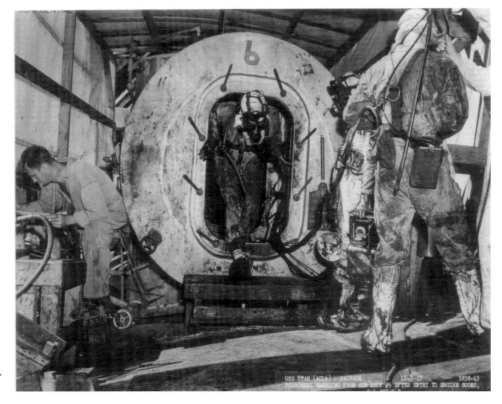

231

Seventeen wooden righting head frames recovered from the successful Oklahoma *salvage operation were erected in place on* Utah's *hull by 15 November 1943, but construction ashore for the pulling winches and their foundations had proceeded slowly and were not ready yet. During this interim divers were closing watertight hatches, removing guns, ammunition and stores. The pair of F-11 mooring quays were removed to clear the area for the ship to roll over. They were never replaced.* NA 80G-410700

The righting operation finally commenced at 0806 on 8 February 1944. The pulling continued over the next three days suspended at various times to adjust tension lines, the winch drums or lubrication of gear. When the ship reached the position of 68-degrees the headframes were being pushed upwards by the mud thus preventing the righting cable from lifting clear. Pulling operations were on hold for the next three weeks while the Pacific Bridge Company removed the headframes and shifted the righting cables. NA 80G-410701

Pulling operations were on hold for the next three weeks while the Pacific Bridge Company removed the headframes with carefully placed dynamite charges. They were replaced with 3-inch steel cables welded to the main deck and looped around the hull. Cables were also wrapped around the four barbettes and the conning tower. Pulling resumed at 0820 on 3 March 1944, lasting over the next nine hours with short interruptions, but things were starting to go wrong. The Utah continued to sink deeper in the mud and slide towards shore while barely turning. USN NH 64301

All winches started pulling at 0846 and halted after only 22-minutes on 5 March 1944. The Utah *would not turn but continued to slide and sink deeper in the mud. Since the maximum safe operating tension was exceeded on most lines, operations were secured until a final decision is made whether to continue or not. Work was officially stopped for good on 13 March 1944 with the wreck left in its final position of 38-degrees. The Navy Department had decided that further work was too costly for a ship no longer valuable to the war effort. The epic salvage operations that began after the infamous attack on 7 December 1941, was officially ended.* NA 80G-276789

Hours after the attack Utah *survivor Pallas Brown S1/c, was transferred over to the USS Argonne. That night he would become* Utah's *fifty-eighth casualty. He was killed when nervous gunners mistakenly opened fire at six planes from the USS* Enterprise *trying to land on Ford Island during the blackout. Today* Utah *is a war grave, the final resting place for the 6 officers and 51 men never recovered. On December 9, 1950, a plaque was mounted on the ship's wreck. The inscription reads: "In Memory-Officers and Men-USS UTAH-Lost in Action-7 December 1941.* NA 80G-484354

On Memorial Day May 27, 1972, a crowd of about 200 persons, many of them misty-eyed with emotion, stood at attention as America's newest war memorial was dedicated. A U.S. Marine Corps rifle squad fired a 21-gun salute over the rusted hulk of the Utah *followed by a lone Marine bugler playing "Taps" The Utah Memorial was built at a cost of $141,000 dollars. The open structure is a 40-foot by 15-foot reinforced cement platform connected to Ford Island by a 70-foot walkway with a tall stainless steel flagpole placed in one corner. The ceremony of colors, hoisting the national ensign, is performed daily.* EA

U.S.S. UTAH

AG16/
(Serial No. 3)

Pearl Harbor, T.H.,
December 15, 1941.

From: The Commanding Officer.
To: The Commander-in-Chief, Pacific Fleet.
Via: (1) The Commander Train Squadron SIX
         (2) The Commander Base Force.

Subject: *U.S.S. Utah* -- Loss by Enemy Action.

Reference: (a) Art. 1712, U.S. Navy Regulations, 1920.

Enclosure: (A href=#EnclA>A) Statement of Lt.Comdr. S.S. Isquith, U.S. Navy.

1. The *U.S.S. Utah* was attacked by Japanese torpedo planes and bombing planes at about 0813, December 7, 1941, and was lost by capsizing at about 0813 that date.

2. The *Utah* had been engaged in operations as a bombing target and all of her 5" and 1".1 guns were covered with steel houses. All .50 cal. and .30 cal. machine guns were dismounted and stowed below decks in storerooms. The ship was covered with two layers of 6" x 12" timbers for protection against practice bombs. All ammunition was in the magazines and secured. Because of this, it was impossible to make any effort to repel the attack.

3. The Commanding Officer was on shore on authorized leave during the action. The Executive Officer, Commander John F. Warris, U.S. Navy was on shore on authorized leave during the action.

4. The senior surviving line officer who was on board during the attack is Lieutenant Commander S.S. Isquith, U.S. Navy, and his report is forwarded herewith as enclosure (A).

5. Statements have been obtained from all officers on board at the time of the action, and from a review of these statements, it is the opinion of the Commanding Officer that Lieutenant Commander Isquith's report is accurate.

6. Reports of dead, missing, and survivors have been forwarded to the Commander-in-Chief, Pacific Fleet.

7. The Commanding Officer concurs in paragraph 11, of the enclosure, and makes the following recommendations:

a. That VAESSEN, John B., 413 35 79, F2, V-6 U.S.N.R. be awarded a Navy Cross.

b. That the following officers and men be awarded letters of commendation:

Lt.Comdr. S.S. Isquith, U.S. Navy.
Lt.(jg) P.F. Hauck, U.S. Navy.

Ensign B.C. Moyer, U.S. Naval Reserve.
Machinist S.A. Szymanski, U.S. Navy.
MACSELWINEY, Terrance, 320 90 45, CMM(PA), USFR.

8. That the following officer and men who lost their lives while ensuring that others escape be awarded the Navy Cross posthumously:

Lt. Comdr. Rudoph P. Bielka, U.S. Navy.
Lt. Comdr. Charles O. Michael, U.S. Naval Reserve
Lt.(jg) John C. Little, III, U.S. Navy.
Lt.(jg) Harold A. Harveson, U.S. Navy.
Lt.(*jg) John E. Black, U.S. Navy.
Ensign David W. Jackson, U.S. Naval Reserve.
TOMICH, Peter, CWT(PA), U.S. Navy.

[signed]
J.M. STEELE

U.S.S. UTAH

AG16/ Pearl Harbor, T.H.,
December 14, 1941.

From: Lieutenant Commander S.S. Isquith, U.S. Navy.
To: The Commanding Officer.

Subject: Report of Loss of the *U.S.S. Utah.*

On Sunday, December 7, 1941, while moored at Berth FOX-11 Pearl Harbor, T.H., 3 planes whose identification were not questioned but taken for U.S. planes maneuvering, were observed just as colors were being hoisted at 0800, heading northerly from the harbor entrance. They made a low dive on the southern end of Ford Island and each dropped a bomb.

1. Immediately thereafter the air was filled with planes clearly distinguished as yellow colored planes with brilliant red Rising Sun insignia on fuselage and red wing tips, flying low at about 100 knots speed and dropping aerial torpedoes and bombs. They appeared to [be] Henkle 113, or similar type, with very silent engines. The general alarm was immediately rung and word was passed "All hands to bombing quarters". At about this time, 0801, a severe under water hit, at approximately frame 84, port side, was felt and the ship immediately commenced to list to port. Another underwater hit was felt almost immediately thereafter in about the same general location and the listing of the ship increased immediately to about 15 degrees. At this time I realized that the ship would capsize and word was passed "All hands on deck and all engineroom and fireroom, radio and dynamo watch to lay up on deck and release all prisoners.

2. All hands were ordered to the starboard side, which was the high side, to escape danger of loose timbers pinning men down. Word was passed for all hands to equip themselves with

life jackets but due to the fact that the life jackets were stored in canvas bags in the air castle, it was not practicable for many men to obtain life jackets due to miscellaneous gear stored in the starboard aircastle moving and bomb explosion in the port aircastle which took place at that time. At about that time the engine room reported that steam had dropped and that they were unable to cut in the drain pumps, that the port engine room was flooded and that the starboard engine room was taking water rapidly, the water at that time being above the high pressure turbine and reduction gear. The lights were still on in the engine room. The engine room watch cleared the starboard engine room. No. 2 fireroom, No. 4 boiler steaming, reported steam dropping rapidly and additional burners cut in to hold steam. The second hit put out all fires. The fireroom watch then abandoned the fireroom, closed the quick closing fuel oil valve, leaving the auxiliary feed pumps operating but slowing down due to lack of steam.

3. By about 0805, the ship had listed to about 40 degrees to port. Lights were still on., No report had been received from the dynamo room; word was again passed "All hands on deck and abandon ship, over starboard side." The crew commenced getting over the side, the ship con tinuing to list but somewhat slower. The attacking planes were now returning from a northerly direction flying low and straffing the crew as they abandoned ship. The loose timber about the decks were moving to port, interfering greatly with the efforts of the crew to abandon ship.

4. Observing the straffing and the moving of the timbers and loose gear in the aircastles, I directed that the crew divide into three groups, one group going up the ladder leading from the starboard aircastle to the Captain's cabin, one going up the ladder from the star board wardroom country to the passage inboard of the Captain's cabin stateroom, and one going up the ladder leading from the starboard wardroom country near the wardroom pantry to the forecastle. A large number of these men escaped through the ports in the Captain's cabin.

5. Lieutenant (jg) P.F. Hauck, Machinist S.A. Szymanski, and myself were the last to leave the ship going through the ports in the Captain's cabin. At this time, about 0810, the ship was list- ing about 80 degrees to port and the planes were still straffing the ship. mooring lines were parting and two motor launches and the motor whale boat were picking up men in the water. Many men were observed swimming to the north and south keys of Pier FOX-11, and as planes were still straffing the men were ordered to the sides of the keys for some protection.

6. At about 0812, the last mooring lines had parted and the ship was capsized, the keel plainly showing. All men picked up by ship'[s boats were taken ashore to Ford Island and boats ordered to return and pick up any men still swimming about.

7. On reaching shore on Ford Island, all hands were ordered into the trenches that had been dug there for some Public Works Project, in order to protect themselves from the straff- ing planes. Noting that many men were injured and wounded, Commander G.H. Larson, (MC), U.S. Navy, with KERNS, Jean W., HA1c., U.S. Naval Reserve, who had brought a first aid kit ashore with him, set up a first aid station in the quarters of Lieutenant Church (CEC), Building No. 118 Ford Island. Commander Larson, GRAY, CPHM., and two other pharmacist's mates proceeded with the first aid treatment of all men who had been injured and necessary cases were sent to the Naval Air Station Dispensary in Naval Air Station trucks supplied for this purpose.

8. While in the trenches, a short time later, knocking was heard on the ship's hull. At this time planes were still straffing and dropping bombs. I called for a volunteer crew to return to the *Utah* to investigate the knocking heard. Machinist Szymanski and a volunteer crew consistingof MacSelwiney, CAM, and two seaman, names unknown, returned to the ship and located the tapping coming from the void space V-98, under the dynamo room. They answered the knocking with knocks on the outside which in turn were answered by knocking within the ship.

9. The following personnel are especially recommended for exceptional conduct under fire:

   Lt. (jg) P.F. Hauck, U.S. Navy, for assisting in getting men safely out of the ship without thought of his own safety.Ensign B.C. Moyer, U.S. Naval Reserve, for especial coolness and assisting men out of the ship without thought to his own safety.

   Machinist S. A. Szymanski, U.S. Navy, for rescuing VASSEN, John B., F2c, V-6, USNR, by cutting a hole in the bottom of the ship while planes were still straffing.

   VAESSEN, John B. F2c, V-6, USNR, for remaining at his post in forward distribution room and in order to keep lights on the ship as long as possible while realizing that the ship was capsizing and without thought of his own safety.

   MACSELWINEY, Terrance, CAM (PA), USNR, for operating a motor whale boat making trips to and from the ship during the cutting operations without regard to his own safety from straffing planes and for inspecting the engine room. clearing out the watch and securing the engineering plant prior to abandoning ship while well realizing that the ship was capsizing.

   Tomich, Peter, CWT(A). (MISSING), for insuring that all fireroom personnel had left the ship and the boilers were secured prior to his abandoning the ship which resulted in the probable loss of his own life.

10. All other officers and enlisted personnel are to be commended for the initiative and prompt execution of all orders during the entire period and I am of the opinion that the coolness and lack of excitement as well as the small loss of life was due to a great extent to the training they had received during the previous nine weeks of duty as a bombing target. The boat crews acted in a manner well worthy of commendation, picking up men from the water during the entire straffing period.

S.S. ISQUITH.

U.S.S. ARIZONA (BB-39), BATTLESHIP

There was no thought of raising Arizona because of her military value, but the divers and other salvors spent a lot of time investigating the wreckage. At one time it was believed that the after part of the ship was reasonably intact and that it could be raised if the underwater cutters could satisfactorily disconnect this portion from the rest of the ship.

The Ordnance Section was successful in removing from Arizona in the early days a great deal of the anti-aircraft battery with its ammunition. Much other ordnance material was recovered from the ship even as late as November 1942. The oil which fouled the harbor was gradually removed as it was released from the ship's opened tanks.

Practically all of the survey conducted in the summer of 1942 had to be performed by divers, mostly from the inside of the ship. It was found that the bow portion was buoyant, the after portion relatively intact, but the central portion of the ship was badly wrecked. Lieutenant Ankers, assisted by Ensign Beauchamp-Nobbs and Carpenter Urbaniak make a thorough survey. Gunner Manthei recovered considerable ammunition from turrets III and IV. The 14-inch guns, except from turret II, were removed and offered to the Army.

It was decided that nothing further should be done toward salvaging Arizona, but that the ship should remain as a memorial to the men who lost their lives at Pearl Harbor. The hull of the ship is the final resting place of about 1100 men, including Rear Admiral Isaac C. Kidd.

In due time the topsides of Arizona were removed, and all projections from the hull were cut off by divers. A memorial structure was built transversely over the hull of the ship. It is supported by two concrete girders which weigh 250 tons each. This rests on concrete piling. The structure is 185 feet long with a width of 27 and 36 feet respectively at the ends to 14 feet at the center. The assembly area accommodates 200 people.

The memorial is reached by a boat landing, and access is gained by formal stairs at the harbor end. Included is a carillon and a shrine. The shrine has a marble wall on which are inscribed the names of the men who were lost on Arizona on 7 December 1941.

This structure is a fitting memorial to the 2335 service men who were lost and the 1143 who were wounded on 7 December. It is painted white and is surmounted by the American Flag which flies day and night. The memorial is visited by many Americans and foreigners visiting Pearl Harbor.

December 7th was a quiet Sunday morning on board the Arizona. *Some of her crew were still at breakfast while others were getting ready for liberty ashore or church call. On the ship's quarterdeck at 0755 a 4-man Marine Color Guard waited for the signal to hoist the Stars and Stripes for morning colors. They noticed some planes approaching when they heard explosions at the seaplane-hangers on Ford Island. General Quarters was sounded as the Marines hurriedly raised the flag. The ship's complement responded immediately and rushed to their battle stations. The* Arizona *was about to fight the first and last battle of her life.* USN

Around 0805 Japanese high level bombers dropped ten 1,760-pound armor piercing bombs on Arizona and the repair ship Vestal tied up alongside. Two bombs crashed into Arizona with several close near misses. One projectile struck near the starboard side of turret #2 penetrating deep into the ships innards before detonating in the forward powder magazine. The resultant cataclysmic explosion of ammunition and fuel oil showered the harbor and nearby Ford Island with tons of debris. The forward section of Arizona was demolished causing turrets #1 and #2 to collapse down into the hull forcing the bridge superstructure and foremast to tilt forwards at an eerie 45-degree angle. NA 80G-32427

The fires on Arizona would burn and smolder for three days before they were finally extinguished. When it was safe, work parties went aboard to remove as many of the 1,177 dead as possible. Of the 233 bodies eventually recovered in the following weeks only 109 could be identified. Ahead of Arizona work is already under way to free the lightly damaged Tennessee which had been wedged against the mooring quay when the West Virginia sank. At sunset that evening, after long hours, some of the rescue crew were relieved from firefighting duties. As they were walking toward the Ford Island Bachelor Officers Quarters for a quick bite and some rest a bugle sounded evening colors. The men, tired and exhausted, snapped to attention and saluted. NA 80G-32609

The broken Arizona *had settled to the harbor bottom in less than nine minutes with the quarterdeck barely level with the harbor waters. Just before sunset on that tragic day Lt. Kebler Masterson and Ensign Leon Grabowsky got into a motor launch and went over to the still burning hulk of their ship. The American flag, though stained with fuel oil, was still there hanging from the sternpost. They lowered the oily flag and brought it over to the battleship* Maryland *and handed it to the Officer-of-the-Deck telling him that they wanted the flag saved as a memorial to the* Arizona. *Sadly, the flag was never seen again.* NA 80G-32761

Six days after the attack, some preliminary dives were done to survey the extent of damage to the ship's hull. The forward section of the ship back to about Frame 70 was completely destroyed. Cmdr. Ellis Geiselman, senior surviving officer from the Arizona *submitted the ship's action report to Admiral Kimmel. It read: "The USS* Arizona *is a total loss except the following is believed salvageable: 50-caliber machine guns in maintop, searchlights on after searchlight platform, the low catapult on quarterdeck and the guns of Number 3 and 4 turrets."* USN

243

There was never a real expectation that the shattered wreck of the Arizona could be raised and returned to service. The Navy Department decided that raising the Arizona during war time would not be practicable to the war effort and the cost would be prohibitive. Thus the ship was placed low on the priority list for salvage. Only work necessary to continue removal of any useful equipment and scrap metals from the wreck was ordered. All major work in Pearl Harbor will be focused on salvage and repairing the lesser damaged ships that could be used in the war. PHP

Looking aft on the starboard side during early salvage work on 17 February 1942. On the boat deck are the twisted remains of the metal shields for the 5-inch anti-aircraft guns that had been removed earlier. Divers were able to enter the Paymasters Office located one deck below the main deck on the starboard side. The soaking wet money recovered from the safe amounted to nearly $480,000 dollars. They also recovered the ship's muster roll and Service Records from the Executive Officers office on the portside. They were still readable with only a few pages smeared with oil. PHP

A clock belonging to the ship's Chaplain, Capt. Thomas L. Kirkpatrick, was recovered from his quarters. It was stopped at 0805, the moment when the Arizona blew up. The recovery of bodies from the wreckage was a priority in the days and weeks following the attack, but these efforts were constantly hindered during salvage operations by the enormity of the devastation. By the time all work had ceased on the Arizona in October 1943, the remains of only 235 of the 1,177 casualties, nearly all unidentifiable, were eventually removed from the ship. For those not recovered the Arizona was now their final resting place. PHP

The Arizona's quarterdeck was now 10 feet underwater as the ship continued to slowly settle deeper in the soft mud. In early February 1942 the tops of the two aft turrets were removed. The Salvage Division Ordnance Units first priority was to remove and save the 14-inch guns and then dissemble the turrets. Turret #3 was rotated towards Ford Island and within a week all three guns were lifted free and placed on a barge. A few days later turret #4 was also trained to starboard to remove the big guns followed by preparations to salvage the after catapult and crane. PHP

When the burnt and blackened foretop of the tripod mast was finally cut away by welder's torches, it was lifted off the leaning bridge superstructure on 5May1942 by the 150-ton heavy lift floating crane, YSD-25. The foretop was loaded on a barge and moved to Waipio Point. Throughout the summer months of 1942 welders continued cutting away the remnants of the tripod mast, the bridge and other salvageable wreckage for scrap metal and also barged over to Waipo Point for further disposition. NA 80G-64595

Detail view of the boat deck amidships of Arizona on 18 May 1942, with much of the debris cleared away. The 5/25-inch antiaircraft guns have already been removed. The crumpled metal over the large circular area is all that remains of the ship's stack. Some witnesses believed that a bomb went down the stack. This proved to be false when the uptake armor grating of the stack on the main deck was examined and found completely intact. PHP PR-411

Looking forward from the mainmast over the tilted superstructure on 18 May 1942. A work barge is in the process of building the staging and supports prior to removing the 14-inch guns of turret #2. At the top is all that remains of the crumpled bow section. Divers found that the sides of the bow area had been blown outward to almost a horizontal position. The crew on the dive boat (right) are handling the life lines for divers working below inspecting damage on the starboard side. The diver's air bubbles can be seen rising to the surface nearby. PHP PR-404

During operations removing powder cans from turret #3 on 1 July 1942, note the work crew wearing gas masks. The greatest hazard for men working in interior spaces on the sunken ships was the presence of deadly gases formed by the decay of numerous organic substances in confined spaces found aboard a sunken ship. This decay is intensified in the tropics such as at Pearl Harbor. Salvage personnel were required to wear gas masks or similar breathing apparatus. Before a compartment could be safe for workers to enter, it had to be "unwatered" to a safe level and properly ventilated to draw off any toxic fumes. Fuel oil, filth and wreckage also complicated the task. USN

By 17 July 1942, looking forward, the bridge superstructure has been completely cut away leaving only the armored conning tower (top), with one of the ship's boat cranes and tons of scrap metal waiting to be lifted off. The work barge (upper right) is preparing the guns of turret #2 for removal. Work was held up for good on turret #1 as it was determined that the guns and equipment were too badly damaged from the heat of the explosion and were never salvaged from the hulk. The armored conning tower would not be lifted off until the last day of 1942. PHP

USS ARIZONA 5/18/42

REMOVING PROJECTILES FROM TURRET #4
FANTAIL CRANE IN BACKGROUND.

After the main battery guns had been removed from the aft turrets #3 and #4, salvage crews now had access to the inner chambers of the barbettes to remove ammunition, powder cans and miscellaneous machinery. The navy yard work force erected shoring and work platforms on the turrets to support the men and equipment in their work. In late 1942 several of Arizona's refurbished 14-inch guns from forward turret # 2 were back in service on the battleships Nevada *and* Pennsylvania *to replace guns that were worn out.* USN

By August 1942 workers from the Navy Yard had removed all useable equipment from the Arizona's charred 120-foot high upright mainmast. The ship's pair of heavy duty boat cranes (partially visible lower right) were also removed. The services of the 150-ton floating crane, YSD-25 were used again on 23 August to remove the cranes and sections of the mainmast as welders cut away each level for easier handling. Of no further use other than scrap value, the parts were barged over to Waipio Point to be cut up and shipped to the mainland for use in the war effort. NARA

Each turret contained approximately three hundred 14-inch projectiles stored on the shell decks and in handling rooms. Also stored in the magazines of each turret were over six hundred cans of smokeless powder. Hoisting the shells and powder cans up from below was a time consuming and tedious process. Some of the elaborate system of piping for ventilation can be seen. Work began in early February 1942 to remove all ordnance from the turrets was not completed until 25 October 1944. USN

U.S.S. ARIZONA   10/5/42   4261-42
REMOVAL OF AMUNITION AFT - VENTILATION BLOWER
TO MAGAZINES THROUGH TURRET #3.

The decks in the forward section from Frame 70 to Frame 38 had been reduced to a mass of crumpled metal. The forward turrets and the conning tower had collapsed about 25-30 feet down into the hull. Most of turret #2 was salvaged but there were no plans to salvage turret #1. The huge openings in the deck are the uptakes from the engine room to the stack that was destroyed in the opening attack. USN

OFFICIAL PHOTOGRAPH
NOT TO BE RELEASED
FOR PUBLICATION
NAVY YARD PEARL HARBOR, T. H.
CONFIDENTIAL

U.S.S. ARIZONA-SALVAGE   12/11/42   5330-42
VIEW FORWARD FROM ABOUT FRAME 70 SUPERSTRUC-
TURE DECK SHOWING STATUS OF REMOVALS.

Temporary piers were built on the portside of the wreckage. A large one was built across turret #1 to the forward quay and another alongside of turret #3. They were necessary for vessels to tie up bringing in work crews and equipment daily. Sheds and lean-to structures were built on the piers for the work crews to stow their gear and to clean-up and shower at the end of their shift. Barges also moored there to load up with useable equipment or tons of scrap metal recovered from the wreckage and then towed to designated areas for disbursement. NA 80G-451256

The Arizona's thick armored conning tower was lifted off the hulk in January 1943 by the YSD-19, a seaplane wrecking derrick, and placed on a barge with other metals salvaged from the wreck. The scrapped materials was then towed over to the scrap piles alongside of Berth 23 in the Navy Yard for eventual shipment to the West Coast. The supporting tube of the tower had to be cut away next to clear the area behind Turret Two before work could begin to recover the 14-inch guns. NA 80G-77921

S ARIZONA (BB39) — SALVAGE   4-19-43
AR VIEW OF UPPER SECTION OF ROTATING PORTION OF TURRET #3 SUS-
PENDED FROM 150-TON CRANE

The rotating section of turret #3 was lifted off the Arizona *on 19 April 1943. When the Navy officially announced in 1942 that the hulk could not be raised, the Army expressed interest in using turrets # 3 and # 4 as coastal defense emplacements on Oahu. Two sites were selected, one on Mokapu Point to cover the eastern approaches to Oahu and named Battery Pennsylvania. The other, Battery Arizona was positioned off Kahe Point in the Waiane Mountains on the western shore of Oahu. Neither achieved combat readiness but Battery Pennsylvania did fire a test salvo four days before Japan surrendered on V-J Day, 14 August 1945, marking the end of World War Two. No longer needed with the advent of peace, both emplacements were dismantled after the war.* PHP PR-408

Looking inside of turret #3 barbette on 19 April 1943 after the upper section of the rotating portion was removed. Notice the roller-path cylindrical bearings on which the turret rotated when in operation. All materials and equipment salvaged from inside the barbette were in need of preservation or repair. The outer shell walls of the barbette were not removed and left on the hull and can still be seen today. PHP PR-409

After the upper section of turret #4 was lifted off, a wooden cofferdam was built around the barbette by the yard work force. Divers assisted in sealing off any leaks. This allowed for the unwatering of the barbette so work crews could enter the lower compartments to salvage machinery and the inner workings that could be reconditioned for later use. The cofferdam was removed after all salvageable materials had been recovered. PHP PR-409

The huge floating crane, YSD-25, prepares to hoist up the center gun from turret # 2. Once out of the water guns were immediately sprayed with a rust preventive coating. The three main battery 14-inch guns recovered from Arizona's turret # 2 during 1943 were shipped to the Naval Gun factory on the mainland and refurbished for further use. The three guns were later installed on the battleship Nevada at the Norfolk Navy Yard. Arizona's guns were fired in anger for the first time during the invasion of Iwo Jima in February 1945. PHP

On September 1943 the gunslide of turret # 2 and the slide assembly would be the last sections lifted off the wreck. Time and wartime priorities were now an issue. Since the guns had already been removed from turret # 2 and much of the equipment from the gun chamber, the Navy Department (Bureau of Ships) ordered that all salvage work on the Arizona will be halted as of 11 October 1943. Turret # 1 was believed to have been so badly damaged from the heat and blast of the explosion, none of it was ever salvaged. Turret # 1 and the shell of turret # 2 were left underwater and are still on the Arizona today. PHP

With the end of salvage operations, what remained of the Arizona would be left alone at her berth as the war went on around her. The work platforms, cofferdams, pumps and other equipment would be dismantled for usage on other ongoing salvage projects. No ammunition or powder cans were ever recovered from turret's # 1 and # 2. The Navy Department had no plans to preserve the ship or save any part of the ship as a memorial. The ship was left as a war grave and the final detail for her crew "still on Eternal watch" PHP

256

Throughout the war the wreckage of the Arizona would serve as an unofficial memorial for the men still entombed in their ship. Navy ships in passing the remains of the Arizona would have the crew "man the rails" to render Passing Honors of saluting the wreck just as had been done in peace time when the proud battleship Arizona was still in service and flying her colors. This tradition continues to this day in memory of their gallant shipmates who lost their live on 7 December 1941. NA

In March 7 of 1950 Admiral Arthur W. Radford, Commander-in-Chief, Pacific Fleet, directed that a small platform and a flagpole be built atop the ship's main deck house as a Memorial to the men of the Arizona. At the dedication he said; "From today on the USS Arizona will again fly our country's flag just as proudly as she did on the morning of December 7, 1941." At 0800 hours every morning a Navy Color Guard raises the national ensign of the United States over the Memorial and lowers it at 1600 hours in the evening as if the Arizona is still in commission. PHP

By 1956 time and weather had taken its toll and the structure was becoming unsafe for the daily ceremony of raising and lowering colors. In 1958 President Dwight D. Eisenhower signed legislation to create a national memorial. The Pacific War Memorial Commission, established in 1949, was asked to sponsor a campaign to raise funds for a permanent memorial worthy of the ship. The funds to build it came from both the public sector and private donors, including one unlikely source. In March 1961, popular entertainer Elvis Presley performed a benefit concert at Pearl Harbor's Block Arena raising over $60,000 dollars. USN

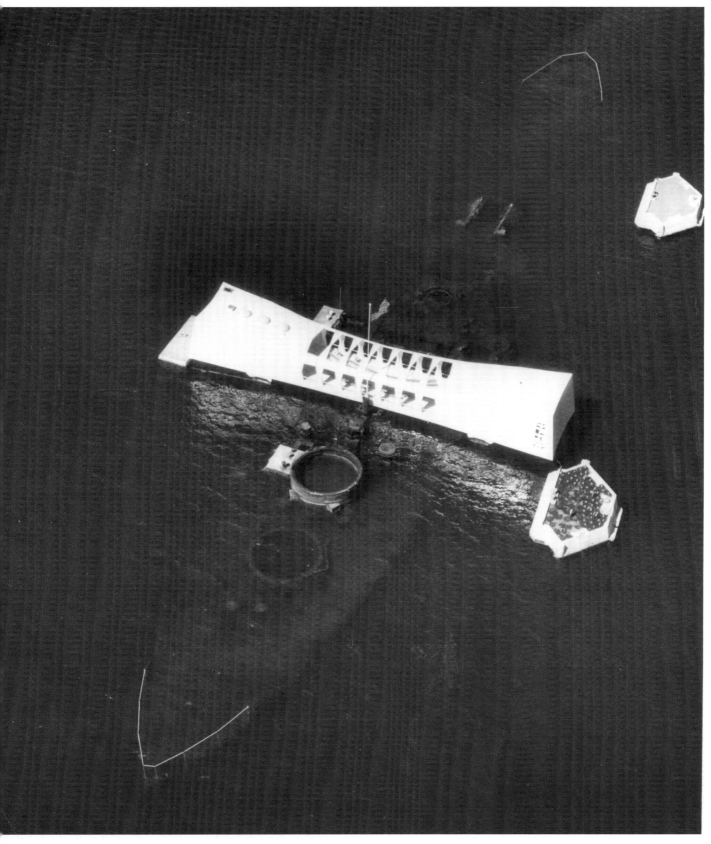

The graceful structure of the Arizona Memorial is seen spanning over the slowly decaying battleship Arizona *that is still faintly visible beneath the waters of Pearl Harbor. Each year nearly 1.4 million people from all around the world come to the Visitor's Center. They can tour the Museum and then board a U. S. Navy launch for the short ride out to the memorial where the can look down on the remains of the* Arizona *and in the Shrine room read the names of the men who went down with their ship on that "Date which will live in Infamy" The* Arizona *lives on, if only in memory, her heritage will endure long after all who served in her are gone.* PHPC

BB39/A16/

U.S.S. ARIZONA

Receiving Barracks, Pearl Harbor, T.H.

December 13, 1941

From:	The Commanding Officer.
To:	The Commander-in-Chief, U.S. Pacific Fleet.
Subject:	Action Report *U.S.S.* Arizona (BB39) December 7, 1941.
Reference:	(a) CincPAC Conf. Despatch 102102 of Dec. 1941.
Enclosures:	(A) Statement of Ensign Jim D. Miller, U.S. Navy.
	(B) Statement of Ensign G. S. Flannigan, USNR.
	(C) Statement of Ensign D. Hein, U.S. Navy.
	(D) Statement of Ensign R. J. Bush, U.S. Navy.
	(E) Statement of Ensign A. R. Schubert, U.S. Navy
	(F) Statement of Ensign H. D. Davison, U.S. Navy.
	(G) Statement of J. A. Doherty, CGM, U.S. Navy.
	(H) Statement of Lt. Commander. S. G. Fuqua, U.S. Navy.

1. In accordance with reference (a) the following report is submitted.
    1. **Offensive measures taken**:

The air raid alarm was sounded immediately when the attack was apparent. General quarters was sounded and word was passed to set material condition Zed. The antiaircraft battery and 50 caliber machine guns fired on the enemy planes as long as personnel at the guns were alive. It is believed that condition Zed was only partially set before the ship was irrepairably damaged.

    2. **Damage to enemy**:

While it cannot be definitely established it is believed that machine guns from this vessel shot down two Japanese planes.

    3. **Own losses**:

Personnel losses and casualties have been submitted to the Commander-in-Chief, U.S. Pacific Fleet under separate correspondence.

    4. **Damages**:

The *U.S.S.* Arizona is a total loss except the following is believed salvageable: fifty caliber machine guns in maintop. searchlights on after searchlight platform, the low catapult on quarter deck and the guns of numbers 3 and 4 turrets.

2. Statements regarding the action of personnel who were on board during the attack are attached as enclosures.
3. The Executive Officer, the senior surviving officer, was not on board at the time of the attack.

[signed]
E.H. GEISHLEAN

BAND 22

COURTESY ROGER HARE

Of all the legends surrounding December 7, the story of USS *Arizona* Band 22 endures in a fog of semi-truth. Popular history presents a thumb-nail sketch: They were a hot-shot band that dominated the famous "Battle Of The Bands" competition. Adept at playing popular swing tunes, they were said to have won the Saturday, Dec. 6 finale. Their reward-sleeping late the next morning. All perished.

The real story is better and late in life, my Father revealed a personal connection to this legendary band.

Band 22 was, indeed, a hot-shot unit and they were favored to win the Battle of the bands competition. They did not, however, win the December 6 finale because, in truth, it wasn't scheduled until December 21. The Saturday finale was actually a semi-final round they did not play.

This unit band was not awarded the luxury of sleeping late on Sunday and if they had, General Quarters would take precedence over any privilege. In the Navy, a call to battle stations means "you too, Mister".

Unfortunately, their battle station was handling ammo in the forward powder magazine.

After December 7, the battle of the bands was cancelled and Band 22 proclaimed the winner by consent of the participants. The trophy was named for their ship and retired forever.

Somehow history has presented blissful sleep in victory as their demise instead of hard work at their battle station.

When I first learned of this band I asked my Father if he knew any members. He changed the subject. Then in 1995, my mother told me an author had contacted Howard and interviewed him about Band 22.

Molly Kent's Brother, Clyde Williams, perished with the group. Her research ("*Arizona's* Last Band") revealed an early band roster listing Howard Hare as a drummer. She contacted our family expecting second-hand memories and was surprised to speak with a live Howard. He helped explain their school experience as they were all classmates.

So he was in the band! What happened? He simply said "Yes I was assigned to the band but missed classes and practice time due to an illness, so when I arrived at the *Arizona*, they told me I'd been bumped to the *West Virginia*, Band 17." Same classmates, though."

Through a fluke, is my Father the only surviving member of Band 22? How could one graduating class produce so many bands?

The answer lies in the amazing class of 1941 Navy School of Music, Washington DC. This was a group that would suffer more than any other. A group current Fleet Bandmaster, Ralph Barrett, calls his "Navy Fathers".

CLASS OF '41 MOTHER OF ALL NAVY BANDS

Fleet unit band 17 of the USS *West Virginia* and Unit 22 of the *Arizona* were all trained in Washington DC at the Navy School of Music during the 1940-41 school year. The class of '41 was the largest class yet graduated from this school; Formed in 1935.

Numbered in sequence, the Navy school had produced bands 1-16 by 1940, but this class was different. Throughout the year more students were added until membership swelled to 160.

Students were put through a strict regimen until the "cream rose to the top". Boatswains Mate James M. Thurmond was the taskmaster under Director and founder, Charles Benter.

Thurmond tolerated no "show-boating" or individual flair. His stated purpose was "To put iron in the soul, steel in the muscles and seafaring sense in the head"

As students progressed, they were assigned to full 20-piece orchestras in a numbered band. This school trained all Navy bands, but unlike other billets, Sailor/Musicians stayed together for their entire hitch. A group would train, then ship out in whole to a ship. If duty called elsewhere, they moved as one unit.

The reasoning for unit assignment was sound: Band mates learned others' playing skills and nuances and worked together much like an intricate watch. Cohesive playing and lasting friendships resulted.

All large Navy ships had a band - it was tradition. They played ceremonial functions and for the pleasure of the crew. Therefore, they must know traditional and popular music.

Band 17 was the class of '41, but rapid expansion meant it was soon large enough to support two full orchestras. Administration soon listed it as band 17/18. The leader for this class was Fred Kinney.

Kinney was a strict Bandmaster but his pupils were the best players. His technique? Drill the incompetent mercilessly.

Band leaders shipped-out with their students and anyone placed in Kinney's eventual billet were assured a good assignment-probably a battleship.

When rosters were listed, Fred Kinney was given Band 21 of the USS *Tennessee*. Howard was placed as a drummer. But something unusual happened on their way to Pearl Harbor that summer of '41-Band 21 of the *Tennessee* suddenly became Band 22 of the *Arizona*.

The Bandmaster of the original Unit 22 was not happy with assignment to the *Arizona*. He had a relative stationed on USS *Tennessee* and in pre-Sullivan law Navy, he sought transfer to this ship. Would Kinney swap bands with him?

Fred Kinney had worked hard to place the best of the 1941 class in Band 21 and would not entertain the thought of losing them. Knowing the Navy would never change band assignments once made, a deal was struck-they would simply swap numbers. Band 21 was now Band 22 and vice versa.

Howard arrived at Pearl Harbor in the Summer of '41 and reported to the *Tennessee* only to be told to report to the *Arizona*. Here he was informed he wasn't needed: "Report to the *West Virginia*, Band 17" He was told. "Bandmaster T G Carlin will take care of you."

An illness had meant he had missed too much practice time and Fred Kinney decided he wasn't good enough for the new Band 22. Such are the vagaries of fate. My Father confessed "I thought I was the drummer for Band 21, and they all went off and died as Band 22.

The class of '41 populated Battleship row that Sunday morning. Musicians from the USS *West Virginia*, *Oklahoma, Nevada* and *California* became known as "Orphan bands". Band 22 of the USS *Arizona* was now a sad memory.

Most of these men were absorbed into newly formed code-breaking units. An interesting fact grasped by the Navy is that knowledge of music lends itself well to the rhythm of code-breaking.

Class of '41 survivors became early Pioneers in an elite unit responsible for deciphering the Japanese "purple" code. The Japanese Naval code remained elusive, but was eventually understood in fractions;read much as a musician observes his part and understands its place in the whole composition.

The class of '41 helped win the war.

Band 17 of the *West Virginia* remained as the only unit left intact. I suspect some Navy Official decided the class of '41 had suffered enough and a plum billet was granted-This band would run a R&R joint in Honolulu named "The Breakers" for the duration of the war.

The Breakers was little more than a large shack that catered to returning Sailors; Fresh from South Pacific battles. Band 17 played music, served food and beer, removed drunken Sailors and maintained the structure. It sure beat a hot battle-zone.

Band 17 had lost their instruments aboard "WeeVee", so Hawaii natives were urged to donate any they could spare. Howard somehow managed to locate a Ludwig Super snare drum he kept his entire life.

(In later years a retired Ludwig worker restored it for him out of respect). Other band members were not so lucky and a motley assortment of instruments were the hallmark of this group.

Old equipment aside, this Fleet unit band was proud of its heritage and played with travelling Band leaders such as Artie Shaw when they passed through Hawaii in USO shows. The last playing members of the class of '41 had the time of their lives. Their only regret was Band mate Gene Lish had perished next to Howard on December 7 and wasn't there to enjoy their reward.

PLAYTIME EDITION B - - -

MY WEEKLY READER

Title Reg. U. S. Patent Office

- - - *THE JUNIOR NEWSPAPER*

| Volume XII | Week of June 21-25, 1943 | No. 3 |

Uncle Sam's Ships Sail Again

Water rushes from the deck of the battleship *California* as she rises to the surface at Pearl Harbor where she was sunk by the Japanese, December 7, 1941.

When the Japanese made their attack on Pearl Harbor, nineteen ships belonging to Uncle Sam were sunk or damaged. "The ships will be repaired and used again," said the men in the Navy.

Divers, engineers, and other workmen have been bringing these "dead" ships to life. Fourteen ships are already at sea. Only three ships will not sail the seas again. Materials from these ships are being used to build other ships.

Bringing the ships to life has been very hard work. Divers were sent down to find out just how badly the ships were damaged. Ships that were not so badly damaged were taken care of first. Work on these ships helped the men to plan how to take care of badly damaged ships.

The *Oklahoma* was upside down. Divers made charts of the ship to show the damage that had been done. The man who had charge of this work said, "Any diver can find his way around in a ship that is right side up. When a ship is upside down, nothing is familiar. The diver walks on the ceiling."

A model, or pattern, of the *Oklahoma* was built. The model was turned in exactly the same way the *Oklahoma* lay under the water. The parts of the model could be lifted away so that each part could be studied. Before going into the ship, the divers studied the part of the ship into which they were going. The divers often worked in darkness and felt their way about. The divers carried telephones so that they could talk with the men on shore.

All holes in the ship were closed and sealed. Then great cables were slung over the *Oklahoma*. A cable, you know, is a strong rope made of wire. The cables were fastened to electric motors. Slowly and carefully, the motors pulled the ship upright. This work took six weeks. After the *Oklahoma* was righted, the work went on in much the same way as on the other ships.

All the water was pumped from the ship so that it would float. Then it was taken to a dry dock. Here it is being cleaned inside and out. The ship is being rewired. New parts are being put into the ship where new parts are needed. The parts of the ship that cannot be used are scrapped. They will be reworked and used in other ships.

Slowly but surely the ships which the Japanese thought were dead are coming to life. One by one, they are sailing out to sea to help win the war.

The Navy has proved that the statement it made right after Pearl Harbor was true. The ships have been repaired and are being used again. Even those ships that can never sail the seas again have been put to use. They are giving materials for new ships that will take their places.

The diving crew has just come up out of the water-filled *U. S. S. Arizona*. Usable parts are being taken from the ship daily. They are being used in new ships.

PEARL HARBOR BANNER

Vol. 1, No. 47   CHA3—NAVY YARD, PEARL HARBOR, HAWAII • DECEMBER 7, 1943   *Price Twenty-Five Cents*

Special December 7th Edition

SELECTED BIBLIOGRAPHY

BOOKS, ARTICLES AND ARCHIVAL SOURCES:

Alden, John. "Up From The Ashes" *The Saga of the Cassin and Downes*. US Naval Institute Proceedings. (Article: page 33-41) January 1961.

All Hands Special Supplement: "*Comeback at Pearl; an Amazing Record of Salvage*" December 1958 (pages 57-63)

Arroyo, Ernest. Pearl Harbor. New York, New York, Metro Books, 2001

Bartholomew, Capt. Charles A. *Mud, Muscles and Miracles; Marine Salvage in the United States Navy*. Naval Historical Center, Washington, DC 1990

Cohen, Stan. *East Wind Rain: A Pictorial History of the Pearl Harbor Attack*. Missoula, Montana. Pictorial Histories Publishing Co. 1991

_____ *Attack on Pearl Harbor: A Pictorial History*. 2001

Di Virgillio, John F. "*Japanese Thunderfish*" *Naval History*. (Article: page 61-68) Winter 1991

Featerman, Maurice. "*The Ship That Sank From Fright.*" U.S. Naval Institute Proceedings. (Article: pages 84-87) December 1972.

Goldstein, Donald M. and Katherine V. Dillon. DEC. 7, 1941: *The Day The Japanese Attacked Pearl Harbor*. McGraw-Hill Book Co. 1988

_____with J. Michael Wenger. *The Way It Was "PEARL HARBOR" The Original Photographs*. Brassey,s (US), Inc. 1991

Hone, Thomas C. "*The Destruction of the Battle Line at Pearl Harbor.*" U.S. Naval Institute Proceedings. (Article: pages 49-59) December 1977

Hyde, J.P. *Pearl Harbor: Then and Now*. After The Battle issue No.38. Plaistow Press Magazines Ltd. London E153JA, 1982

Jasper, Joy Waldron. *THE USS ARIZONA: The Ship; The Men; The Pearl Harbor Attack and the Symbol That Aroused America*. Truman Talley Books, New York, New York. 2001

Karig, Walter and Wellbourn Kelley. *Battle Report: Pearl Harbor to Coral Sea*. Farrar and Rhinhart, Inc. New York, New York. 1944

Lord, Walter. *Day of Infamy*. Henry Holt and Company. New York, New York. 1957

Madsen, Daniel. *Resurrection: Salvaging the Battle Fleet at Pearl Harbor*. Annapolis, Maryland. Naval Institute Press. 2003

McLaughlin, Mike. "*A Magnitude Never Imagined.*" WW II History (article: pages 70-79, 89-90) November 2002

Miller, John A. *Men and Volts At War – The Story of General Electric in World War II*. Whittlesey House a Div. of McGraw-Hill Publishing Co. New York & London

Morrison, Samuel Eliot. *The Rising Sun in the Pacific, 1931-1942*. Boston, Massachusetts. Little, Brown & Co., 1958

Navy Department, Naval History Division. *Dictionary of American Naval Fighting Ships* Volumes. 1-8. US Government Printing Office, Washington, 1959-77

Naval Historical Center. *Dictionary of American Naval Fighting Ships*. Volume I-Part A. Department of the Navy, Washington 1991

Newell, Gordon R. *"Tug Boats Are Tough Little Guys: Last struggle of the Oklahoma."* Ships and the Sea. Fall 1957 (Article: pages 24-25, 46-48)

Pearl Harbor Banner. Official weekly newspaper of Civilian Housing Area III (CHA III) Navy Yard, Pearl Harbor, Hawaii. Various issues July 1942- December 1945

Pearl Harbor Bulletin. An official news publication for personnel of the Navy Yard, Pearl Harbor. Published twice monthly. Various issues June 1942- December 1946

Penfold, John B. *"Out of the Deep: The Navy's Greatest Salvage Job."* Our Navy. (Article: pages 32-34)

Phister, Jeff with Thomas Hone and Paul Goodyear. *BATTLESHIP OKLAHOMA BB-37.* Norman, Oklahoma. University of Oklahoma Press. 2008

Raymer, Edward C. *Descent into Darkness: Pearl Harbor 1942—A Navy Diver's Memoir.* Novato, California. Presidio Press. 1996

Schrader, Grahame, F. *"The Oklahoma's Last Voyage"* Copy of article of unknown source received from past historian of the PHSA, Robert A. Varrill.

Sheehan, Ed. *One Sunday Morning.* Norfolk Island, Australia. Island heritage Press 1961

Simon, Mayo. *"No Medals for Joe"* Readers Digest. December, 1990

Slackman, Michael. *Remembering Pearl Harbor: The Story of the U.S.S. Arizona Memorial.* Honolulu, Hawaii. Arizona Memorial Museum Association. 1984

_____ *TARGET: PEARL HARBOR.* University of Hawaii Press, Honolulu, 1990

Smith, Jr., Myron J. *The Mountain State Battleship USS West Virginia.* West Virginia Press Club. Richwood, West Virginia. 1981

Stillwell, Paul. *Air Raid Pearl Harbor: Recollections of a Day of Infamy.* Annapolis, Maryland. Naval Institute Press. 1981

_____ *Battleship Arizona: An Illustrated History.* Annapolis, Maryland. Naval Institute Press. 1991

Trumbull, Robert. New York Times correspondent, a six part un-published manuscript of the salvage at Pearl Harbor. December 1942. Manuscript Division, Library of Congress.

Utley, Jonathan G. *An American Battleship At Peace and War; The USS Tennessee.* University Press of Kansas. 1991

Wallin, Homer N. *Pearl Harbor: Why, How, Fleet Salvage and Final Appraisal.* Washington, D.C. Naval History Division. U.S. Government Printing Office. 1968

_____ Report: *"The Repair and Salvage of Naval Vessels Damaged at Pearl Harbor December 1946"* by Capt. H, N, Wallin, USN July 13, 1942

_____ *"Rejuvenation at Pearl Harbor"* Article from US Naval Institute Proceedings. December 1946 (pages 1520-1547)

Whitaker, Francis H. *The Salvage of the U.S.S. Oklahoma.* The Society of Naval Architects and Marine Engineers, Transactions volume 52. 1944

Zimmerman, Gene T. *Return of the Mighty Oklahoma.* Sea Classics magazine September 1974 (article pages 44-53)

REPORTS:

Action Reports U.S. Navy, RG 38 at National Archives II, College Park, Maryland, Records of the Bureau of Navigation.

Commandant, Navy Yard, Pearl Harbor, T.H. War Diaries January 1942 to March1944

Commandant, Pearl Harbor Navy Yard, USS Arizona "War Damage Report" to Chief of the Bureau of Ships, 7 October 1943. RG 19 at National Archives II

USS California Damage Report No. 21. October 28, 1942

USS Cassin and *Downes* Damage Report No. 13. May 28, 1942

USS Curtiss Damage Report No. 11. Un-dated.

USS Helena Damage Report No.4. February 21, 1942

USS Helm Damage Report No. 6. March 15, 1942

USS Nevada Damage Report No. 17. September 18, 1942

USS Oglala Damage Report No. 2. February 14, 1942

USS Oglala—Report of Salvage of. July 3, 1942
   (a) Salvage Officer's Report of Progress March 20, 1942
   (b) Salvage Bulletin No. 36. April 9, 1942.
   (c) Salvage Bulletin No. 35. April 22, 1942.
   (d) Salvage Bulletin No. 41.June 4, 1942.
   (e) Salvage Bulletin No. 43 June 23, 1942.

USS Pennsylvania Damage Report No. 14 Un-dated

USS Raleigh Damage Report No. 9. March 31, 1942

USS Shaw Damage Report No. 7. March 15, 1942

USS Tennessee Damage Report No. 22. November 25, 1942

USS Vestal Damage Report No. 12 May 25, 1942

USS West Virginia Damage Report. June 15, 1942

Deck Logs U.S. Navy, RG 24 at National Archives II, College Park, Maryland.

White, Capt. William, USN, Salvage Report *USS West Virginia*.
  West Virginia Division ofCulture and History. 2015

ERNEST ARROYO, a retired production manager for a national printing firm has been a student of U.S. Naval history for more than 50 years. In 2001 he wrote the acclaimed book "PEARL HARBOR" published by Pacific Historic Parks (formally: The Arizona Memorial Museum Association) and a co-author of "ATTACK ON PEARL HARBOR" (formally EAST WIND RAIN) a highly popular pictorial account of the Pearl Harbor attack. He is co-author of "MY PEARL HARBOR SCRAPBOOK – 1941"

Mr. Arroyo maintains a large collection of U.S. Navy ship photographs and a personal reference library and has received acknowledgments for contributions of numerous photos and associated data in over two dozen books on naval and maritime subjects.

Mr. Arroyo lives and writes at his home in Stratford, Connecticut.

STAN COHEN is a native of Charleston, West Virginia, and a graduate geologist. After many years as a geologist, in the ski business, and director of a historical museum, he established Pictorial Histories Publishing Company in 1976 in Missoula, Montana and has authored or co-authored 71 books and published over 350 more. He is the director of the Museum of Mountain Flying in Missoula, and involved with several other historical associations. His other Pearl Harbor book—*Attack on Pearl Harbor* has been in print since 1981.

APPENDIX

PACIFIC HISTORICAL PARKS. *The new Arizona Memorial Visitor Center was dedicated in December 2010, replacing the original center opened in 1980. It includes a much-expanded exhibit area, gift shop and theater. The memorial is part of the World War II Valor in The Pacific National Monument created in December 2008 by President George W. Bush by Executive Order. The monument honors several aspects of America's engagement in the Pacific during the war. It also includes the USS Utah and Oklahoma memorials, six Petty officers bungalows on Ford Island and the Mooring Quay F6, F7, and F8 which formed part of Battleship Row. In Alaska the sites include sites on Attu and Kiska islands and the crashed B-24 on Atka Island. In California is the Tule Lake Segregation Center. Pacific Historic Parks supports and funds various activities at this site and Kalaupapa Historical Park on Molokai, America Memorial Park on Saipan and War in the Pacific Historical Park on Guam.* COURTESY PACIFIC HISTORIC PARKS

Entrance to the museum.

USS Arizona *anchor.*

The Utah Memorial was dedicated on May 27, 1972, by Utah Senator Frank Moss, who led the fight for its approval and construction.

The 184-foot gleaming white structure that spans across the width of the Arizona *today was designed by architect Alfred Pries. No part of the memorial touches the ship itself. The low 14-foot high center of the Memorial rises to 20-feet high at each end signifying America's low point in World War Two and her rise to ultimate victory. There are seven large openings on each side and seven on the roof of the Memorial to give the impression of a continuous 21-gun salute. The Arizona Memorial was officially dedicated on Memorial Day May 30, 1962. The final cost of the Memorial was $532,000 dollars and attracts over one million visitors a year.* PHP

Since 1982 former crewmembers of the USS Arizona *that survived the attack can request, that upon their death, to have their remains interred inside the ship's hull to be with their fallen shipmates. When that day happens and with members of the family in attendance a full military funeral service is performed on the Arizona Memorial. After the ceremony the urn containing the ashes is solemnly handed to a team of three divers who swim slowly and reverently down to the* Arizona *to place the urn into the base of turret #4.* PHP

THE WESLEY BOLIN MEMORIAL PLAZA

The plaza was established on March 9, 1978 by the Arizona Legislature in honor of Gov. Wesley Bolin, who had died five days earlier. It had previously been a part of the Legislature Governmental Mall. The plaza exists only as a part of the mall. The plaza holds 27 memorials dedicated to topics of *Arizona* history.

A portion of the original signal mast from the battleship is on display, For a time during the war, ships leaving Pearl Harbor for battle saluted the flag that flew defiantly from the sunken ship's mast, still visible above the waterline. Later it was removed along with the remaining superstructure. Until 1980, the mast served as a training mast at the Navy Academy in Lorain, Ohio. After that it was offered to the city but was refused and ended up on private property for 10 years. The *USS Arizona* Signal Mast Committee purchased the mast and moved it to the plaza and dedicated it on Dec. 7, 1990.

The anchor of the battleship was dedicated on Dec. 7, 1976 at the plaza. Thousands of school children, businesses and individuals paid to place the anchor, forged in Chester, Pennsylvania in 1911, with a weight of 19,555 pounds. Plaques around the base last the casualties from the December 7 attack.

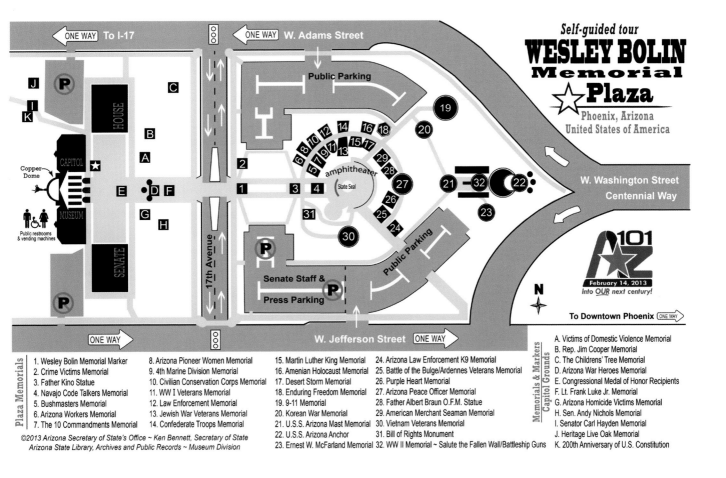

Self-guided tour
WESLEY BOLIN
Memorial
☆Plaza
Phoenix, Arizona
United States of America

February 14, 2013
Into OUR next century!

To Downtown Phoenix ONE WAY

Plaza Memorials

1. Wesley Bolin Memorial Marker
2. Crime Victims Memorial
3. Father Kino Statue
4. Navajo Code Talkers Memorial
5. Bushmasters Memorial
6. Arizona Workers Memorial
7. The 10 Commandments Memorial
8. Arizona Pioneer Women Memorial
9. 4th Marine Division Memorial
10. Civilian Conservation Corps Memorial
11. WW I Veterans Memorial
12. Law Enforcement Memorial
13. Jewish War Veterans Memorial
14. Confederate Troops Memorial
15. Martin Luther King Memorial
16. Amenian Holocaust Memorial
17. Desert Storm Memorial
18. Enduring Freedom Memorial
19. 9-11 Memorial
20. Korean War Memorial
21. U.S.S. Arizona Mast Memorial
22. U.S.S. Arizona Anchor
23. Ernest W. McFarland Memorial
24. Arizona Law Enforcement K9 Memorial
25. Battle of the Bulge/Ardennes Veterans Memorial
26. Purple Heart Memorial
27. Arizona Peace Officer Memorial
28. Father Albert Braun O.F.M. Statue
29. American Merchant Seaman Memorial
30. Vietnam Veterans Memorial
31. Bill of Rights Monument
32. WW II Memorial ~ Salute the Fallen Wall/Battleship Guns

Memorials & Markers Capitol Grounds

A. Victims of Domestic Violence Memorial
B. Rep. Jim Cooper Memorial
C. The Childrens' Tree Memorial
D. Arizona War Heroes Memorial
E. Congressional Medal of Honor Recipients
F. Lt. Frank Luke Jr. Memorial
G. Arizona Homicide Victims Memorial
H. Sen. Andy Nichols Memorial
I. Senator Carl Hayden Memorial
J. Heritage Live Oak Memorial
K. 200th Anniversary of U.S. Constitution

©2013 Arizona Secretary of State's Office ~ Ken Bennett, Secretary of State
Arizona State Library, Archives and Public Records ~ Museum Division

USS ARIZONA MEMORIAL ON FORD ISLAND. *In 1938 the Navy Club of the United States of America was established. On Dec. 7, 1955, members of the Navy League dedicated the first permanent memorial in honor of all servicemen killed during the Pearl Harbor attack. The monument was placed on Ford Island adjacent to the sunken USS Arizona. It consists of a large bronze plaque, placed on a bluestone 27-ton lava rock, standing 10 feet tall. It is now in an area seldom visited, in the island's foliage. It is important, however as it inspired the Navy to start the process of placing a permanent memorial over the sunken battleship.*

NATIONAL MEMORIAL CEMETERY OF ARIZONA. *Located at 23029 North Cave Creek Road in Phoenix. A state law was passed in 1976 and signed by Gov. Raul Castro authorizing the development of a state veteran's cemetery. It was dedicated on Dec. 9, 1978 and the first burial occurred on March 19, 1979. The cemetery was officially transferred to the VA on April 1, 1989. The cemetery consists of 225 acres and will not reach capacity until well after 2030. The Department of Veterans Affairs spent over $13 million for Improvements in 1999. The project included three new committal shelters, maintenance building, visitor center, founder's plaza, assembly area, columbaria, and extensive landscaping. Monuments and memorials since 2003 include 18 including a large monument to the USS Arizona.*

USS ARIZONA STUDENT UNION MEMORIAL EXHIBIT. *A major display of USS Arizona has been incorporated in the University of Arizona Student Union bookstore in Tucson. The USS Arizona Memorial Lounge was dedicated on Feb. 19, 2003. One wall replicates the curve of the bow of the ship.* COURTESY LESLIE JOHNSON

LAKE ISABELLA PARK. *A large granite monument and two sections of the USS Arizona ship's tripod mast legs and a section of the drive shaft for the training gear of the B & A cranes and a "Duc" tank and a Walker "Bulldog" tank are located at Lake Isabella Park, 30 miles northeast of Bakersfield, California. The park is located at Elizabeth Norris Road and Lake Isabella Boulevard.* COURTESY LAKE ISABELLA CHAMBER OF COMMERCE

USS ARIZONA BELL, UNIVERSITY OF ARIZONA. *The bell in the University of Arizona Student Union in Tucson is one of two original ship's bells salvaged from the battleship after the December 1941 attack. In 1944 Wiber L. "Bill" Bowers, UA Class of 1927 discovered the bell, about to be melted down at the Puget Sound Navy Yard. Bowers was instrumental in saving the bell and in acquiring it for the university. On Nov. 17, 1951, the bell rung for the first time in the clock tower of the new Memorial Student Union. The bell was rung on special occasions for the next 50 years until the clock tower and student union was razed for the present facility in 2002. Bowers, at age 99, was given the honor of ringing the bell for the first time in its new building on Sept. 11, 2002. This bell is rung seven times on the third Wednesday of every month at 12:07pm in honor of the servicemen who died at Pearl Harbor and to honor the outstanding achievements at the university and its community. The bell is in a tower on the south end of the Student Union.*

273

REMEMBER PEARL HARBOR MONUMENT. *Dedicated December 7, 1947 by Karl Post No. 16, American Legion.*

A flagpole with a Remember Pearl Harbor marker at its base is located on Civic Court in Stockton, California, across from the entrance to the city hall. Its inscription reads: On December 7, 1941 the country's unpreparedness invited a surprise attack on Pearl Harbor. Which plunged us into a costly war and taught us the price of peace is preparedness.
PHOTOS COURTESY SYD WHITTLE, SACRAMENTO, CA

USS ARIZONA AND USS MISSOURI GUNS. *A 14-inch gun from the* USS Arizona *and a 16-inch gun from the* USS Missouri *were stored in Virginia. The Arizona Capitol Museum raised money and transported these guns, weighing nearly 200 tons from Virginia to Arizona. The guns have been refurbished in Arizona and were placed in Wesley Bolin Memorial Plaza as a memorial to the beginning and end of World War Two on December 7, 2013. The project was sponsored by the Arizona Secretary of State and a website was established for fund raising along with social networks Facebook and Twitter. www. gunstosalutefallen.com.*

CITY OF GLENDALE, ARIZONA VETERANS MEMORIAL. *The city of Glendale, Arizona acquired artifacts from the* USS Arizona *and placed them in the Glendale Veterans Memorial, located at the intersection of 59th Avenue and Brown Street at the north end of Sahuaro Ranch Park, east of the Glendale Public Library. The rusted metal pieces are from a portion of the potato locker in the ship's gallery. The steel rings were cut from the ship's flagpole.*

The original flag that was on the USS Shaw *during the attack is now on display at the US Naval Academy in Annapolis, Maryland.* COURTESY SCOTT HARMON

THE USS OKLAHOMA MEMORIAL

The *USS Oklahoma* Memorial Committee and the National Park Service hosted a joint dedication ceremony for the *USS Oklahoma BB-37* on Dec. 7, 2007 on Ford Island. The memorial honors the 429 sailors and Marines who lost their lives on December 7, 1941. It was designed by Beck Associates Architects of Oklahoma City and sits on a 3,700-square-foot plot of land just outside the entrance to Foxtrot 5, now home to the *USS Missouri* Memorial.

The memorial is constructed of 429 pieces of three-dimensional white marble columns engraved with the name of each crew member who perished during the attack. The columns are arranged in a "U" shape to resemble sailors manning the rails. Black marble slabs surround the colums and are etched with quotes from the ship's survivors. Seven survivors along with family members attended the groundbreaking.

THE USS OKLAHOMA ANCHOR. *The anchor from the* USS Oklahoma *is on display at Campbell Park, a small patch of land at 13th Street and North Broadway Avenue, just north of downtown Oklahoma City. It is only a few blocks from the Murrah Building Memorial. The 10-ton anchor was recovered and for years was mounted on a pedestal outside the Skirvin Hotel. It was temporarily moved in 2005 when the hotel underwent renovation, but was permanently placed at its present site. The anchor has been in Oklahoma City since 1960, originally located near the Civic Center at Couch Park and Robinson Avenue, due to the efforts of Rear Admiral John E. Kirkpatrick USNR. The text on the anchor reads: This anchor was one of three that was added during the Navy's modernization of the* USS Oklahoma *in 1927. Manufactured in 1919 by Baldt Anchor Company in Chester, Pennsylvania. The anchor weighs 19,860 pounds.*

USS OKLAHOMA MAST. *A 45-foot portion of the ship's mast, the largest artifact recovered from the sunken ship was dedicated in July 2010 at the* USS Batfish *& War Memorial Park in Muskogee, Oklahoma. An unusual site for a World War Two submarine, the* Batfish *sank three enemy submarines and 11 enemy ships during the war. The sub and crew received nine Battle Stars, one Navy Cross, four Silver Stars and 10 Bronze Stars. The park also includes an army tank, cannons, missiles and other military memorabilia. There is also a Walk of Honor in tribute to all veterans. The battleship turned over but was righted in 1944 and sold for scrap. In 1947 it was being towed to the West Coast when it was sunk again. The mast was recovered in 2006 and was going to be scrap, placed back in the water for preservation or given away. The park was able to obtain the mast and place on display in the park.* COURTESY RICK DENNIS

THE USS CALIFORNIA BELL MEMORIAL. *The bell from the* USS California *is located on the grounds of the state capitol park in Sacramento. Gov. Earl Warren officially accepted the 350 pound cast bronze bell on Oct. 27, 1949. On the left side of the base the inscription reads: Only battleship built on the Pacific Coast. Launched at Mare Island Navy Yard, Nov. 20, 1919. (It was later found that five other battleships were built there.) Despite a resolution sponsored by three Navy veteran assembly members in 1954, the inscription was never corrected. The right side inscription reads: World War 1, Pearl Harbor, Marianas, Leyte Gulf, Surigao, Lincayen Gulf, Okinawa, Japan.* COURTESY SYD WHITTLE, SACRAMENTO, CA

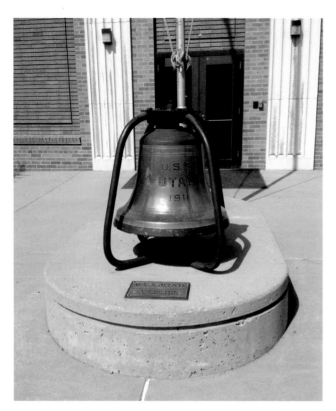

THE USS UTAH BELL. *The bell from the* USS Utah *was located at the Utah State Historical Society Collection in Salt Lake City but has been moved to the Naval Sciences Building at the University of Utah in Salt Lake City.* COURTESY MONICA SIMONS

This monument to Pearl Harbor on the Texas State Capitol grounds was erected in 1998 by the Pearl Harbor Survivors of Texas. COURTESY MICHELLE LAMBING, STATE PRESERVATION BOARD

USS MARYLAND BELL AND HELM. *The bell is on the grounds of the Maryland State House grounds in Annapolis. The helm is in storage at the Maryland State Archives.*
COURTESY ELAINE RICE BACHMANN

BATTLESHIP PENNSYLVANIA GUNS. *Two 14-inch/45 caliber gun barrels, each weighting in excess of 66 tons were set in front of the Pennsylvania Military Museum in Boalsburg, three miles east of State College in 2009. In a 1945 overhaul, both of the guns were removed and eventually placed in storage at the Navy Surface Warfare Center in Dahlgren, Virginia. They were re-discovered by a retired naval officer working at the facility. It took from 1999 to 2009 to get them in place. The PMM and the 28th Infantry Division Shrine is administrated by the Pennsylvania Historical & Museum Commission.*

The USS Pennsylvania *Bell is on display at Pennsylvania State University at College Park.* COURTESY JOSEPH HORVATH

THE USS TENNESSEE MUSEUM

The *USS Tennessee* Museum, which holds the largest collection of the battleship's artifacts is located on property of Scott High School in Huntsville, Tennessee. School students were instrumental in building and designing the museum.

Items include the 1920 bell, a five-foot model of the ship built by the Navy, and a six and one-half foot model built by historian Cliff Simmons. Also on display are many other original artifacts and the largest private collection of ship photos.

The Museum of Scott County is a complex of three acres and the only museum in the nation designed, built and curated by high school students.

Contact museumofscottcounty@gmail.com.

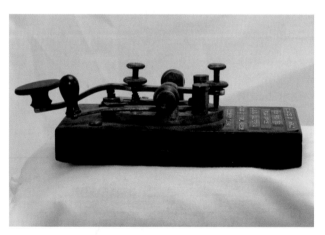

THE CALIFORNIA KEY. *The wireless key off the* USS California *now is in the collection of the Antique Wireless Association Museum in East Broomfield, New York. It was donated by Louise Moreau, a Pennsylvania collector. During the refitting of the ship, Capt. Thomas W. Regers, in charge of the ship's repairs removed and kept the radio key. He passed it on to a fellow naval officer, Ray Meyers. In 1972 he passed it to Moreau who decades later donated her entire collection, including the key to the wireless association.* COURTESY BOB HOBDAY, ANTIQUE WIRELESS ASSOCIATION

USS NEVADA BELL AND WHEEL

A bell from one of World War II's most famous ships—one that rang when the badly damaged USS Nevada escaped the Pearl Harbor attack and survived to clang during the invasions of Normandy and Iwo Jima—was returned to Nevada's historic collection in September 2011.

The return came 61 years after Sen. Pat McCarran gave the bell to the Kiwanis Club of Las Vegas.

In a ceremony attended by three Pearl Harbor survivors, Gov. Brian Sandoval gratefully accepted the silver-plated, brass bell from the club's president, Willard Wooten, who dinged it with his gavel one last time before sending it to retirement at the Nevada State Museum in Carson City.

Sandoval promised to "guard that bell with my life" and make it available for all Nevadans to see. The USS Nevada's master bell is already at the State Museum. Sandoval retrieved the ship's wheel from storage for display at his office along with a watercolor painting of the ship undergoing repairs at the Puget Sound Navy Yard after it was torpedoed and bombed by Japanese warplanes during the Dec. 7, 1941, Pearl Harbor attack.

"I'm just very proud that this Kiwanis Club is willing to share this original bell from the USS Nevada with all the people of the state," he said. "It's going to have a proud place in Carson City at the Nevada State Museum for all the kids to see."

Kiwanis Club of Las Vegas officials decided to retire the bell to the state's custody because it had served a long-standing tradition of being rung by the club's presidents at meetings since McCarran presented it to the community organization during the club's 25th anniversary year in 1950.

The bell was one of several from the historic ship and survived not only Pearl Harbor and other major sea battles but also the 1960 fire at the El Rancho Vegas, where the Kiwanis Club held its weekly Wednesday meetings, board member Owen Lloyd said.

LAS VEGAS REVIEW-JOURNAL

USS Nevada *bell*

USS Nevada *wheel*

THE RALEIGH COUNTY VETERANS MUSEUM. *Founded by a group of Raleigh County, West Virginia veterans in 2001, the museum is located in a former home with a modular addition facing Harper Road, a short distance off of the West Virginia Turnpike's Harper Road exit. There are thousands of artifacts from the mine wars in 1921 to the present war in Afghanistan. Among these is a 1:32 scale, 20-foot-long scale model of the USS West Virginia. It was built over a 17-year period by retired teacher James Toler, who runs the museum.* COURTESY JAMES TOLER

THE USS WEST VIRGINIA CLOCK. *When the* USS West Virginia *was raised in 1942, this eight-day clock was found in a compartment along with the bodies of several sailors who had lived for several days trapped in the compartment. It was salvaged and donated to the West Virginia State Museum in Charleston.* COURTESY MATT BOGGESS

USS SACRAMENTO *(PG-19) was a World War One-era gunboat. In August 1941 it was stationed at Pearl Harbor, berthed next to a couple of destroyers across from Battleship Row. Its crew shot down two enemy planes and helped rescue dozens of sailors from the USS Oklahoma. The Sacramento was decommissioned in 1946. Some of the ship's artifacts were saved, including its bell, which was placed and dedicated on Oct. 16, 1984, at the Old Sacramento Docking Barge at L Street.* PHOTO COURTESY SYD WHITTLE, SACRAMENTO, CA

THE USS WEST VIRGINIA BELL. *This bell was on the* West Virginia *motor launch that took the captain of the ship from ship-to-shore and shore-to-ship. After the war it was rung at ship reunions to commemorate the sailors who died. It was donated by shipmate Louis Grabinski to the West Virginia State Museum.*

CEMENT PLANT IN NEW ZEALAND

David Teele, an author in New Zealand explains: "virtually every male over the age of 40 knew something about the history of our local concrete plant. Each one would say something like, 'You do know that the batching plant came from Pearl Harbor after World War II?' We didn't, but we do now."

In 1939 the US Navy recognized that support facilities at its bases in Hawaii were inadequate. Gigantic efforts were made to rush these works to completion. Amongst the equipment used were at least two huge concrete batching plants. Their job was to build new dry docks and supporting buildings. In many iconic photographs showing the destruction of the Japanese attack, close inspection reveals a concrete plant standing sturdily amid the smoke and flames near the *USS Shaw*.

Shortly after the war ended, one plant from Pearl Harbor was sold to New Zealand, specifically to build the dam at Roxburgh. The plant could mix a huge amount of concrete and no such equipment had been seen in New Zealand before.

What the plant did en route to its present home in Queenstown is an important part of New

Zealand's history. It mixed the concrete for virtually all of the South Island's major hydroelectric dams except for the Clyde Dam. When the projects and the upper Waitaki Valley were complete the government deemed the plant surplus to the government. The plant was purchased "for a song" and fortunately the decision was made to keep it intact. It has been put up for sale.

COURTESY OF DAVID TEELE, NEW ZEALAND

283

Pearl Harbor commemorative stamp.

THE PEARL HARBOR MEMORIAL PARK.
A vacant lot at the intersection of Nautway and Maple Streets in Morrison, Kansas was turned into a memorial park to honor the survivors of the Pearl Harbor attack. It has a pergola and engraved marble benches with the names of the 54 surviving Pearl Harbor veterans from eastern Kansas at the time of the dedication in 2004. The anchor is on permanent loan from the US Navy and a granite marker with the inscription *Pearl Harbor, December 7, 1941* and dedicated *V-J Day, August 15, 2004.*
COURTESY DAVID TETTERS AND MARTHA SUMRALL

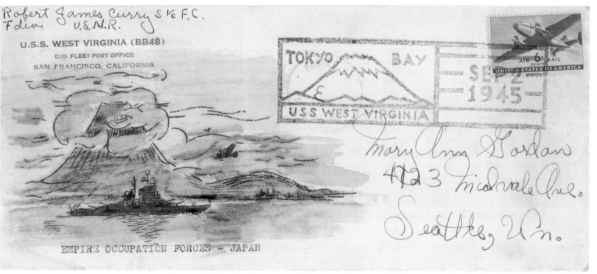

This cachet envelope w created for the Septem 2, 1945 surrender of t Japanese. The USS We Virginia, *the only ship* Tokyo Bay that was a at Pearl Harbor Decer ber 7th, was suppose t be the signing site. But instead, President Har S. Truman picked the USS Missouri, *as Mis-souri was his home sta and it was newer and could accommodate m people for the signing.*
COURTESY DAVID KENT
NEW BRITAIN, CT

284